PUSHING THE LIMITS

Encounters with **BODY WORLDS** Creator **Gunther von Hagens**

[handwritten signature and note: 08.08.2008 - Body Worlds Exhibition]

Arts & Sciences | Editor
Angelina Whalley

GUNTHER VON HAGENS

On His 60th Birthday

CONTENTS

facet – a particular part or aspect of sth

Preface

This volume on Gunther von Hagens will shed light on previously unknown facets of this famous anatomist and creator of the BODY WORLDS exhibition. It will do so through accounts of people who have accompanied von Hagens for some part or other of his life, beginning with his childhood and adolescence (reported on by his former classmate, *Dietrich Wagner*) to his imprisonment in the Cottbus penal institution (as remembered by his fellow prisoner, *Bernd Wolfram*) and on to his first anatomical workplace, the Medical Faculty of Heidelberg. *Wolfgang Koser* and *Klaus Tiedemann* describe the beginnings and first successes of plastination that they contributed to, medically and technically, not only as experts and coworkers, but also as friends. *Wilhelm Kriz*, back then von Hagens' supervisor at the Anatomical Institute, writes about the balancing act between medical education and lay information that eventually failed, not without speculating on von Hagens' motivation. Von Hagens' further development is reflected on by *Karine Oostrom* and *Bernd Hillebrands* from the viewpoints of a former plastination student and family friend, as well as a coworker and executive officer of the BIODUR company, respectively. *Rurik von Hagens*, his son, and *Angelina Whalley*, his second wife, contribute very personal impressions of the father and husband von Hagens. *Wolfgang Heindl*, his financial advisor and friend, and the journalists *Nyschanbek Kotschkorov, Harald Biskup* and *Stefan Rathgeb* accompany the exhibition producer through high and low points in the history of his enterprise BODY WORLDS, that, by now, has expanded to Kyrgyzstan, China, and the U.S.A. Eventually, *Bazon Brock* and *Franz Josef Wetz*, one an artist, the other a philosopher, both of them friends of Gunther von Hagens, take a step back and paint a portrait of von Hagens as a spiritual ascetic and describe his path of life up to now as the forceful movement of a highly controversial and much admired breaker of boundaries and envelope-pusher.

granle

The Editor   *Heidelberg, January 2005*

push the envelope – to go beyond the limits of what is allotted or thought to be possible

9

The Parents

Gunther von Hagens

Ingenious Scapegoat–Stages, Pathways, and Goals

Gunther von Hagens is born as Gunther Gerhard Liebchen on January 10, 1945, in Alt-Skalden near Posen (Posznan) in what today is Poland but then was Germany. When he is only five days old, his parents put him in a laundry basket and begin their flight west from the approaching Russians. Their travels are to last six months. They pass through Berlin and Gera and end up in Greiz/Elster. In this Thuringian town in the Vogtland area of (East) Germany, Gunther von Hagens grows up as the middle one of five children.

Gunther Liebchen comes from a non-academic family. His father, Gerhard Liebchen, had first trained as a bank clerk, then as a miller, and prior to their flight had managed his own mill for several years. In the GDR, he worked for many years as the head of a coal store and later ran a gas station. Not a party member, his professional life in the GDR was not easy. Eventually, he worked as a beekeeper because bee colonies cannot be collectivized GDR style. Gunther's mother, Gertrud Liebchen, née Knaack, on the other hand, was a convinced communist, true to the party line, and strongly influenced her children in this way. She was a nurse by profession.

In Gunther's early childhood, a bleeding disorder causes frequent hospital-izations, often for several weeks at a time. They make him an outsider and eccentric. Fascinated by his close encounters with the medical profession, he decides early on to become a physician.

From 1951 to 1961 Gunther attends the ten grade Polytechnical High School in Gera and Greiz. His academic achievements are consistent with the class average and he passes his final exams with a grade of "good." Having graduated with the intermediate German high school diploma of *Mittlere Reife*, he starts his career as an "untrained person" at the county hospital of Greiz, initially working as a doorman, mail carrier, elevator operator, and eventually as assistant to the nursing staff. However, none of these occupations satisfy him, and he attends adult school to obtain the higher level high school diploma, the *Abitur*. He passes the requisite exams with good results in 1963. In 1964, he first works as a pharmacy aid at *Elster-Apotheke* in Greiz and later, until he enrolls in medical school, in the Greiz county hospital.

In 1965, he registers as a student with the Medical School of Friedrich Schiller University in Jena and receives a monthly stipend of 200 marks. An excerpt from an informational report supplied later for the preliminary proceedings against von Hagens reads:

"However, Gunther Liebchen is a personality who does not approach tasks systematically. This characteristic and his imaginativeness, that sometimes let him forget about reality, occasionally led to the development of very willful and unusual ways of working–but never in a manner that would have harmed the collective of his seminary group. On the contrary, his ways often encouraged his fellow students to critically review their own work."

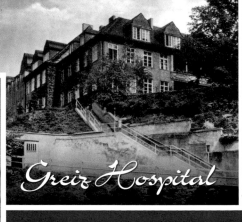

Greiz Hospital

The adolescent Gunther is very much shaped by his political environment. He himself readily acknowledges today that "I was raised in a very communist manner. To me, as an atheistically brought up *FDJ-Pimpf*[1], socialism was my ersatz religion." When he is 17 years old, he applies for party membership in the ruling SED (*Sozialistische Einheitspartei Deutschlands*, German Socialist Unity Party). The older he gets, and the more he acquires the ability to judge things for himself, however, the more he doubts the system. He begins gathering information from Western news reporting on radio and television and eventually develops a very negative attitude towards the organization of society in the GDR. When the Warsaw Pact troops invade Czechoslovakia in 1968, he decides to leave the German Democratic Republic.

He pretends to be planning a vacation trip to Bulgaria and Hungary and applies for a passport for this purpose. He tells his family that he intends to visit friends in Czechoslovakia during the semester break. On January 5, 1969, during his return trip from Budapest to Bratislava, he obtains an entry visa for Austria from the Austrian embassy in Bratislava. On January 7 he takes a tour bus to a Czechoslovakian-Austrian border checkpoint near Bratislava, but is rejected by the Czechoslovakian immigration officials without stated reasons. On January 8, 1969, he again tries to cross the Czechoslovakian-Austrian border, this time by train and via the checkpoint Devinska Nova Ves. Border controls, however, reveal that he has no exit visa from the GDR for the trip to Austria, and the travel date noted in his passport has already expired. He is arrested, extradited, and transported back to the GDR.

Gunther Liebchen is taken into custody in Greiz, is tried and, on April 25, 1969, is sentenced in the county court of Greiz to one year and nine months imprisonment for "attempted unlawful crossing of the border" and

---

[1] Translator's Note: Member of the GDR youth organisation „Freie Deutsche Jugend" (Free German Youth).

Ausfertigung

Urteil ist seit dem 26.4.19 69 rechtskräftig!

Greiz, den 2.5. 1969

Der Schriftführer der Geschäftsstelle des Kreisgerichts

Aktenzeichen: S 41/69 -KIA 32/69 Gr

BStU

FA 000048

Im Namen des Volkes!

In der Strafsache

gegen d en ehemaligen Studenten
Gunther **L i e b c h e n**,
geb.am 1o.1.1945 in Kalmen,
wohnhaft in Greiz, Am Roth 1,
-lt. Strafregisterauszug nicht vorbestraft-
seit dem 8.1.1969 in Haft

wegen ungesetzlichen Grenzübertritts u.a.

hat die Strafkammer des Kreis. gerichts Greiz

in der Hauptverhandlung vom 25.4.1969 an der teilgenommen haben:

Direktor Schulze
<u>als Vorsitzender</u>

Angestellte Ronniger

Papierarbeiterin Waldmann
<u>als Schöffen</u>

KStA Himmer
<u>als Staatsanwalt</u>

•/•
<u>als Verteidiger</u>

•/•
<u>als gesellschaftlicher Ankläger / gesellschaftl. Verteidiger</u>

J.-A. Richter
<u>als Protokollführer</u>

für Recht erkannt:

Der Angeklagte wird wegen mehrfachen Vergehens, des versuchten
ungesetzlichen Grenzübertrittes, der versuchten Verletzung
der Geldverkehrsordnung (§ 213 Abs. 1u.2, Ziff. 2, Abs. 3 StGB
i.V.m. § 7 Abs. 1 und 2 Geld -VO) zu einer Freiheitsstrafe von
-1- einem Jahr und -9- neun Monaten
verurteilt.

Der Geldwert in Höhe von 2o7,76 M wird entschädigungslos einge-
zogen.

Der Angeklagte hat die Auslagen des Verfahrens zu tragen.

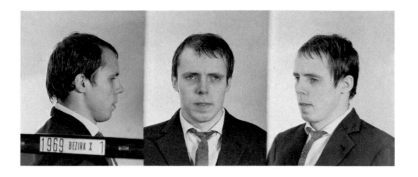

"attempted violations of the currency regulations" of the GDR. He serves his sentence in the Cottbus penal institution, where he first learns from fellow inmates of the possibility of being "traded" to the Federal Republic of Germany for hard Western currency. Back then, such exchanges of prisoners for money were unofficially practiced between the German Democratic Republic and Federal Republic on a rather regular basis. On one of the following visiting days, Gunther manages to pass on to his father a secret note that he had managed to hide behind his upper lip. In it, he asks his father to see a lawyer, Dr. Vogel, in Berlin, and to apply for his exit visa. His father complies and the application is successful. About one month before his scheduled release from prison, Gunther is transferred to the Secret Police prison in Chemnitz.

For the amount of 40,000 German marks, Gunther Liebchen's freedom is bought, and on August 27, 1970, he sets foot on Federal German soil for the first time. It takes him more than one and a half years to get used to the thousands of aural and visual stimuli in the cities. He continues his medical studies at Lübeck university and passes his exams there in 1973. He receives his practical training at the smallest German community hospital, on the island of Heligoland, where he works in the Department of Emergency Medicine and Anesthesia. On "Liquor Rock," as the duty-free

Left: Judgement against Gunther von Hagens, sentencing him to 1 year and 9 months in prison for the attempt to unlawfully cross the border of the GDR and for the attempt to violate currency regulations.

island was called by its inhabitants back then, he treats many alcoholics, often among them kids who drink schnapps from Coke bottles with their teachers looking on. Besides drunken kids, he mainly works on knees, for his supervisor also is the sports doctor for the Hamburg soccer club HSV.

In 1974 he obtains his medical license and the same year accepts a position as an intern in the Department of Anesthesiology and Emergency Medicine of Heidelberg university. There he works on his doctoral thesis, titled "The Effects of the Intravenous Narcotics Etomidate, Propanidide, Methohexital and the Inhalational Narcotics Laughing Gas, Halothane and Ethrane on the Lower Esophageal Sphincter (Studies on the Issue of Regurgitation Under Conditions of Anesthesia)."

On June 20, 1975, he marries his former fellow student Cornelia von Hagens. After one year of married life, Cornelia Liebchen is sick of constantly being teased as "das Liebchen," the German equivalent of "little darling," and the couple considers a name change. However, under Federal German law, the processing of such a change is so complicated that they decide instead to divorce and remarry. In August 1976 they are married for the second time, now choosing the family name of "von Hagens." Later, they will have three children: Rurik Gunnar, Bera Anuk, and Tona Gerrit.

While working at the hospital, Gunther quickly discovers that the profession of physician, with its tedious routines, is not for him after all. "I have a pensive mind," he analyzes. He would rather work for an international organization such as the World Health Organization (WHO), and he decides to prepare for the prerequisite certification by the US Educational Commission for Foreign Medical Graduates (ECFMG). That, however, takes time—more time than his work at the hospital allows. Thus, he decides to switch to the slower-paced field of anatomy and accepts a position as scientific assistant at the Anatomical Institute of Heidelberg university in July 1975. In 1977 he passes the ECFMG certification exams, but his career will take a different path than planned.

As an anatomical assistant, von Hagens sees, for the first time, specimens embedded in plastic blocks, and he wonders why the plastic has been poured around the specimen in block shape instead of being inside the specimen, stabilizing it from within. This question keeps nagging at him. Weeks later, he needs to produce serial slices of human kidneys for a research project. Embedding the kidneys in paraffin and cutting them into a series of extremely thin slices, as is customary, seems to him a waste of time and energy, since he needs only every fiftieth slice. While watching the sales clerk in the university's tiny grocery store slicing ham, he has an exciting idea: Why not use a sausage slicing machine for slicing the kidneys? Thus, a "rotational slicing machine", as he refers to it in his application to the university to buy such an item, becomes the first investment in plastination. He embeds the kidney slices in liquid Plexiglas. The air bubbles introduced while stirring in the hardener have to be extracted under vacuum. While watching these bubbles he has another, decisive, idea: It should be possible to impregnate an acetone soaked renal piece with plastic under vacuum conditions simply by extracting the acetone in the form of bubbles, just as is done in degassing.

The experiment is initially successful. Many acetone bubbles are, indeed, extracted from the specimen; but after one hour, the renal piece is pitch black and has shrunk. Most would have considered the result of the experiment a failure. But not Gunther von Hagens. Thanks to his basic knowledge of physics and chemistry, he understands that the black coloration stems from the special refractive properties of the Plexiglas, and that the shrinking is due to a too quick impregnation process. So he repeats the experiment a week later, this time using liquid silicone rubber. He conducts the impregnation slowly and, in order to avoid premature hardening of the silicone bath and specimen caused by exposure to air, he pours fresh silicone in three subsequent baths. After hardening the specimen in an incubator, he holds in his hands the first presentable plastinate. It is January 10, 1977, his 32nd birthday. In March of the same year he submits this process to the

German Patent Office under the title "*Konservierte biologische verwesliche Objekte und Verfahren zu ihrer Herstellung.*" In 1980, he published the first corresponding US patent titled "Animal and Vegetal Tissues Permanently Preserved by Synthetic Resign Impregnation."

Gunther von Hagens realizes that this invention is the opportunity of a lifetime, one he will never let go of. Its practical implementation and further development require numerous nights of brooding. It takes many, many experiments to find a method for removing water and lipids from biological tissues at room temperature, and for replacing them with plastic without causing the specimens to shrink. His increasing commitment, however, collides more and more strongly with the interest of his boss, Professor Wilhelm Kriz, who urges Gunther to return to his "regular" research tasks, and eventually forces him to choose. Gunther persists. He leaves the Anatomical Institute and accepts a position as an assistant at the Institute of Pathology of the Heidelberg university in October 1977. At the same time, he is offered a position at the Anatomical Institute of the Aachen university with the intention of enabling him to further develop the plastination method and even to obtain the German formal requirement for professorship, *Habilitation*. Apparently, this offer is not without effect at the Heidelberg Anatomical Institute, and Gunther is offered another position there as well. He accepts it, and on October 1, 1978, he is once again in the service of the Heidelberg Anatomical Institute. From then on, his special task will be the "development of new methods for the production and preservation of macroscopic and microscopic specimens."

He will spend the next twenty years at the Anatomical Institute of the Heidelberg university as lecturer and scientist. During this time, he continuously enhances the method of plastination, and makes further inventions, such as the hardening of silicone through gas, which allows him practically unlimited time for processing silicone impregnated specimens.

Another invention is the plastination of thin translucent slices of bodies or brains, requiring not only the refining of many aspects of the technology, but also the development of appropriate plastics systems. Many patents follow in various countries, especially in the U.S.A.

His technology is noted at professional conferences, and at the beginning of the 1980s the media for the first time report on Gunther von Hagens and his invention. But in order to achieve a breakthrough of his method in the field of anatomy, the special plastics have to be made commercially available to other universities as well. Negotiations are conducted with, among others the *Merck* company, but eventually no-one is interested for fear of an insufficient market. Thus, in 1980, Gunther von Hagens himself, while still working at the university, founds a small business, BIODUR, that will sell plastics and later other plastination supplies and equipment as well.

Slowly, but steadily, plastination spreads around the world and finds users on all continents. It is especially well recognized in the U.S.A. In April 1982 the first Conference on Plastination is held in San Antonio, Texas, and the International Society for Plastination (ISP) is founded. From then on, every two years international plastination conferences are held, and the ISP publishes an annual journal. In addition, Gunther von Hagens regularly holds workshops for interested scientists, from all over the world, in order to spread his technology. Often, the workshop participants are far more qualified or higher in rank than he is. With the increasing worldwide interest in his invention, Gunther von Hagens achieves the international status that he sorely missed in the petty bourgeois GDR.

[handwritten annotations:]
sorely, very much
thus - tak ; u ten sposob
thus far - jak dotąd
petit bourgeois - a member of the lower middle class in society, especially one who thinks that money, work and social position are very important

This urge for international work and recognition also is responsible for Gunther von Hagens' later cooperation with other universities outside of Germany. One such instance is with the *State Academy* in Bishkek, Kyrgysztan, where he founds a Plastination Center at the Morphological Center in 1995. In 1999, the Bishkek Academy awards him an honorary title of Professor.

The plastination method continues to evolve and eventually reaches dimensions that stretch the limits of its university home. Thus, in 1993, Gunther founds the *Institute for Plastination* in Heidelberg. To this end, he cuts back his university hours by half. Together with his second wife, Angelina Whalley, whom he met as a young colleague in 1987 and married in 1992, he now conducts plastination increasingly on a commercial level.

The great breakthrough, however, is not achieved until a few years later, when the plastinated specimens are publicly displayed for the first time. In 1995, Gunther von Hagens is invited by the Japanese Anatomical Society to participate in an exhibition at the *National Science Museum* in Tokyo, Japan. The exhibition will celebrate the Society's 100th anniversary, and Gunther is to show some of his plastinates. The exhibition is surprisingly successful–it is visited by more than 450,000 people in only four months. It is followed by other successful exhibitions in Japan, until, in 1997, the plastinates are shown for the first time in Germany as well, namely in Mannheim.

Unlike in Japan, in Germany the BODY WORLDS exhibition, as it will be called from now on, is accompanied by stark public controversies that are triggered again and again by later exhibitions. BODY WORLDS finds supporters and opponents in all segments of the population, and even the Anatomical Institute in Heidelberg is split into two fractions. The disputes make it impossible for Gunther von Hagens to continue working there, and so he leaves the university at the end of 1997. At the same time he is refused recognition of his private Heidelberg institute as a research in-

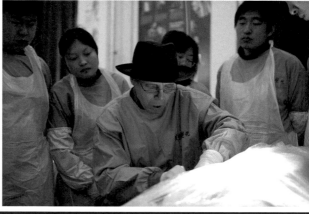

DER SPIEGEL

Nr 4/19.1.04
Deutschland: 3,00 €

Dr. Tod

Die horrenden Geschäfte
des Leichen-Schaustellers
Gunther von Hagens

stitution by the German government. Consequently, he turns his back on Germany and in 1996 accepts a guest professorship at *Dalian Medical University* in China. Here he is given an entire building on the university campus, and he establishes the *Institute for Plastination at Dalian Medical University*. In 2000 he additionally founds a private institute, the *Von Hagens Dalian Plastination Company, Ltd.* As of this writing, the company has about 200 employees and is funded mainly by the revenue from the BODY WORLDS exhibitions. *Plastination City*, as Gunther von Hagens likes to refer to his Chinese company, gives plastination another enormous lift. By 2002 enough material for a second exhibition is created there. The new exhibition tours Asia and is shown for the first time in Seoul, Korea, with overwhelming success. There is no public criticism whatsoever. Quite to the contrary, the exhibition in Asia is even officially supported by science and education departments.

In Europe however, especially in Germany, the controversy surrounding the exhibition refuses to die. It focuses more and more on the person Gunther von Hagens, culminating in personal disparagement early in 2004. From then on, von Hagens concentrates on his work in the U.S.A., taking his exhibition there in that same year. In the United States, just as in Asia, no public criticism of BODY WORLDS is heard. Since January 2005, Gunther von Hagens is visiting professor at New York University's *College of Dentistry*.

Encounters with
Gunther von Hagens

Dietrich Wagner as confirmand in 1954 and today. Together with Gunther Liebchen he attended Greiz high school (Goetheschule) in Greiz until 1961. After his apprenticeship as an electrician and his university studies in mechanical engineering and electrotechnics in Zwickau, he worked in various technical fields until he and his family, after significant problems with the "instruments of state," were released from "GDR citizenship" and "expelled from GDR state territory" in 1985. From 1986 until his early retirement in 2004, he worked as an engineer in middle management at SiemensVDO Automobil-Elektronik. Since then he has been a consultant to an import-export business on their Central America project. As of this writing, Dietrich Wagner lives with his family in Regensburg, Germany.

Dietrich Wagner

My days with Gunther Liebchen in Greiz

Our Hometown

I have fond memories of my childhood and adolescent years spent in the 1950s in my hometown of Greiz in Thuringia, Germany. The town is often referred to as the "gem of the Vogtland area," most likely because it is beautifully situated among rolling hills, in the glorious valley along the river Weiße Elster, and because of the two palaces that call it home. Greiz used to be a royal seat, where the princes of the older and the younger lines of the Reuß dynasty ruled. Today Greiz has only 26,000 residents, but after World War II there were more than 45,000 people living there.

Whenever I think back to those times, one image comes to mind: the image of Gunther. He is the one with whom I spent most of my time back then. We were young during the post-war years, and that was a special historical era. On the one hand, those years were characterized by political turmoil and the founding of the GDR, the German Democratic Republic. On the other hand, life was simpler, quieter, and there was more human contact back then. At least that is the way it seems to me in retrospect. I also have unpleasant and painful memories, especially of my school years, but they are outweighed by the interesting and exciting ones.

The Homes We Grew Up In

Gunther did not join my class at *Goetheschule* until the mid-1950s. His family was originally from an area that today belongs to Poland, and had come via Cottbus to Greiz. That was, I believe, when we were in fourth grade. Our homeroom teacher decided that Gunther was to sit next to me. This, but also the fact that we shared the same route to school, was why we quickly got to know each other. Gunther always met me at our house, for he was ten minutes further away from school (by foot, of course) and passed by our house every day. My family had a small piece of land with a garden, and on most days Gunther and I met at the garden gate. He lived on Laagweg, from which a small side street, named "Am Roth" led directly into the woods and to the *Pulverturm* tower, where we had some exciting adventures–but I will get back to that later.

During the week, Gunther's father worked and lived further east in the GDR, I believe it was in Cottbus, and came home only for the weekends. Gunther's mother, Gertrud Liebchen, was a very resolute woman who gave the orders in the family. She was a nurse by profession and worked as ward sister at the old age and long-term care home "Anna Seghers." That home had been built by its founders, Ernst and Lina Arnold, on a rise right next to my family home. Before the Communists, it had been called "Ernst und Lina Arnoldstift." Mrs. Liebchen was well liked there, but also knew how to hold her own among co-workers and residents.

The Wagner Home

The Liebchen family had a giant apartment at "Am Roth 1"–the entire upper floor–which was very much tailored to the needs of the children. They each had their own room. Gunther had four siblings: his two older sisters Gudrun and Siegrid Oda, his younger brother Gero, and Sunhild, the little sister, a late arrival. I often wondered about the names their parents chose for them, especially because such Germanic names were not common in the GDR.

The Liebchen Apartment, Am Roth 1

Although I often visited Gunther, we spent only a little time upstairs, but instead went into the woods. This may have been due to the fact that the ambiance in Gunther's home was very much communist. His brother Gero later became a very high ranking officer. My family, on the other hand, was inherently dissident because we had owned a large company that had been seized by the state. Also, my father had died of the consequences of his imprisonment by the Russians. Therefore, my mother was rather critical of Gunther, but Gunther never acted like a follower of the party line. I was much freer than he, and had, I believe, a lot more family support.

These differences never became an issue for us. At the Liebchen home listening to Western radio stations was not allowed, so we did not do it. Gunther's later escape and my expulsion from the GDR eventually demonstrated that we had similar views. Gunther just had had to work hard and fight for a different attitude that was not tolerated at his home. Back then, Gunther lived between two worlds. The older he got, the clearer his political views became.

Goetheschule

Being together in the same class and spending a lot of time together led to friendship. Even though I am careful today with using the term "friend," I think I can say that we were school friends. But we were not always close. There were times when the cliques in school changed, but I was with Gunther most of the time. We both were very introverted and

GREIZ · THÜR.

complemented each other. Thus, we often became the scapegoats for our classmates, for people notice quickly when someone is not able to fight back very well. We were different from the others, and that was enough. Gunther's nickname back then was "Bull," for he was somewhat stocky back then, of a heavy build. Although he was very much annoyed by it, that name stayed with him almost until the end of his school days. Gunther also suffered from a severe bleeding disorder. Whenever he had a nosebleed in school it turned into a medium-sized catastrophe. He had to get to a doctor as quickly as possible. One always had to take care that he did not fall. When people teased him, this care was not always taken, and injuries resulted. It was awful.

Goetheschule at that time was a so-called "polytechnical high school," which compares to the intermediate form of German high schools (*Realschule*) today. Students who would be allowed to attend the higher level high school were selected after the eighth grade. The selection criteria changed from year to year and were determined by "party and government" officials. Crucial factors were the student's social background (workers and peasants, of course, were especially distinguished), the student's political work, the social commitment of the student, membership in social organizations (Pioneer Organization, Free German Youth, German-Soviet Friendship) and lastly the student's performance in school.

Gunther was different from all his classmates, even back in our school days. I knew him as a "cerebral person." He always had ideas and proceeded to defend them against anything and anyone. His topics and subjects would change over time, but not his commitment and enthusiasm. We often discussed, sometimes disputed, social and political issues, for Gunther was exposed to a different political climate at home than I was. He evaluated the daily events of political life with a lot of thought. However, we would discuss these issues only when we were by ourselves, on the way to or from school. At home, as in school, he had to act very differently during discussions. For although we were only adolescents, high school students, our critical thoughts created a danger that was real both for us and our parents.

cerebral person —

From the files—about 15 binders full—that the secret police had kept on me and that were made available to the subjects of these investigations after the Wall came down I learned that some of my fellow students had spoken negatively of me. But Gunther Liebchen was not among them. He never made any statements against me. Back then he certainly was not a full-blown dissident, for his homelife always put him in an in-between position, and it is even possible that his parents questioned him. But I would have learned of any betrayals from my files. Gunther obviously had not passed on anything that he had learned and heard at my house—a sign of good character.

Sputnik

Whenever Gunther got hooked on one of his hot topics, he really got going. The older he got, the more clearly he got into his own element, medicine, which he is still active in today. But medicine was not what it started with; back then, he was interested in more general topics. I especially remember when, on October 5th, 1957, the first Russian sputnik was sent into space. Gunther was so enthusiastic that he almost freaked out. He collected everything that was even remotely related to space, rocket science, and man-made satellites. He was in a delirium-like state and worked obsessively by himself. With the sputnik issue I was not able to help much, anyway, for most of the information was in Russian, which I did not understand. Neither was I allowed to talk about it at home, for it was a Russian event, and was therefore not acceptable as a topic of conversation.

Gunther created a wall newspaper in school and filled folders with materials he collected on this topic. He got the information from books and magazines. In the GDR that was not easy, for it was hard to get your hands on these sources. There was no Internet and virtually no TV back then. Gunther's urge to study and to gain knowledge has to be appreciated even more given those conditions. Slowly, Gunther became *the* authority on this topic at our school, and his projects netted him recognition and praise from our teachers. Many of his characteristics today—as one can see in his interviews—were already present back then. For example, he was able to get incredibly worked up about something, to get obsessed about it and really get down to it—but rhetorically he never was really good, that was not one his strengths, even back when he was a child. So his special way of trying to impose his ideas and opinions on teachers and fellow students often offset the brownie points he got for all the work he put into his projects.

When Gunther focused on school subjects for a change, he composed extensive homework assignments and essays. It was actually contagious, and so we often spent an entire afternoon sitting in the kitchen at my home, writing, discussing, and writing some more. Our teachers probably

Goetheschule *High School*

were pretty surprised by these sudden attacks of hard work. I remember that on some afternoons we produced 15, even 20, pages, even though only about one tenth of that was required of us. We extended these essays on purpose, in order to win our teacher's recognition and our fellow students' admiration the next morning. After such an outburst of activity, they would always leave us alone for a while.

Joint Activities

In school we both were slightly above average in our academic performances. The older he got, the more Gunther improved. His special subjects were biology and chemistry. But most of the time he was not focused on school or studying–they merely served as inspiration for his own activities. I especially remember his chemical experiments. We worked with sulfur, magnesium, and other not really harmless substances. Sometimes we would turn my kitchen into a laboratory–at his home, it seemed, Gunther had already outstayed his parents' welcome of his experimental work. But after one of our counters had been stained with a permanent burn and soot stain, we had to transfer our "laboratory" to the woods, near the *Pulverturm* tower.

The Pulverturm *Tower*

Those woods also bore witness to Gunther's first attempts at dissection, done on beetles, frogs, and other small animals. Gunther set up a number of hiding spots in the woods, where he buried his specimens. But Gunther not only worked with his knife, he also gathered all the information that he could get a hold of, and he knew a lot of stories about all his little discoveries. Even back then he had already cultivated his special way of getting his listeners interested in his subject by way of explanations and the sharing of his knowledge.

Gunther always chose our school lessons as the forum for his "presentations." Unfortunately, Gunther's disease led to his downfall: He cut himself with his knife and his mother had to take him to the Greiz hospital for treatment. I do not know what happened next, because after a conversation between both our mothers, I was no longer allowed to participate in Gunther's experiments. I believe, however, that he continued them. Gunther always needed an assistant, and another fellow student of ours (Günther Meinhard), who also lived near him, later filled this position. For quite some time I was no longer allowed to leave our house or our garden after school. In spite of this, Gunther often came to our house, and we continued walking to and from school together.

We often went on afternoon bike tours, exploring our immediate surroundings. One of our main routes was along the Elster River towards Neumühle, a community about five miles north of Greiz. We went there because Neumühle was the nearest destination on our side of town. The way led us through beautiful woods, and we had to climb a mountain with a 13% slope. That was hard work–but on the way back, we rode down at breakneck speeds. Sometimes we also would ride further. Next to the train tracks there was a narrow footpath on which we biked. This tour led through two train tunnels, and we loved it for that–a kind of test of courage, entirely unimaginable today. For it was very dark inside those tunnels, and we had to take great care to stay on the footpath alongside the tracks. When a train approached, we had to press ourselves against the tunnel walls. What was interesting was the fact that the weather often was different on one end of the tunnel than on the other. That, too, was another source for Gunther's lectures and fantasies.

Another one of his fields was chess. He liked to compete with his fellow student Reinhard Postler, who always was at the top of his chess class. Certainly, Gunther did not beat him every time, but he was proud of every partial success. It could be said that he was the second best player at our school.

Medicine and Technology

The older we got, the more Gunther got interested in medicine. During one of my visits one day, I noticed a roll-up anatomical poster of the human skeleton in his room, probably a gift from his parents, who had always supported him in these things as best as they could. Gunther would tell us more and more detailed stories about the human body and its development. This was in part due to his extraordinary interest in this field, and in part due to the fact that, in his mother, he had a nurse and thus a discussion partner within the family.

Later, our interests diverged. We no longer saw each other that often. My own development led me more towards technology; I had never been very much into Gunther's medical passion. Today, too, I often have a critical opinion on that. Gunther's experiments sometimes were disgusting to me, for my interests were very different. My subject is technology–I preferred experimenting with electron tubes and later became an electronics engineer. That, on the other hand, was of no interest to Gunther.

Our ways parted, basically, after we left school at the end of tenth grade. We each started an apprenticeship, and although we occasionally stopped to chat, we no longer spent the intense hours together that we had during our school years. We had a good neighborly relationship. Both Gunther and I would later go to adult school in order to obtain a higher level of high school diploma, the *Abitur*, but because we were assigned to the schools based on the locations of our work places, we went to different schools.

Afterward, Gunther studied medicine. During his university years, he earned his keep by working at the Greiz hospital. Once, I saw him there, sitting in the nurse's room with a book, studying. I no longer remember whether that was during a semester break, because those were usually given to mandatory missions such as leading harvesting teams or serving in a military student unit. I had not served in the armed forces and neither, by the way, had Gunther, because of his bleeding disorder.

I learned of Gunther's attempt to leave the country from my mother, who worked at the same old age home as Gunther's mother. The two did not really like each other, mostly because of their differing political views. My mother worked at the home as an independent podiatrist. But even though they did not talk to each other directly, my mother obtained information via the other nurses. Gunther's parents were apparently deeply saddened by his attempted escape.

I myself left Greiz after completing my engineering studies, and spent a mandatory year as junior engineer in Denim, a town in the North of the GDR. Afterward, I worked for many years in management positions for the social institutions of the Lutheran church, and for the state owned company Carl Zeiss, Jena, in Brandenburg and Sachsen-Anhalt, respectively. I had more and more conflicts with the police state–I was accused of spying activities and of helping people to escape–and in 1985 my family, i.e., my wife and our four kids, were expelled from the GDR as "Traitors to our country." Police cars came to pick us up from work and school, respectively, and then we were, as it was called in the GDR, "released from GDR citizenship." That made us "foreigners," and we had to leave the country immediately. They gave us five hours to do so. Quickly, we had to write a list of items we would be allowed to take with us. My eldest daughter, almost 18 years old at the time, in the rush forgot to list her shoes. Sure enough, they were taken from her at the border and she had to make do on the train with her socks until we reached Fulda in West Germany, where the traveler's aid office managed to find a pair of shoes for her.

„Harvest Captains"–Gunther on harvesting duty

Our High-School Reunion

In 1999, two students (Hannelore Proft, née Bonitz, and I) of our high-school class organized a reunion. We found the current addresses of almost all of our former classmates and invited them, including, of course, Gunther. He drove all the way from Heidelberg to Greiz to attend the meeting and, naturally, gave a presentation on his work and the technology of plastination. That was my first real encounter with Gunther's work of today. His name is known in Greiz, and the inhabitants of Greiz have been following his development. At the reunion, Gunther was completely relaxed, very open and friendly. He liked to talk and was not shy or reserved, was very communicative and did not think himself too good for anything. He was a true asset to this event. However, he did not go anywhere without his notebook and palmtop. And he carried a little box with index cards containing the words he was busy studying. During a walk we took, he explained to me how he comes up with mnemonic aids for difficult-to-remember words. He associates the words with images, and when he needs a word, he thinks of that image. It reminded me of our high-school mnemonic that we had created together for Ohm's Law: Unsere Italien-Reise, "our Italian trip."

Of course, I am in no position to judge Gunther's work from an expert point of view. But I do believe that every person is entitled to learn about his or her body, and to get to know its "structural plan." For technical devices, drawings, photos, and so-called "exploded views," are available. But when dealing with the human body, popular-science "doctor's books" are supposed to make do. When comparing those with the lavishly produced publications on, say, new car models, they appear very scant. And this gap is filled by Gunther, with the technology of plastination he has developed. Now the human body becomes understandable, even to medical laypersons. Gunther has achieved this by continuously working and researching, and by staying focused on this goal. This human greatness and scientific competence of his certainly were not foreseeable in our school days. However, in retrospect, his development appears to be linear–detoured

perhaps a little, involuntarily, by the GDR regime and his imprisonment–
but always single-minded and successful.

For his 60th birthday, I wish Gunther good success with his future work.
I would be happy if it were possible for him to continue to bring the results
of his work to people all over the world. I always enjoy reading or hearing
about the progress of his scientific work. At an age when others begin
thinking of retirement, he still is on his way. I cannot wait to see his new
successes in research and in his work on humans–benefiting all of us.

So, Gunther: All the best, good luck, and may you stay healthy so you will
be able to reach many more goals!

Bernd Wolfram in 1971 and today, fellow inmate of Gunther von Hagens in the Cottbus penal institution. Bernd Wolfram today lives in Dreieich in Hesse. After leaving the GDR in 1975, he found a job with the Fleissner company in Egelsbach in 1979. The company is the leading producer of machines for the production and processing of fibers and fleece. After years in the field, he now works in their research and development department. He lives with his wife and three sons in a nice house in the Sprendlingen district of Egelsbach.

Bernd Wolfram

Our Cottbus Days

Political Prisoners

That part of the our lives that Gunther and I walked together is now more than 35 years behind us, and it was not spent under a very lucky star. We first met in 1968 in the Cottbus penal institution in the GDR. In spite of the circumstances, I got to know Gunther as a very intelligent person of absolute integrity. He has left indelible impressions in my memory and I have never forgotten him. My impressions of him are what I would like to describe here. However, in order for the reader to fully grasp the situation that we prisoners were in back then, I first will try to give some insights into those days, our escape attempts, our criminalization, sentencing, and imprisonment.

The Cottbus institution was, next to Bautzen II, one of the largest prisons in which people were incarcerated for what the GDR regime called "political offenses." As political prisoners, so called "new criminals," we were worth less than criminals who had committed theft. When I arrived in Cottbus in September 1968, there still were some common criminals detained there but they were separated from the "politicals" by the prison management, who feared our anti-system influence. The common criminals still were considered to be true to the state. They said, "We'll be better, it will never happen again;" they worked hard and fulfilled what was expected of them.

For them the world was in order, they knew what they had done wrong, and they also knew that if they behaved properly they would be released when two thirds of their sentence was up. The political police actually said, "The politicals will ideologically spoil the criminals." And to prevent that from happening, the criminals were separated and we were grouped in politicals-only cells. We always said, "We accept this. We will sit out our sentences until the last day, unless we get to go where we want to be." And what was our goal? The West, of course. And almost all of us made it.

From that time on, that is, from late October, early November 1968, there were only two offenses known in Cottbus. There were the so-called "agitators," who had protested against the 1968 invasion of the Czechoslovakian Republic by the Soviet Union, and then the "escapists." Gunther and I belonged to the group of "illegal emigrants from the GDR."

The Cottbus Penal Institution: "Gate to the West"

Failed Attempt at "Illegal Emigration from the GDR"

All of us failed illegal emigrants had our own stories about our attempted escapes, and usually they differed only regarding the date and the checkpoint chosen. Eventually, we all had met the same fate, namely, that our escape had been discovered, and that we had been arrested, sentenced and imprisoned. Our motives, too, were largely the same. We did not have extraordinary plans, but simply wanted to leave the GDR. And because that was not legally possible, we had to resort to illegal attempts. On August 21, 1968, the so-called "parties to the Warsaw Pact" had invaded Czechoslovakia. With the Prague Spring it had seemed the overall political situation was becoming more relaxed. But as early as the beginning of the summer we began to suspect that an invasion or something similar was going to happen, and so we wanted to take our last chance. An

escape via the Czechoslovakian Republic seemed the logical approach. My "accomplice," as he was called in GDR jargon, and I left on July 7, 1968, towards Stubnach, where we wanted to head towards Zwiesel in West German Bavaria, passing between the Rachel and Arber mountains. Gunther's attempted escape was similar to mine, but he wanted to travel via Bratislava, i.e., to cross the border into Austria.

We all had to overcome the border control facilities aimed at keeping people from crossing to the West. As the name "Iron Curtain" suggests, those were rather tight: There were towers in the countryside at the border, from which the area before the border was watched. All of them were equipped with telephones so that an alarm could be immediately raised. Just before the border there were plain-clothes patrols that stopped anyone they encountered and checked papers. Then there were the border fences. One fence was braided in squares, the other one in longitudinal strips, with about three yards between them. The ground in between the fences was always neatly raked so every footprint would stand out. And at intervals of no more than 300 yards along the fences were additional towers, equipped with floodlights, that enabled the border guards to see everything. Finally, there was another broad strip of land, protected by patrols with dogs, that extended to the actual border. The actual border itself was equipped with automatic firing devices.

So, all of us in Cottbus had suffered their own fates during their attempts at escape. Still, there was a lot we had in common. Most of us fled under the protection of the darkness of night. Not all of us ran into friendly border patrols. Some had sustained gunshot wounds. My own attempt at escape had been by train and on foot. One of our fellow inmates had tried it by car, and his vehicle was confiscated. His escape attempt was discovered because of a state police spy who had pretended to be going along. At one point or other, all of our attempts at escape had failed. Some were discovered in the area before the border protection facilities. My "accomplice" and I were discovered by one of the border patrols with dogs, i.e., we had overcome most of the security facilities and had almost made it. For us that was very unlucky, but the patrolling guard was lucky and happy, because they were praised for every arrest at the border. But that is a whole different story.

Eventually, we all were transferred to the state police after our arrest, and were transported to Gera. Everyone from the Gera region was taken there. Gunther, too, ended up there. In Gera we were questioned,[1] taken into custody for three and a half months, and then sentenced to 22 months because of our attempt to "illegally emigrate from the GDR." The time spent in custody was counted towards the sentence, and we then were taken to Cottbus where we spent the remaining time of our imprisonment.

Truck for the transport of prisoners with extremely narrow cells, disguised as civilian vehicle, photos: Florian Falcke

1. *Frequently, suspicions have been voiced that those questioned in Gera were exposed to radioactivity from an x-ray device installed behind a chair used when photographing detainees that was screwed into the ground, and that was hidden by a curtain. The Jena artist Frank Rub, who started legal proceedings after his friend, the writer Jürgen Fuchs, had died of cancer, triggered a public debate and investigations in the late 1990s. In addition to Fuchs, Gerulf Pannach, the former songwriter of the GDR rock band "Renft", and the regime opponent Rudolf Bahro had fallen ill with and died of cancer. All three of them had been imprisoned in the mid-1970s in Hohenschönhausen. Even though a report by Michael Beleites, the official of the State of Saxony in charge of the former State Police files, has declared the suspicions of radiation damages inflicted in Gera "as far as possible cleared" (cf. for example http://www.havemann-gesellschaft.de/info10. htm), it must be stated that both Bernd Wolfram and his "accomplice," Bernd Gruber, were diagnosed with cancer in the early 1980s. Today, both of them are considered cured.*

Das **Kreis-** gericht   Gera , den 15. 01. 1969

Fernruf

Aktenzeichen: 1/69
(Bei Eingaben stets anführen)

Haftbefehl

er Student LIEBCHEN, Gunther, geb. am 10. 01. 1945 in Kalmen,
D wohnhaft in Greiz, Am Roth 1

ist in Untersuchungshaft zu nehmen

Er wird beschuldigt bzw. steht im dringenden Tatverdacht, versucht zu
haben, ohne Genehmigung der staatlichen Organe der Deutschen Demokratischen Republik nach Österreich auszureisen.
Der Beschuldigte war im Besitz eines Reisepasses und erhielt die Genehmigung durch ein entsprechendes Visa nach Bulgarien und Ungarn zu
reisen, wobei die Durchreise über die CSSR und Rumänien eingeschlossen
war.
Der Beschuldigte hat seine Urlaubsreise nach Ungarn und Bulgarien am
21. 12. 1968 angetreten. Auf seiner Rückfahrt von Budapest nach Bratislava am 5. 1. 1969 hat er sich in der österreichischen Botschaft in
Bratislava ein Einreisevisum nach Österreich ausstellen lassen. Von
den Sicherheitsorganen der CSSR wurde er auf der Fahrt zur österreichischen Grenze festgenommen. Aus seinem Ausreisevisum der DDR wurde ge-
schlußfolgert, daß er bis zum 7. 1. 1969 wieder in das Gebiet der Deutschen Demokratischen Republik zurückkehren mußte.

Entgegen den gesetzlichen Bestimmungen hat somit der Beschuldigte versucht, die Deutsche Demokratische Republik ohne behördliche Genehmigung
nach Österreich zu verlassen.

Straftat nach § 213 (1) und (3) StGB
Der Erlaß des Haftbefehls stützt sich auf Fluchtverdacht, was sich aus
der konkreten Handlung des Beschuldigten ergibt.

gez. Pöthig
Richter am Kreisgericht

Gegen diesen Haftbefehl ist binnen einer Woche das Rechtsmittel der Beschwerde zulässig

Ausgefertigt:

Gera , den 15. Januar 19 69

Pöthig

Best.-Nr. 220 16 Haftbefehl – I. Instanz – (§§ 141 ff. StPO)   VLV Spremberg Ag 310-66-DDR-5133 I-5-20 1235

"Admission" in Cottbus

At the Cottbus penal institution, all the newly arrived prisoners first had to pass through the so-called "admissions" area. There, the infamous "Jailer of Cottbus" wreaked havoc. His name is Hubert Schulze, and he tormented, hit, and kicked many political prisoners with sadistic joy and out of his inner socialist convictions.[2] He was the "Red Terror," "RT" in short, as we Cottbus prisoners referred to him. None of us have ever forgotten him. We witnessed terrible things. There were escapists with both legs shot. They had to walk in circles on crutches with casts on both legs. "RT" was the worst of all the prison guards. We had ample opportunity to provoke him, but we tried to avoid him whenever possible. We always knew: "Those are the ones who do not know how to think; all they can do is follow orders." We saw what resulted from that, and we are still paying dearly for it.

As far as I remember, however, most of those in our cell were lucky enough to have had to spend only a brief period of time in "admissions." I myself was there for only two days. That's because behind the well-known very high walls, on the grounds of the Cottbus penal institution, there were the production facilities of two companies that urgently required workers. One of them was Anker-Werke, were armature coils were produced, and the other was Pentacon, the company that manufactured the then world famous cameras. Thus, we were quickly passed on to the regular prison so we could be used as workers for Pentacon.

2. *Hubert Schulze is only one of about 300 prison guards in Brandenburg who have been accused of abuse. But his unique brutality, that lasted for more than 20 years until the collapse of the regime, has by now been legally proven. On May 14, 1997, he was sentenced by the Cottbus regional court to two years and eight months in prison because of continuous prisoner abuse. The court imposed a sentence that was only minimally below the maximum of three years allowable under GDR law.*

Left: Arrest warrant for Gunther Liebchen, issued "because, based on the concrete actions of the accused, there is suspicion of an attempt to escape."

The "Application Cell"

Within the regular prison those political prisoners who, after their arrest and sentencing, continued to try to leave the GDR were grouped together. Many, but not all, of the inmates continued to apply for exit permits. And everyone who did ended up in the "application cell." All the cells were of different sizes. The "application cell" measured roughly five by ten yards, and there were twenty-two of us living there, all with bunk beds. Every cell had a room leader and a steward, and for about three quarters of my imprisonment I held those two posts.

I met Gunther when he was put into our cell. That meant that he, too, had tried to escape and that he continued to want to leave, and so he was one of us. He told us that he had studied medicine in

Jena and had been sentenced to two years. In the beginning, Gunther was rather withdrawn and inconspicuous. He was, after all, rather young, only twenty-three years old, and tended to keep to himself. But when one talked to him, wanted to know something, one immediately noticed that he was someone special. Gunther always did the work he had to do, as did everyone else who was at least a little intelligent. But we all realized right away: he had his own opinion on everything. There was no doubt about it. Gunther knew exactly why he was in prison; there was no turning back. When Gunther was on his own, he was pretty much preoccupied with himself; he was a well-balanced person. But when he sat at the table with us, he, of course, joined in the conversation and had interesting stories to tell.

„Man is born free, and yet is everywhere in chains." (Rousseau), photos: Florian Falcke

We "Maybugs"

Just so you can understand what we went through, to give you an idea of the atmosphere in which we lived: Inside the prison we were under the continuous watchful eye of the political police. Outside our working hours we were always locked up in our cells. The police were in charge of "security." In GDR nomenclature, the jailers and guards were called "educators," in itself schizophrenic. Well, at least they thought they could educate us through these people.

We had strict daily schedules. We were awakened at 5:00 a.m., including Saturdays, for we had to work at least 54 hours per week. The waking procedure, the unlocking of the cells in the morning alone, the steady sound of insulting drill sergeant's barks—they treated us like fifth class humans. At six we were off to work. We were marched in a group stretching out 20 to 25 yards, always watched by the police. Each wore

Behind bars, photos: Florian Falcke

a blue prisoner's uniform with thin yellow stripes on the sleeves and on the back that distinguished us as "new criminals." Almost like the Nazi-imposed Star of David. Everyone knew it. We were called "Maybugs." At four in the afternoon we were marched back. Afterwards, we had half an hour of free time to be spent in the prison yard, the only time of the day we spent outdoors. Two prisoners at a time were allowed to walk in circles next to each other. Afterward they locked us back into our cells. We had time for our personal things until 9 p.m., and at 10 p.m. the lights were turned off. After seven hours of sleep, the whole routine started over again. Every day except Sunday.

Our food was miserable and of inferior quality. Only watery soup, sometimes a few pieces of potato, always fat of inferior quality. We had no vitamins, no vegetables, no fresh fruit, nothing. The biggest problem was staying physically healthy under such conditions. Some prisoners got sick, sustaining lasting damage. Our medical care, if one can even call it that, consisted of a sick station with a lab that seemed to be from the 1800s and that was equipped with only the most primitive medical devices. After our imprisonment we all were emaciated. I weighed only about 150 pounds.

But it was not only about physical humiliation. We also had to take great care not to lose our personalities, our self-confidence. For that was their goal, to break one's self-confidence, one's personality. There were full-time employees of the state police working at the prison. The so-called "Department K 1" of the political police wanted to make sure that there always was pressure on us. You could never speak freely. There always were things one kept to oneself, because there always was the risk that someone else, to gain personal advantage, would have made certain statements, had he know certain things. Fortunately, in our cell we stood together and resisted this kind of pressure.

The fresh air area, photos: Florian Falcke

The "Tiger Cages"

The smallest offense carried with it the risk of being locked up in a detention cell. We called them "tiger cages," a prison inside prison; cells that had grates on the left and the right, no daylight. Inside them, one could take merely seven steps back and forth, all day long, that's how small the cell was. Extending one's arms, one could touch both grates with one's hands. At 10 p.m. the plank-bed was lowered down for the night, and at 5 a.m. it was locked back up again. There was only water and bread to eat. It happened that in addition to this treatment, disagreeable prisoners were locked with handcuffs to the top bars of the grates, hands above their heads, and had to stand on tiptoe for hours until their arms and legs were completely numb. At night, the thus tortured prisoners were stretched out and had one arm and one leg chained to their plank-bed. Fortunately, this happened to no one in our application cell. Prisoners were allowed to be locked in the "tiger cages" for a maximum of 21 consecutive days. The fact that these cells existed has long been denied, both in the East and the West.

One example: Once we sang a Christmas song on Christmas. Immediately, one of the "educators" who had heard us showed up. We called him "Iron Gustav," and if you are familiar with Hans Fallada's novel by the same name, you will know what he was like: stubborn, pig-headed, bowing to his superiors, kicking his inferiors. "What is going on here?"

Eberhard Fischer, a teacher, said: "Today is Christmas, so we are singing a Christmas song." – "You may not sing here." – "Why aren't we allowed to sing?" – "You are in a penal institution. It is not my fault that you are here. I pity you." – "What's one got to do with the other?" – "You have to do as you are told here. And I forbid you to sing." The situation escalated when Eberhard said to the jailer: "You know, you actually are the one to be pitied. You yourself are in a penal institution." – "Why?" And Eberhard replied: "We will leave when our time is up. But you are here for life."

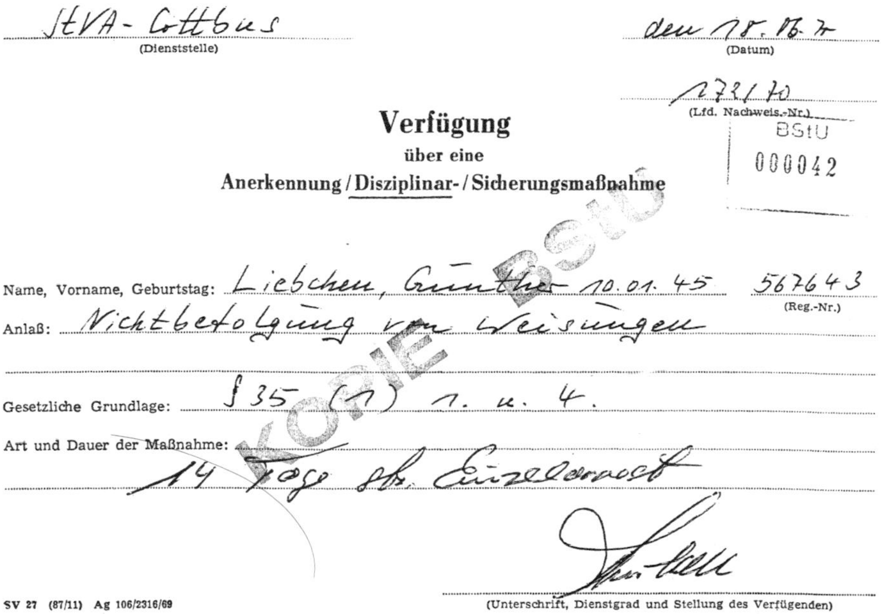

StVA - Cottbus
(Dienststelle)

den _18. 12. 7_
(Datum)

_273/70_
(Lfd. Nachweis.-Nr.)

Verfügung
über eine
Anerkennung / **Disziplinar-** / Sicherungsmaßnahme

Name, Vorname, Geburtstag: _Liebchen, Günther_ 10.01. 45   _567643_
(Reg.-Nr.)

Anlaß: _Nichtbefolgung von Weisungen_

Gesetzliche Grundlage: _§ 35 (1) 1. u. 4._

Art und Dauer der Maßnahme: _14 Tage str. Einzelarrest_

(Unterschrift, Dienstgrad und Stellung des Verfügenden)

SV 27 (87/11) Ag 106/2316/69

Order of a disciplinary measure of 14 days solitary confinement for refusal to follow orders.

But "Iron Gustav" thought of himself as a socialist, as one who educates people. He had nothing further to say and locked us up again. But the following morning at 6, the cell door opened: "Prisoner Fischer, 21 days of detention." That netted you the maximum "sentence." But Eberhard was lucky – only three days later he was prematurely released from prison. His freedom had been bought, and he went "on transport" as we called it, to the West.

I also spent 14 days in detention. Here is how that happened: One morning, as our cells were being unlocked, a fellow inmate said–stated in a rather vulgar, but factually accurate way–very quietly about the jailer on duty: "That really is the most stupid cop running around here." The jailer heard it, but could not tell who had uttered the statement, and so asked: "Who said that?" We all knew exactly who. But one "political" ratting out another one– that simply did no happen. Thus, I as the room leader was held accountable. When we returned from work that afternoon they tried to get a name from me, but I remained steadfast and was locked into the "tiger cage" that same afternoon. Why did I do that for a fellow inmate? There was a police rule: Four weeks prior to someone's scheduled release that person was not allowed to be locked up in the "tiger cage" any more, because those who came back up after two weeks without daylight and with hardly any food looked like concentration camp inmates. The "guilty" party in this case still had six weeks to go, so he would have been locked up. Thus, I agreed with him to take his place, and after I came back up after 14 days he would admit his guilt. By then, he would have only four weeks in prison remaining and would not be locked up anymore. Since I had been sentenced in spite of my innocence, I immediately filed a complaint with the prison management. We were entitled to that, but it took 13 days for the director of the prison to ask me the reason for my complaint. So I said: "Now I don't need you any more. That one day extra I can wait out." My fellow inmate kept his word. When I came up after 14 days in the dark he confessed. And the police and their treatment of us prisoners were exposed, and I had to be rehabilitated.

Working and Quotas

The entire prefabrication for the Pentacon company was located in Cottbus. Pentacon had its headquarters in Dresden, where the final assembly of the prefabricated pieces took place. At that time, the space research competition between the U.S.S.R. and the U.S.A. was on: who would send the first rockets into space, who would obtain the first photographs of the dark side of the moon. Hardly anyone knew back then that those pictures were taken with Pentacon cameras. And in the slammer, if I may say so, we inmates produced all the required parts.

Production- drilling, turning, and deburring–was located on the second floor of the factory building, the final inspection was located one floor below. Inspection was an extra department that did the final check on all parts produced. That was where Gunther worked. I was employed upstairs in production, and so we spent little time together during our working hours. Because I had come from the Zeiss company–I was fully trained as a precision engineer–and had been trained there as well, I fulfilled certain requirements. When the term of the so-called "brigadier," some kind of head worker in production, was up, the civil engineers put me in his position. Due to the different lengths of our sentences, there was a steady coming and going. Over the course of my prison term I was able to form arrangements with two of the civil engineers so that they left me alone for the most part. I had six setters working for me, and even a separate room where all the equipment for the machines was stored and where there was a desk where I keep my books. The entire production was under the administration of the prisoners, as had been customary in Nazi times.

Although we prisoners had to work for Pentacon, the work as such was a kind of "mark of distinction." For prison and work were two different worlds. The task of the police was to watch us, to get us to work and back to our cells according to plan. At work, no police were present, only the civil engineers. We had three civil engineers who were also in charge of handing out the tools. We had a rather good relationship with them. They did not know why we were in prison because they were not allowed to für den Strafgef. Liebchen Gunter.............. geb. .10.1.1945....

I.

Schwerpunkte der Erziehungs-
arbeit

Besondere Merkmale der Persönlichkeit hinsichtlich des sozial- und
Leistungsverhaltens - mögliche Erscheinungen im SV
Der SG Liebchen stammt aus einer Arbeiterfamilie.Er erreichte in der
Allgemeinbildung das Abitur.L.wurde im Elternhaus im Sinne der Politik
unserer Partei u.Staatsführung erzogen.Er war Mitglied der SED.Führte
in der FDJ an der Universität die Funktion eines FDJ Gruppensekretärs
aus.Sein bisheriges Verhalten in der Aufnahmestation sowie wärend der
U-Haft gab in keiner Weise Anlaß zu Beanstandungen.
Hauptrichtung der Erziehung:
Anknüpfend an die in der Vergangenheit positiven Entwicklung des SG ist
dem SG in den Gesprächen an Hand von Gegenwartsnahen Beispielen bewußt
zu machen,daß seine strafbare Handlung eine grobe Verletzung der Rechts-
normen unserew Staates war u.die angewndte Erziehungsmaßnahme des FE
den Strafrechtsnormen entspricht.Dem SG ist im weiteren Verlaufe der
Haft ein entsprechendes Klassenbewußtsein anzuerziehen um dadurch zu
erreichen,daß er für sein künftiges Leben in unserem sozial.Staat die
Normen u.Regeln unserer Gesellschaft beachtet u.nichtmehr straffällig
wird.

II.

Maßnahmen zur Erziehung

(auch unter dem Gesichtspunkt des Setzens einer pädagogischen Perspekt.

Unterbringung:
Der SG wird entsprechend seiner Vollzugsart im SV in einem dafür vor-
handenen Stationsbereich untergebracht.

Arbeitseinsatz:
Der SG wird entsprechend seiner Fähigkeiten u.Fertigkeiten innerhalb
der StVA - Cottbus zur Arbeit _unverlang_ eingestzt.

Staatsbürgerliche Erziehung/Bildung - Aus- und Weiterbildung -
Presse u. Literaturbezug:
Ausgehend von den Festlegungen der Hauptrichtung der Erziehung ist der
SG Liebchen unverzüglich in das System der staatsbürgerlichen Erziehung
u.Bildung einzugliedern.Ausgehend von seiner strafbaren Handlung ist dem
SG nochmals die Gefährlichkeit seiner Handlungsweise zu verdeutlichen,
wobei es besonders daruf ankommt,dem SG aufzuzeigen welchen Gefahren er
sich sowie seinen Mitmenschen durch seine Handlungsweise ausgetzt hat.
Dabei sind besonders die Schlußfolgerungen für den SG für sein künftiges
Verhalten als Bürger unseres sozial.Staates herauszuarbeiten.
Er wird für seine persönliche Weiterbildung in polit-idiol.Richtung das
ND abonnieren.

Mögliche Formen der Mitwirkung an der Erziehung:
Der SG wird auf der Grundlage des §§ 48 in XXXX Verbindung mit 44 der
ersten DB in eine entsprechende Funktion innerhalb der Station eingestzt.

Bes. Hinweise für Kontrollmaßnahmen:
1.Wie übt er seine zukünftige Tätigkeit aus.
2.Wie arbeitet er im System der staatsbürgerlichen E u.B mit.
3.Wie verhält er sich gegenüber den Angeh.d.SV
4.Welche Diskussionen führt er unter seinen Mitgefangenen.

Pers. Verbindung / entspr. der Vollzugsart:
Der SG wird entsprechend seiner Vollzugsart mit seiner Mutter in
brieflicher Verbindung bleiebn.Von einem Besuch bittet er wärend der
Zeit der Strafverbüßung Abstand zu nehmen.

Verbindung zum Betrieb u. gesellschaftl. Kräften:
Nach Klärung der Frage in Verbindung mit dem Offizier für Wiedereingl.
sofortige Verbindungsaufnahme.

III.
Regelung pers. Belange

Familien-, Wohnungsprobleme u.a. (die die Erziehung beeinträchtigen
können bzw. in Vorbereitung der Wiedereingliederung zu regeln sind)
Der SG wird nach der Haft XXXXX Wieder bei seinen Eltern wohnen.
In Verbindung mit dem Offizier für Wiedereingliederung ist zu klären,
wo der SG nach der Haft arbeiten wird.Die Vorstellungen des SG gehen
dahin,entweder im Institut für Verhaltensforschung Berlin oder als
Übersetzer in einem Med.bzw.Sprachinstitut tätig zu werden.

Teilnahme am Gottesdienst: nein

IV.
T e r m i n e

- 1. Erziehungsgespräch: .Oktober.1969..
- 2. Prüfung gem. § 349 StPO: .Februar.1969.

Aufnahmekommission:

.Stelmaszyk.   .Rosenthal.   .Hauditz.
Ltn.d.SV   Ob.-Ltn.d.SV   Ltn.d.SV

"Educational program" for Gunther Liebchen during his GDR imprisonment.
See next page for a translation.

Educational Programm

For the prisoner Liebchen Gunter................... DOB .01/10/1945.......

I.
Educational Priorities

Special personality traits with respect to social behavior and performance—possible expressions while imprisoned

Prisoner Liebchen comes from a working-class family. In general education he obtained the Abitur. At home L. was raised according to the policies of our party and our government. He was a member of the SED*. Filled the function of FDJ** group secretary within the FDJ organization at his university. His behavior during intake and while in custody has not given rise to complaints so far.

Main Direction of Education:

Using his positive development in the past as a point of reference and using current examples, the prisoner is to be made aware in formal conversations that his punishable act constituted a gross violation of the legal standards of our state, and that the educational measures applied during his imprisonment are in accordance with those legal standards. Furthermore, as his imprisonment continues, the prisoner is to be trained to develop an appropriate class-consciousness so that it may be achieved that in his future life in our social state he will follow the standards and regulations of our society and will not commit an offense again.

II.
Educational Measures

(also in terms of establishing a pedagogic perspective)

Placemant:

The prisoner will be placed according to his type of imprisonment on an appropriate ward.

Work Assignment:

In accordance with his skills and capabilities the prisoner will be assigned to work within the Cottbus Penal Institution as house worker/janitor.

Citizenship Education – Continued Education – Media and Literature Subscriptions:

Based on the stated main direction of education, prisoner Liebchen is to be integrated immediately into the system for citizenship education. Based on his punishable act, the prisoner is once more to be made aware of the dangerousness of his way of behaving. In this, it is especially important to point out to the prisoner the dangers to which he exposed himself and his fellow human beings by acting the way he did. In doing so, the prisoner's conclusions for his future behavior as a citizen of our social state need to be established.

For the purpose of his personal continued education in the area of politics and ideology, he will subscribe to the Neues Deutschland newspaper.

Possible Ways of Contributing to his Education:

Based on article 48 in conjunction with 44 of the first implementing regulation, the prisoner will be placed in an appropriate function within his ward.

Special Notes on Monitoring Measures:

1. How is he practicing his future occupation.
2. How does he cooperate in the system of citizenship education.
3. How does he behave towards the staff of the penal institution.
4. What discussions does he have with his fellow prisoners.

Personal Contact/Appropriate to Type of Imprisonment:

In accordance with the type of his imprisonment, the prisoner will remain in written contact with his mother. He has asked not to be visited while in prison.

Contact with his Place of Work and Social Forces:

After settling this question in cooperation with the rehabilitation officer, contact is to be initiated immediately.

III.

Setting of Personal Affairs

Problems with family, living quarters, etc. (that might affect his education or need to be settled in preparation of rehabilitation).
The prisoner will return to live with his parents when he has served his term. It is to be determined in cooperation with the rehabilitation officer where the prisoner will work after he has served his term. The prisoner is considering working either for the Institute of Behavioral Studies in Berlin or as a translator for a medical or language institute.

Participation in religious services: No

IV.

Dates

=	1. Educational discussion:	..October 1969..
=	2. Exam in accordance with article 349 of the Penal Code:	.February 1969..

* SED: *Sozialistische Einheitspartei Deutschlands,*
German Socialist Unity Party, party ruling the GDR during its entire existence
** FDJ: *Freie Deutsche Jugend,*
Free German Youth, party-led youth organization in the GDR

have personal conversations with us. They only wondered: There is a student, there a doctor, there's a geographer, there a teacher... If we did our work, i.e., fulfilled the quotas, then we prisoners would occasionally have the opportunity of chatting with each other. Because we were distributed across the various departments we saw relatively little of each other, but sometimes we were able to meet. We also saw the inmates from other cells at work, and so always were in touch with each other.

The work could not be called forced labor because it was possible to refuse it. There were a few prisoners who said: "For this State I am not going to do anything anymore." But as non-workers they had to stay in their cells all day and were fed even more poorly. Stubbornness was not a way of damaging the State. One had to take care to at least keep one's health intact. Because there was no use for physical wrecks in the West (after one's release).

Working had another advantage. If we worked and fulfilled the quotas, we received 20 marks a month for our personal expenses. The 20 marks were like gold to us. We were able to buy a few groceries that we normally would not get: a pack of margarine–"Goldina," more like baking fat of inferior quality, butter was completely out of the question, a little sugar or canned applesauce. That way we were able to at least stay afloat.

This is how the quotas worked: There was one for every task. But there were tasks for which the quotas were unattainable. And when someone did not make their quota the difference was taken out of their expense account. Our goal was to make sure that, as far as was possible, everyone fulfilled his quota and received his 20 marks. As brigadier, I was in a position to organize this, for I had to give an account of everything that had been produced throughout the day. I knew exactly who was fast and good with his fingers, and who was not. A roofer has different fingers than a medical lab technician. So I gave bad jobs to the clumsy ones, and good jobs to the skilled ones. For a less skilled person would not have made the norms even doing the good jobs, the jobs in which a skilled person was able to produce 16 hours worth of work in a single day. So I said to the skilled workers: "Listen, I will write down 12 hours for you, and the other four hours you let me play with." I credited those four extra hours to inmates who could not meet their quotas. Thus, we juggled and compensated in such a way that all the quotas were filled. It was "teamwork," so to speak, and outsiders were not to know, of course. Thus, we were able to reach a good level of production, and the less skilled prisoners were also able to receive their much-needed expense account deposit.

Sticking Together in a Time of Need

All I can say about this terrible time is that we made the best of it. There was no use in resisting in any way. Any resistance would have been broken and would have been only harmful to those attempting it. In other words: Resistance would not have changed a thing, not the system, and not the doctrines of socialism and communism that were propagated at the time. We did not agree with that ideology. But to fight our "educators" over this would have been senseless; we were living in different worlds. It also would have been fateful for our cell community, for we certainly would have been separated.

We prisoners always agreed and we always encouraged each other. I did not experience a single fight or argument during my entire imprisonment. And there is no one about whom I could say anything bad. There was Gerhard, a medical doctor from Leipzig, Manfred Berleth, Gunther–back then still Liebchen, Steinbeis, Reiner Teuber, Klaus Karl, Peter Hellmund, Robby, and Eberhard the teacher. I still remember most of the 22 from our application cell by name. All of them were wonderful–fine and intelligent people. One of them was a mathematical genius. During our time in prison Apollo 11 flew to the moon. Our genius worked out all the calculations and gave us mathematical lectures on gravity. And there were several chess experts. Gunther, too, often played. All of them were strong personalities who knew what they wanted, and there was a strong bond between all of us.

To this day it probably is not documented how big of an error it was to put all of us exit visa applicants into one cell. When we started our time in prison, hardly any of us knew about the political practices back then. We were not even aware of the possibility of having our freedom bought. But during our imprisonment we taught each other everything, and also helped each other, for example by writing applications, and smuggling information in and out of prison. We learned all the required tricks and passed them on to new prisoners. Nothing was ever leaked to the police or prison management. No one gave someone else away. We "politicals" all stuck together. That was something that strengthened us morally and strengthened our personalities.

We learned all the legal finesses: To officially leave the GDR one had to simultaneously apply for the deprivation of GDR citizenship and for expatriation under article 10 of the GDR penalty code. In addition, one could refer to article 213 of the UN's Human Rights Declaration according to which everyone has the right to leave his or her country–and to return to it. The GDR did not ratify the UN Declaration until 1974, but the state police never was interested, anyway. Our applications had to fulfill certain formal requirements, had to contain certain phrases and arguments, and we helped each other with those.

The state police was solely interested in the trades–a modern slave trade–and arranged everything for the Federal German government to pay for our freedom.[3] We learned from well-informed inmates who, prior to their arrests had been close to the GDR elite, that Dr. Wolfgang Vogel was the lawyer whom we had to contact in the East. Dr. Vogel arranged the trades together with West-Berlin lawyer Jürgen Stange. Between the two, there was the state police with whom Dr. Vogel, of course, had to co-operate closely.

3. The Department of Inner-German relations paid up to 100,000 German marks per prisoner into the bank accounts of the GDR. Following the "Change through Approximation" guideline, which was adopted when the Basic Treaty (on the mutual relations between the GDR and the FRG) was signed in 1972, the bought out prisoners were encouraged not to talk about their imprisonment and about inmates still in prison, for they would otherwise complicate their release. This attitude humiliated many prisoners once again, for they were not able to produce any proof of the injustices that had been done to them. The judgments and letters of application could only be looked into after the downfall of the GDR regime, when the files of the state police were opened.

Our Information Service

As prisoners, we were cut off from the outside world. However, information was the most important thing in phrasing exit applications correctly, in getting them to the right places, and in learning who had succeeded in leaving and who had not. For this, we had a great information service. This knowledge was our "performance review," so to speak, and we could adapt our application letters accordingly. When the police came to take someone away, we checked–inconspicuously, of course–where they were taking him. As soon as the police were gone, we asked questions. Then we were told, most of the time, "Yes, he went on a transport." We immediately passed on everything we knew to everyone.

Our outside information service was operated through "spokespeople." Whenever someone had permission to speak to an outsider, we agreed: "If there is something to be passed on, let the person know who is going to be the spokesperson (i.e., will have an outside visitor), and when the moment is right, it will be passed on." That is how we learned what had happened to our former fellow inmates. Within four to six weeks we would know when someone had gone "on transport." And so we were always up to date. Of Klaus, for example, we learned through his "accomplice." He was visited by his mother, who told him: "Klaus has made it to the West." Klaus had informed his mother who in turn had told the mother of his "accomplice," and she had come to our spokesperson. And so we learnt of it. And this is how I knew what was happening when I myself had applied for my exit visa.

If we had more complex information that could not be passed on orally, we still had to get it outside somehow. Legally, that was not possible. So we used cigarette paper and wrote on it with a very fine pencil in the tiniest handwriting possible. Then, secretly, we obtained cables from an electrician and removed the copper wire that was about 1/12 of an inch in diameter. The cigarette paper was tightly rolled up and inserted into the insulating cover of the cable. A maximum of four cigarette papers would fit inside. The outer ends of the plastic were melted shut with a cigarette lighter and thus could be carried in one's mouth, hidden above the upper

STRAFVOLLZUGSANSTALT
Cottbus
Vollzugsgeschäftsstelle

Strafvollzugsanstalt Cottbus · 75 Cottbus · Bautzener Straße 140/141

Frau
Gertrud Liebchen

66   G r e i z
Am Röth 1

Ihre Zeichen	Ihre Nachricht vom	Unsere Zeichen	75 Cottbus Bautzener Straße 140/141
−	13.08.69	60.50.11 Wi.-3	20.08.1969 4741/69

Betreff:

Sehr geehrte Frau Liebchen !

Ihrer Bitte entsprechend erhalten Sie die
Erlaubnis, Ihren Sohn Gunther am Sonnabend,
dem 30.08.69, in der Zeit von 08,00 - 12,00
Uhr für die Dauer von 30 Minuten, zu sprechen.

Dieses Schreiben gilt als Besuchserlaubnis.

Hochachtungsvoll

Haßel

Durchgeführt am 30.08.69

b.w.

Fernruf:
42 41 · 42 42

Bankverbindung:
Industrie- und Handelsbank der DDR Cottbus, Konto-Nr. 8 078

gums. During the obligatory body search before every visit–"Open your mouth!"–they were never discovered.

I, too, for example, had information that had to get to Dr. Vogel. My mother took care of that for me. During one of her visits, at an opportune moment, I took the cable mantle with the information inconspicuously from my mouth and passed it on to her. Then I said, and the attending officer was able to hear, "Open the can carefully at home. And then let Heinz know once you know what is going on." Unnoticed, we passed on information in such mundane statements. My mother knew what she had to do, and she passed on all my information to Dr. Vogel in this manner. While I was in prison, many who had to communicate with the outside used this method. So did Gunther, who communicated with Dr. Vogel through his father in this way. That was his only chance to orchestrate the buying of his freedom.

Gunther–Soul of the Cell

We had experiences that are unforgettable. They really treated us harshly. All of us suffered pretty much in the same way, and during our imprisonment most of us were able to deal with it. But there were some who were broken; not everyone was as tough as we were. But now, afterward, it keeps coming back. I have had nightmares for a long time, still have them. And that will always remain the same. All of us were only in our early or mid-20s. When you have to go through something like that because of nothing–just because you could not identify with the state and did not want anything to do with it–when you are punished like that, you will wonder whether you are really such a great danger to mankind. Everyone I know from those days has made his way and has achieved something. Isn't that a sign that they locked up the wrong ones? Locking up the right ones, that has been forgotten, and many of them are receiving fat pensions on top of it.

Left: Visiting permit for Gunther Liebchen's mother.

There are very few positive moments from the years of imprisonment that I can report on. The only ones worth remembering are when all of us were locked into the cell together and had time to do things. This was only the case on Sundays, when we did not have to go to work. But just those moments ensured our survival, especially our mental survival. And Gunther played a big part in it. That showed how special he was.

There actually were only two types of entertainment. Some Sunday afternoons we were allowed to watch TV. The programs then consisted of children's shows–that was all we were allowed to see, and Gunther never bothered to watch. I cannot remember ever having seen him there; he was not interested. Watching TV was supposed to be a benefit, inasmuch as we were able to look at something other than just the four bare walls in the cell.

The other form of entertainment was reading. There was a library on the locked hall between the cells. We were allowed to read–but only those of us who had fulfilled their quotas. We were allowed to borrow books for a week or 14 days: biographies of artists such as Mozart, the child prodigy, and some science books. Those were the books available, but we would not have read anything else. Had they offered us the "Communist Manifesto," no one would have touched it. Of course, the selection of books was limited to those acceptable under the dictatorship; there were none that were critical of it.

I read a lot about Einstein. You cannot falsify Einstein. Gunther, too, read many books. He often withdrew from the rest of us. He always had something to keep him busy, and we did not always know what it was. Certainly, he kept some things to himself because he thought the others would not be interested. Others, too, kept their minds busy. I myself experienced it when I spent those 14 days in the basement, without daylight: One tries to solve problems one had not solved before. One works on it. And I believe that that is what Gunther did, too. He probably had visions and ideas on which he worked mentally that kept him going.

But whenever something really bad happened, Gunther was there. Before his imprisonment, he had been dancing in competitions or at least in a club. On several of those Sundays he taught us the impetus, the special waltz step for the slow waltz. He demonstrated it to us again and again, maintaining perfect posture—it was great. On several Sundays we practiced for three or four hours. That was something Gunther was good at. He was able to entertain us, to drag us along when we were, once again, mentally down. Those moments were not exactly rare. Gunther was especially pre-destined for this task. Every time the "morale of the troops" was low, he contributed to lifting it up again.

Gunther knew how to distract us. He actually had one skill—and in the beginning I thought it was, well, I would not say, quackery, but I simply could not believe it. Gunther knew how to hypnotize. Up until then I had not even known that such a thing existed. Gunther would say: "Listen. I am going to pick someone now." Then he looked each of us in the eye, chose one, and had him sit at a table. Then he gave his introduction: "You have to do everything I tell you. You must not oppose me. You must listen to me, and think about what I tell you. You have to mentally follow everything I say." Then he proceeded to tell a beautiful story in which he spoke, in the warmest tones, of chocolate. The seated person followed him in everything he said. We all watched with excitement. Then Gunther held out to the seated person, instead of chocolate, a piece of—and this is true, a true story, and where would we have gotten chocolate in prison, anyway?—soap. Then he asked him to taste the chocolate. The seated person would actually eat the soap without making a face. No rejection, no nothing. With apparent pleasure he ate the small pieces of soap. It simply could not be true. Then Gunther brought him out of the hypnosis and it was as if nothing had hap-pened. The seated person would ask: "What, I ate soap?" And could not believe it. But that was what had happened.

I kept telling myself: "That is impossible." Because I had this semi-pri-vate working room as a brigadier, I once was able to test Gunther: "Come up with me today and do that to me. I cannot believe that you can hypno-tize me." And he came, had me sit on a chair, and said: "You really have to believe and follow what I say in your mind. You have to hold on to it." I listened to his calm voice and I slowly realized that I was following along with what he was saying, that I was disappearing, that my mind was growing weak. But that I could not afford to capitulate–after all, at any minute someone could have walked in on us. After ten minutes I was really close to passing out, and I said to Gunther: "Okay, that's it. I believe you." And indeed: just one more minute and I would have been hypnotized.

From Gunther I learned with my own senses that something like that is possible. But I do not know where he had learned it, how he had gotten interested in it. Gunther, with his calm being, took us on a trip with him. His voice, his special way of talking, the way he chooses his words–recently, I spoke to him on the phone from Singapore, and when I heard his voice, I immediately knew: "Yes, Gunther, it is you."

Or at night, when we could not sleep because something had happened that had troubled all of us very much, we would say to Gunther: "Tonight, you have to make sure we sleep." And he was actually able to hypnotize us collectively. Gunther asked us to breathe regularly. Then he told us a nice story that we had to follow in our minds, and then we would automatically fall asleep. Gunther made it happen. He pulled us up from quite a few lows and gave us back our strength. I will never forget that. He was something like the soul of our cell. A person with many ideas. And, therefore, he had a lot to give, was able to do a lot of good, with his entire being. We still are grateful to him for that today.

The End of Imprisonment

Every release happened relatively inconspicuously; only people in the immediate surroundings of the released person would notice. When someone "went on transport," it was always up to the police to take care of it. Releases happened only rarely at night or on the weekends. In most cases the police came to one's workplace: "Prisoner so-and-so, you'll be coming with us!" And then he had to go, immediately. It was never possible to say good-by, for we no longer were allowed to talk to each other. They would then go over to our cells to get our personal belongings. At night, when we returned from work, there was nothing left to see of the released. Occasionally the police would show up on a Sunday. The cell was unlocked: "Prisoner; you'll be coming with us! Gather your belongings!" And then we knew: "Ah, another transport!" There was no time for long good-byes.

I, too, stayed until the last day of my sentence and was released prior to Gunther on May 27, 1970. All the others, including Gunther, were bought by the West or were directly released to the West via Karl-Marx-Stadt, where they were nourished for four weeks so they would not look too miserable when they arrived in the West.

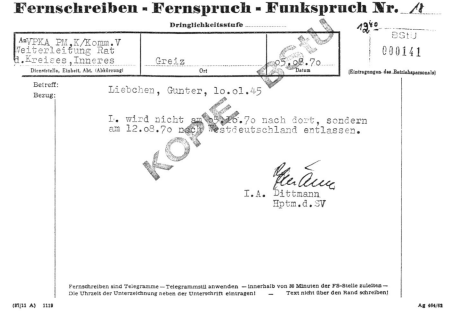

Telex stating that "L. will not be released on 10/05/1970 to there (Greiz) but on 08/12/1970 to West Germany."

Only Gerhard and I, we were the only ones from the application cell who were released back into the GDR. Why the state police would not agree to the trade in our cases? No one knows how those things worked. Of course, it was better for those prisoners who got to the West directly from Cottbus. They did not lose as many years.

Gerhard and I continued to work on our applications to leave. We stayed in close contact. From him I had learned that he had been released two or three months after me; we had exchanged an address where we would meet. After his release we met in Leipzig in August of 1970. He obtained permission to leave in 1972; Dr. Vogel had arranged it with the state police. Gerhard briefly informed me: "I now have my exit permission. Keep pushing it, you, too, will finally get it." He proved himself to be a nice person. He kept writing to me from the West and encouraged me. We remained friends for a long time.

After almost three years of waiting, I, too, finally had mail from Dr. Vogel. He worked hard for my exit permission and that of my current wife. I saw him a total of three times between 1970 and 1975. He worked on it until the end, although he never guaranteed me that I would be freed. All he would say was: "I am trying my best." Whether that would work out or not, that was another question. He was not allowed to make any promises. But with time, I learned to interpret the various statements he made, and so, in spite of all the setbacks, I continued working on plans to leave the GDR.

During the time that I spent in the GDR until I finally was able to leave, I met my current wife. Our first son also was born there. But we were not allowed to marry in the GDR. My wife's father was a political scientist and worked for the county administration of the party. Because I did not give up my plans to emigrate and did not make any attempts to integrate myself into society, I had a lot of problems at work and in similar situations. I was treated as if I were state enemy no. 1, and connections to state enemies were not only disliked but were actively discouraged. They told my now father-in-law, who had to constantly show up at the state police to give statements: "Your daughter need not even go to the registrar's office. We will not approve of her wedding." And I said: "Well, then we will just have to get married once we are on the other side." And that is how it all turned out. In March of 1975 I finally was allowed to leave. And one and a half years later, in September of 1976, my wife and my son also were given exit visas, officially, as part of the program for "family reuninfications," but in reality they also had been bought out via Dr. Vogel. And with that, we finally left the GDR behind us.

Found Again

Ever since I arrived in the Federal Republic I tried again and again to find Gunther. But I never succeeded, because I had wrong information. I thought that he had gone to Lübeck, and I did not know that he had taken his wife's name. So we lost each other. Through my son, Tobias, who learned through his university studies in Heidelberg of this novel plastination method, I heard again of Gunther. I, too, was very much interested in the modern technology. But my son and I initially did not realize that we were talking about one and the same person. Not until I saw a TV discussion about BODY WORLDS and body donors did I recognize Gunther in "Gunther von Hagens." Ever since then we have been in touch again, and sometime we will meet in person, so I will be able to express to him my recognition and admiration for his unique scientific work and his research for us and the following generations.

On the occasion of his birthday, I and my family would like to tell Gunther the following: May his creative power last, so that he will, for many years to come and with great joy, continue to do what is so meaningful to so many people. Everything that he wishes for should come true. When Gunther reads this article he will remember our time in Cottbus, and he will recognize how much he achieved even back then. I hope he will be able to enjoy the fact that the hard time in prison also had a somewhat positive side. The experience there certainly made an impact on him, and made him even stronger in the face of all the resistance he had to overcome over the years. He probably developed his fighting spirit in Cottbus. There, in his early youth, he experienced things that gave him staying power for later in life. Of that I am convinced, especially in view of the far-fetched accusations and the defamation against him. When they threatened to arrest him in England, he said that he was not afraid, for he already had been in prison in the GDR. And I said: "That's Gunther. He has his opinions. Just as back then. He will not be moved." And that I find very admirable.

Now that I know how his life has gone here in the Federal Republic, I am twice happy for him. I am happy about everyone who went through what we went through over there and then made it here, achieved something, stood his ground, and acquired some wealth. All those whom I know from our time together have succeeded at that. But what Gunther has created: He, of course, will go down in history.

As told to Dietmar Töpfer

Engraved stone plate commemorating the "innocent victims of political persecution,"
listing the years during which the Nazi regime ruled Germany (1933–1945) and the
years during which the GDR existed (1945–1989).

Dr. Wolfgang Koser was Head of the Reaction Resin Application Technology Department at BASF AG in Ludwigshafen, Germany, until 1993. He studied chemistry at Stuttgart university where in 1961 he earned his doctorate with a thesis concerning his experimental work on the synthesis of natural substances. He started his career in the mineral oil industry that same year, where he first worked in research in Germany, than in development and applications technology in France and in the U.S. After his return to Germany in 1967, he became chief executive officer of a medium-sized enterprise in the chemical industry in Wiesbaden. In 1969 he joined the Reaction Resin Application Technology Department at BASF. He has authored several patents, industrial designs, and other publications, and in 1980 was elected to the board of The Federation of the German Composite Industry (AVK), where he was in charge of the technology department until 1994.

Wolfgang Koser

From the Beginnings

First Encounter

"There is someone here to see you—he is wearing shorts, an unbuttoned shirt, and health sandals, no socks. He is carrying a wicker basket." The call came from Mr. Kaufmann, back then, head receptionist in the BASF high-rise. He was used to welcoming CEOs, directors, and managers of our major clients, dressed in dark double-breasted suits, and to directing them to the sales or application technology departments. "If that is Dr. von Hagens, it is okay—we are expecting him." A few minutes later our secretary, Ms Lindhof, poked her head in and said: "There is a gentleman here to see you, is that okay?" And there he was, unconventional, but dead-sure of what he wanted. That was in the fall of 1976, and Gunther still is the same—unconventional and dead-sure—except that nowadays he wears a hat.

Gunther had gotten stuck in his experiments with plastics and apparently was concerned that he would not be able to proceed on his own. From his towel-covered basket, he produced organs and tissue parts that had been impregnated with synthetic resins but that did not satisfy his expectations and requirements. Even so, they were—considering the usually poor knowledge in the field of polymer chemistry to be found in physicians—surprisingly well done. We discussed possible improvements, and I led Gunther into the application technology laboratory, where one of our experienced technicians demonstrated to him the proper processing of synthetic resins. Highly satisfied, with new knowledge and some resin samples in his wicker basket, he returned to his Anatomical Institute at

Heidelberg university. Two weeks later, Gunther was in touch again. There still were some uncertainties and problems with hardening. The resin samples simply would not dry properly in a wet environment and inside the fine blood vessels. Another visit to the lab was urgently requested. We discussed the mission of application technology departments in industrial chemical companies. Broadly speaking, I explained that it was to support development that would, as quickly as possible, lead to shipments by the tanker load. In spite of this, I agreed to another visit. It was three more weeks until Gunther called again. The hardening of the polymers still was not working as desired.

Joint Projects

I simply could not justify, to my co-workers, a third visit by Gunther to the lab. They had been instructed to direct inventors and artists who did not represent a large market potential to specially equipped universities and

The results of hundreds of experiments

sales partners. That I did not want to do to Gunther. Besides, I was interested in his work because of his interdisciplinary approach that, at the time, was a rarity in the German research community. And I was intrigued by the idea of working with an extremely motivated, highly innovative, unconventional, and yet very personable scientist. Thus, I suggested to Gunther that we meet at his anatomy lab on a weekend and conduct some experiments together. This was the beginning of a long series of weekends we spent at Gunther's lab–where he also received generous support from the BASF department of university supplies.

On such days, we worked from morning until night, breaking only around noon, briefly, to open a can of peas or the like. Over the following weeks, Gunther, with his untiring exploratory urge, would have conducted hundreds of additional experiments, and whenever I showed up on a weekend, I was greeted by a laundry basket filled with glass vials. The vials contained synthetic resins in all states of hardening, in all colors, with and without organ and tissue samples. Together, we selected the samples that appeared useful both from an anatomical and a practical point of view, and discussed the next steps. Then we would begin the next series of experiments or work on a larger batch.

Ancillary Devices

Once the first plastinates of exhibition quality could be reproduced without errors, Gunther tried to improve the plastination procedures. When he had achieved results that were–within the limitations of the institute–satisfactory and also reproducible, he turned to lowering costs. Here, too, Gunther's inventiveness knew no limits. Everything he spotted–on his way to the institute, while shopping, or in his kitchen–was considered with regard to its usefulness for plastination services and, if appropriate, was acquired on the spot. Thus, it was not surprising to find a meat slicing machine from a butcher shop, glue clamps from the carpenter's, and, taken from a junkyard, the back windows of a Renault R4 in the anatomy lab, side by side with the traditional tools of the trade.

First Public Interest

His success proved Gunther right. As early as April 1977 he exhibited his first specimens on occasion of the annual conference of the German Anatomical Society in Aachen. The media became aware of Gunther, probably not completely without his help, and in May 1977 the weekly news magazine *Der Spiegel* reported in its science section, "Prisma," to the general public on the work of "Heidelberg pathologist Gunther von Hagens."

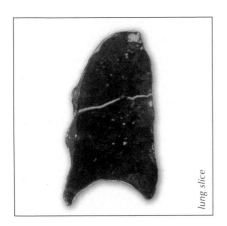

lung slice

smal intestine

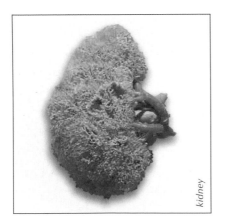

kidney

embryo of a chicken

The first plastinates from Heidelberg (1977)

Filing a Patent, Publications

Towards the end of 1976, after lengthy considerations prompted mostly by the high cost involved, Gunther eventually decided to file a patent. When the selection of examples seemed satisfactory and the patent attorneys had no further requests, he filed his patent application with what was then the German Patent Office on March 9, 1977. From then on he published his scientific work in German and foreign medical journals, referring to it as "surface preserving impregnation of biological objects with plastics."

"Whole-Body Plastinates"

While working together in the lab, we, of course, "fantasized" as well. Gunther always was (and still is) full of ideas relating to polymer chemistry, process engineering, and plastination, of course, and other areas as well. Also, he wanted to become good customer of BASF. In that context, I remember our discussion about driving to Africa in a well-equipped polyester tanker truck in order to preserve an elephant using the perfusion method. But never during all those conversations did we utter the one term that today is the basis for Gunther's success and reputation: "whole-body plastinates." Even though we had the first whole-body plastinate in front of us, namely that of a chicken embryo, we never even thought of the term.

Commercialization

It is well known that research and development are expensive. Add to that patent applications in various countries, and the salary of a scientific assistant working in academia will not go very far. Cutting back on research was out of the question, so Gunther soon had to consider commercialization of his inventions. Thus, he offered the use of his patent to companies that produce plastic reproductions of biological objects for educational purposes. He sent them his most beautiful samples and personally presented his novel specimens. All of the companies contacted recognized the educational advantages of the plastinates and were very interested. However, no agreement was ever signed.

BIODUR

Instead, Gunther received support from what was then the German Federal Department for Research and Technology (BMFT) that enabled him to occasionally buy a new hardening oven for his university lab or to hire a technician. The financial problem thus was alleviated, but far from solved. In his many publications, Gunther not only described the procedures he employed, such as infusion, perfusion, and impregnation, but also gave details of the synthetic resins used, the plastics mixtures he developed, and even his commercial sources. His declared goal was to enable any anatomist, any pathologist, and ultimately any medical student to produce his or her own plastinates. His creed was: "To each child his or her placenta." (1977)

That was where I saw an opportunity for Gunther to make a little money, namely, by selling the resins and resin mixtures along with the ancillary devices required for the procedures. Gunther immediately accepted my idea. During one of our long nights in Grünstadt, we "invented" the name BIODUR together with Dr. Cornelia von Hagens. From then on, all of Gunther's publications referred to the Heidelberg company BIODUR, and to the products available under the new brand name, such as BIODUR E–10, BIODUR P–35, BIODUR S–28.

BIODUR actually turned out to be a worldwide success with anatomical institutes, significantly simplifying the work of many physicians and taxidermists. They no longer needed to ask many different companies for minute amounts of substances, but now had a one-stop shopping source for plastination materials, where they would receive the latest, improved products in the desired small amounts.

Other Activities from the Early Days

In July 1979 Gunther started teaching anatomists and students from all over the world at plastination workshops in Heidelberg. This educational offer was enthusiastically welcomed and yielded not only more recognition, but also some money for further research. But Gunther neither shied away from the less profitable activity of the founding of the International Society for Plastination nor from organizing conferences. They, in turn, led to many requests for plastination of specimens sent to him from around the world. When the number of these requests continued to grow, Gunther suggested, to the Heidelberg university, if memory serves me right, that an institute for the plastination of biological materials be founded.

Closing Remarks

The continuation of this story will be told by competent authors in the following articles. I supported Gunther in a technical manner during his early plastination work, wherever necessary for him and possible for me. Other colleagues, experts in other fields of plastic research, working for other companies, advised Gunther as well. But without his tireless exploratory urge, without his unshakable belief in the technical–and eventually commercial–success of his ideas, his worldwide plastination endeavors never would have become the overwhelming success that they are today.

Klaus Tiedemann, born in 1944, is University Professor at the Institute of Anatomy and Cell Biology I of the Ruprecht Karls University at Heidelberg, Germany. In 1977 in Heidelberg, after a promising start (doctorate in veterinary medicine at 24, Habilitation in veterinary histology and embryology at 31 in Berlin) he joined the ranks of those whose names will not be registered in the great book of history. Self-critically he sees himself as a "VUP," a Very Unimportant Person, in Gunther's terminology.

Klaus Tiedemann

Inventor–Entrepreneur– Exhibition Producer–Gambler

Prolog

Gunther von Hagens turns 60–a heavy blow for an adolescent. I know, for I just experienced something similar. One eye already focusing on retirement, I sometimes wonder what I did wrong in life. No, even at 30 I no longer aspired to become famous, rich, or powerful. But it certainly would have been smarter to have started collecting data early and to have written a book *about* Gunther than to publish a book *with* him. "Profile of a Gambler," would have been the subtitle. But I do not have an archive, nor diaries or old appointment books. And because I seldom can accurately date anything from the past, I am not a good biographer. What I remember is of a more anecdotal nature and is hard to put in chronological order. On the other hand, unlike some biographers, I have accompanied Gunther's development for 20 years, from my arrival at the Heidelberg Anatomical Institute in 1977 (when I came from Berlin as a veterinary anatomist to accept a professorship here) until Gunther left the Anatomical Institute in 1996.

And yet I hesitate, because during the long years in academia I, too, have mutated from an uninhibited, natural person to one harboring doubts about almost everything. That's because my very balanced homage, that also was a critical assessment, and which was published in *"Schöne neue Körperwelten"* (Brave New Body Worlds) by Klett-Cotta Verlag in 2001, apparently has never been read by my mostly anti-Gunther colleagues.

Still, in writing about Gunther I would rather not repeat myself, because that is how one makes a name for oneself in publishing, by peeing again and again in the same corner until it stinks. I do not like to adapt, to fit in; if I publish something, I have to have fun with it, or I will not do it. I am not eager for royalties, I do not need publications for my career advancement or my list of publications, and neither do I have to prove that I am a smart little guy.

But it is fun to once again write about my former lab neighbor. For an entire book on Gunther, that would not be enough. I am–as always with Gunther–only contributing. Gunther has become a person of public interest and has the means of beautifying his own biography, starting with retouching his old photographs so that they show his Beuysian hat.

Beginnings and Periods

My encounter with Gunther resembled that of two celestial bodies with elliptical orbits: Initially far away from him, I soon entered his gravitational field, than ran in parallel with him and finally moved away from him again. For one decade, from 1979 to 1989, I spent so much time with Gunther that my wife jokingly suggested that I had a homoerotic relationship with him. During those fat years Gunther was one of my best friends. A break, initiated by me, came in 1989. I was no longer ready to be involved in plastination all the time, including weekends, days, and nights. Gunther was so shocked that initially he wanted to throw away all specimens and quit plastination. Over the course of the following days we managed to transform our relationship into a coexistence with boundaries. Thus, I was able to work relatively independently with head slices which were published in 1993 in a book that was as beautiful as it was nearly unsellable.

In retrospect, I see three long periods in Gunther's development. The first one, in the 1980s, I would like to title "Inventor." I enjoy reporting about that time; it was preceded by a period in the late 1970s during which Gunther generally was taken to be a chemist and was in close contact with a chemist-friend of his at BASF. The period of the 1990s deserves the title "Entrepreneur" and was accompanied by a certain estrangement.

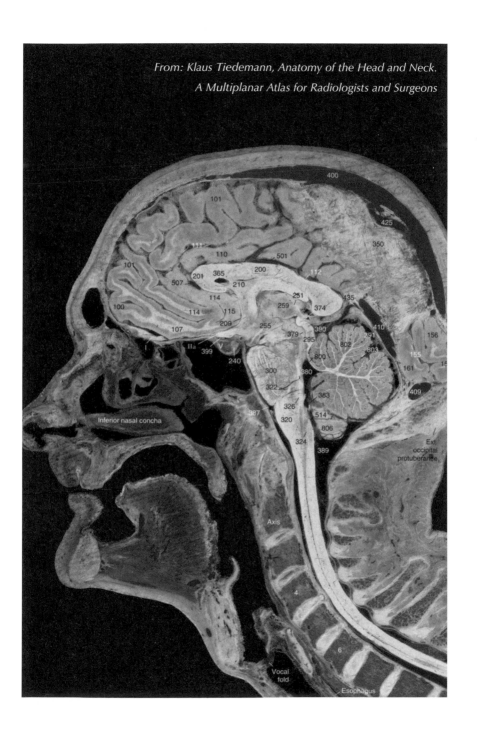

The Mannheim BODY WORLDS exhibition (in 1997) was a turning point. With that exhibition, in my eyes, the period amply described by others as "Exhibition Producer" began. Gunther would set the starting date for this period three years earlier, but we in Germany did not hear that much of his initial exhibitions in Japan. *Tempora mutantur, et nos mutamur in illis* (The times change and we change with them.) For me, it is easy to determine exactly when Gunther was no longer the same: ever since he began walking around with his hat, had people address him as professor, and used the daily revenues as a computational measure.

He used to run his hand over his head, saying that he was standing by his bald plate. And he did not mind not being a professor, for his status as scientific assistant awarded him significantly more freedom. The intellectual narrowness in the minds of quite a few professors of anatomy, that he encountered during various conferences, made it hard for him to completely identify with this particular human species. His attempt, carried out over several years, to promote his technology through exhibitions and presentations at anatomical conferences, came to a standstill after the International Congress of Anatomists in London in 1985 that we attended together. In

People waiting in line to see the BODY WORLDS exhibition in Mannheim, Germany

April of 1987, luxuriously equipped with a work visa, I traveled alone to the Congress of Anatomists in Leipzig, East Germany, carrying with me plastinated slices of heads as advertising media for plastination, so to speak. I presented these slices in front of a light box that was attached to a wall, its power cord hidden behind it for aesthetic reasons. An older East German colleague reverently touched the lit milk glass pane with his fingertip and asked how it was possible for this field to be glowing. Immediately, I was reminded of the mean interpretation of the German acronym for the German Democratic Republic that I had once heard from the left-wing singer-songwriter Wolf Biermann: DDR–*Der Dumme Rest* (the stupid rest).

Looking for a Role Model

Back to the time when anyone who came into contact with this guy who was obsessed by his invention was touched by him. Unlike today, back then he seemed to me to be searching for something. He was searching for a role model, he wanted to follow a hero. Initially, that role was filled by Professor Wilhelm Kriz with his expert knowledge, his leadership qualities, and his didactic capabilities. Then he noted minor weaknesses in his model, for example, when Kriz thought himself incapable of improving his English, especially his pronunciation. Maintaining one's knowledge of foreign languages always has been important to Gunther, and he dreaded poor pronunciation. With me, he discussed semantic details such as the meaning of "seaborn," both with and without an ending "e." Or we would conduct a quiz by blindly opening an English dictionary, pointing to a term, and taking turns in quizzing the other. From his motorized adjustable double bed he operated–also to maintain language proficiency–three TV sets. One showed two German stations at once, another with an additional antenna pointed towards France, and the third enabled him to receive US Army programming–long before the blessings of cable and satellite dish reception. Years later, when he had a professional need for it, he brushed up on his Russian with the help of a Walkman. He conducts his studies of Chinese by the same method, complemented by private lessons, with dogged determination.

The next role model for the young assistant, temporarily, was the Heidelberg pathologist Professor Wilhelm Doerr, into whose institute Gunther switched from anatomy in 1977. Doerr was a fascinating patriarch, a charismatic original with a talent for acting, in a way a kind of living fossil. Gunther wrote down every reference that Doerr quoted in his lectures with impressive precision, suggesting immense knowledge and a gigantic memory. His attempts to read up on those publications failed, the reference information simply was wrong. Had the old gentleman been bluffing, or had he confused the data over the years? In any case, he was playing tricks in his lectures. He gave the impression that the histological sections that were projected onto the wall came from the very body that the students had just dissected that morning. However, histological preparations usually took much longer, the illustrative section was years old and came from a similar case. Doerr, by the way, felt tricked by Gunther's name change (from Dr. Liebchen to von Hagens) and was completely unreceptive to it. Doerr, the seemingly tireless researcher, who would leave notes on the desks of his assistants ("Didn't find you at your work space at 5 (a.m.)"), and who would be at the institute until late at night, had a secret that Gunther revealed: Around lunch time, he would go home unnoticed and rejuvenate by means of an extended nap. In order to suggest their late night presence, his subjugated assistants simply left the lights on. Driving past the pathology institute, one assumed that someone was still working there. One of the cleaning ladies was secretly in charge of turning off the lights. When she was not at work one day, the scam was exposed. After about half a year, Gunther returned to the Anatomical Institute and handed me a list of medical malpractice incidents which he had observed at the pathology dissection table. These incidents served as a welcome introduction to clinical life for his anatomy classes, and were intended to convince his students of the importance of solid anatomical knowledge.

For a brief period of time, I believe Gunther even saw me as a role model. He liked my knowledge of comparative anatomy (that I had acquired through my veterinary education), of terminology, and of histology. Back then, Gunther did not have a firm grasp of microscopic anatomy. When I tested him with unusual specimens (e.g., astrocytes from an elephant) he looked at them and said spontaneously "It's not liver; liver I would recognize immediately." At the same time he was attracted to old microscopes and old microscopic specimens, which, on one occasion, resulted in an awkward situation for him. I was in the middle of a histology class when Gunther rushed in through the door connecting my classroom to his and asked for help because his students had begun laughing at him. I followed him and took a look at the slide in question, which was projected on the wall. Gunther had claimed that it showed an esophagus, but attentive students had detected cilia and complained that that was not possible. Gunther insisted that it was an esophagus, he himself had taken the picture of the specimen. The puzzle was quickly solved: The specimen came from an old box of class materials and was from a frog, and frogs do have cilia instead of the squamous epithelium seen in humans. There was spontaneous applause.

I did not remain a role model for long. During his last visit to my house, in 2002, Gunther looked at my walls that are covered with a tile collection and noted: "Well, one thing is obvious to me: you are not an anatomist." Why not, for heaven's sake? What does a true anatomist have to have on his walls? Body parts, or at least copperplate etchings of old skeletons? No, don't tell me, I do not need to know everything, to understand everything; I do not look inside hearts.

The Early Years

During the early years of plastination, Gunther would ask others for their opinions a lot, more like 20 than 2 times a day. Which plastics mixture looks clearer, should the sawed out slice have rounded edges or not, should the labeling be on the left or right? How much, do you think, would a horseback rider pay for a plastinated horse's hoof that he could use as an ashtray?

In the late 1970s my research interests were oriented towards embryological electronmicroscopic work. The only points of contact with Gunther, who had already made the essential inventions, came about because I had learned about various injection techniques and the assembly of a specimen collection for exhibition purposes in veterinary medicine. While waiting for embryos to reach the developmental stages I required, there were lean periods that drove me into Gunther's lab. Because of my trips to the slaughterhouse, I had access to animal matter that could be used for plastination experiments. At the same time I was interested in the production of educational materials. One of my first specimens I still use today in all of my dissection classes. It is the heart of a calf with a patent oval foramen. It was made by PEM technology (polymerization emulsion), and its only disadvantage is that it is breakable. At the Congress of Anatomists in Hamburg, Germany, in 1981, Gunther gave a paper on plastination methods and slice plastination, and I spoke about the ultrastructure of the mesonephros and about "Plasticization of Heart Specimens and their Use in Teaching." We both expected that we would be able to persuade other institutes of the advantages of this technology, but

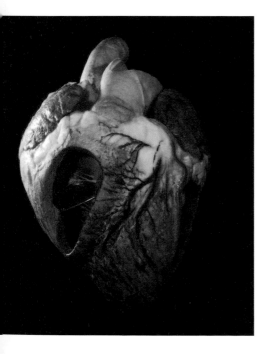

this was only rarely the case, and only as a result of great efforts. Specimens from this extremely fertile time are still displayed today in the showcase of the Heidelberg Anatomical Institute, e.g., the impressive cow's heart that was presented to Professor Hermann Hoepke on his 90th birthday in May of 1979.

But there were spectacular failures, too. I had spent two days dissecting a not yet fixed monkey that we had been given as a present from the zoology department. It was to be im-

"Heart of a calf"

pregnated with PEM in about 30 pounds of plastic. The next morning we found that the exothermic reaction of this large batch (we never had tried it at this order of magnitude before) had led to a very quick and complete hardening—only the monkey's extremities stuck out of a white block of plastic; the precious specimen was completely useless. I also have feelings of guilt when I remember the fetus of a black rhinoceros, another gift from the zoology department, about the size of a dachshund. Owing to my carelessness, its underside remained forever marred by a grid pattern that had been impressed into its skin by a draining grate.

Skin-covered objects, such as fetuses, are hard to impregnate because the very viscous silicone barely penetrates the skin, even under vacuum conditions. To avoid significant shrinking, silicone has to be injected through the orifices of the body, which is very difficult to do because a hand syringe cannot be compressed strongly enough. A mechanic offered to build a small, motor driven pump for this purpose. As talented as he was, however, he misestimated the power and the dimensions required for the cogwheels for the gear ratio so thoroughly that the pump was useless and remained so, even after two attempts to fix it. It cost Gunther about one month's salary. So as not to hurt the mechanic's feelings, Gunther did not complain again, but took the gear part of the pump home, where he turned it into the drive for a cable car running up a string—an expensive toy.

Gunther's experiment in which he tried to operate a vacuum chamber almost the size of a coffin, made from stainless steel plates welded together, was not well thought out. A safety glass plate about an inch think served as its cover. When the vacuum had reached about one tenth of normal atmospheric pressure, the glass plate, which had bent considerably by then, burst with the sound of a hand grenade and covered us with glass crumbs like the ones seen in traffic accidents. Later, I calculated that the force on the plate had been the equivalent of almost 15,000 pounds. A much stronger, much more expensive, and prohibitively heavy glass plate was acquired before Gunther implemented the much better idea of reducing the free span of the plate by inserting a removable crossbar.

The next mishap befell us on a weekend, in the basement of the institute, in some kind of storage room. In addition to reprints, snow tires, and empty coffins that were made from raw wood at the institute, large glass plates were stored there that were left over from when the showcases were built, and that years later were hard to dispose of. We wanted to pull out one of those plates, and in order to do so had to move the coffins stacked in front of them. I stood on one end and grabbed the top-most of three coffins. It was not very heavy, but hard to handle because one could hardly move one's arms out to the sides in the narrow space. Gunther attempted to do the same at the other end, but he slipped, and the coffin that I had lifted on my side up to about the height of my head fell almost vertically down in front of him and hit him. Where exactly I could not see, for he fell down on the floor, rolled around, and screamed so insanely for five or ten minutes that I could not get to him in order to ascertain clearly the type and severity of his injury. Never before had I heard a human scream like that. The edge of the coffin had hit his big toe; I no longer remember how we managed to get his shoe off. For the following days, Gunther was limping pronouncedly, his toenail, lifted up by the hemorrhaging, had come loose.

Speaking of glass plates: Slice plastination required the use of safety glass plates. They were expensive, but inventors like Gunther have to be inventive. Car recycling companies are glad to get rid of old car windows, and so we used them initially. But then it turned out that the different shapes and sizes were irksome to handle and that their surfaces were too scratched. Later, when Gunther had already become a steady customer of a glass manufacturer, he needed extremely thin plates of safety glass to harden polyester resins under UV light. The "purveyor to the court" claimed that they were not available in thicknesses of less than 3 mm (about 1/8 of an inch), not knowing that such a statement would be unacceptable and only prompt Gunther to prove the opposite. He took me in his Volkswagen van to the glass trade fair in Düsseldorf in the Rhineland. Wherever we inquired about safety glass, we were led by brightly smiling people to glass doors in which machine guns bullets were embedded. As we learned, those were made from laminated glass, but what we were actually looking for was single slice safety glass. After being cut to size, it is hardened in an oven and then can no longer be modified. Eventually we got a tip and asked a Belgian company, and they were able to offer us 1.7 mm (about 1/16 of an inch) plates that were pre-tightened by ion removal. So there! On our drive back Gunther surprised me. When he told me that we would have to get gas soon, I got out the map to look for an off-autobahn gas station that would be cheaper. Gunther's unexpected comment was that "a man in my position does not have time to drive off the autobahn just to get gas." The comment tells me that this episode clearly dates from the entrepreneurial period.

As late as 1986 Gunther had been more price-conscious. At the Third International Plastination Conference in San Antonio, Texas, I had to share a motel room with him and another dissector from Munich, Germany, who also was giving presentations. At four o'clock in the morning, Gunther obtained an electric typewriter, complete with extension cord, from the reception desk and began–we were still sleeping, exhausted–to work on his presentations. In the morning we were asked, in Doerr manner, what we had done in the previous hours to keep our minds busy. Even the cheap

Sheet Plastination

motel breakfast seemed too expensive to him, and he walked for a mile along the highway to a gas station to obtain instead of his obligatory quart a gallon of milk, which would last as his only source of nutrition for the entire day.

This eating without joy: "His poor children," I sometimes thought. But he did care about their well-being. Immediately after the Chernobyl disaster, he bought and stored milk powder, fruit juices, and mineral water, enough to fill their entire basement. And, just for fun, he hypnotized his wife Cornelia–she came back upstairs without any water, had missed the hundreds of bottles in the basement. Gunther and his children: His son, Gunnar Rurik (what a strong sounding name) von Hagens, also was used as an experimental object. Gunther had been so impressed by breastfeeding that he invited me and other colleagues from the institute to witness a "suckling session," as he called it. I declined, but he told me how much a newborn follows his reflexes. If one put a finger to his cheek, he would turn his head, hoping to be able to grasp the breast. One could repeat this, he said, switching from left to right until exhaustion. It is never too early, according to Gunther, to gain expert knowledge. At an age at which other kids stutter "ball" or "papa," Rurik was able to say *"musculus sternocleidomastoideus."* When he was about three years old, Gunther had taught him around 50 anatomical terms. If one pointed to a body part, he would, for instance, say "knee joint." The playful guy that I am, I pointed somewhere else and was surprised to get an answer appropriate for a child: "water faucet." His eldest daughter is called Bera Anuk. How do you get a conservative registrar's office (that in Germany has to approve of names before they can officially be given to a child) to accept such a name? Gunther had insiders' tips on these issues. For Bera, he got the Yugoslav embassy to certify that it was the name of a female (that was important) partisan. And the Canadian embassy was willing to declare Anuk an Inuit name. This name quirk has been perpetuated in the family. I know Gunther's current wife as Andrea Whalley, but she changed her first name to the more illustrious pet name that Gunther used, to Angelina. Anything but normal, be different, appears to be their motto.

Teaching Anatomy

Have you noticed? I prefer telling funny little anecdotes to dealing once more with controversial topics. Nor do I want to fight with my colleagues ever again during what remains of my life; they all are wonderful people without blemish. However, Gunther's teaching activities at the Anatomical Institute have not really been mentioned so far. He did hardly any teaching in histology. His domain was macroscopy, which I would like to divide into lectures, dissection classes, and classes for dissection teaching assistants. A scientific assistant, he hardly had to give any lectures–for that we had plenty of professors. He mainly did so by his own request and had favorite topics, such as the inguinal canal or the position of the uterus on the pelvic floor.

Every single one of his hour long lectures was prepared, over several days, by two or three assisting students. And indeed, these single, unforgettable lectures exhibited a choreography like that of theater productions. The main part of each lecture was a simplifying, as plastic as possible visualization of the organs in question, with the help of huge, unusual models. For example, the uterus was represented by a 200-quart plastic barrel, the fringe-like structures of the ovaries by blown-up rubber gloves. A bed

Abdominal muscles and spermatic cords

sheet was used as the peritoneum, tossed by two helpers over the uterus. For the inguinal canal topic, he had dressed his helpers in white paper overalls from the stable. When he motioned them to do so, they opened the door to the lecture hall and pulled a 2-inch-thick and several yards long rope that served as the inguinal ligament into the room. Because only the students in the first rows had a good view of this, the others climbed up on the wobbly folding seats—an atmosphere like on a hay wagon ride. The abdominal muscles extending towards the inguinal ligament were represented by huge flags. For reasons of parity, the less familiar blue NATO flag was fastened with curtain hooks to the inguinal ligament rope behind the red Soviet flag with its hammer and sickle. The main attraction, however, was the spermatic cord: a flexible exhaust pipe from the remodeled air supply of the dissection room, about 12 inches in diameter. It was carried into the lecture hall by additional helpers and was properly positioned in the flag gaps. Pandemonium in the lecture hall, 400 bawling students; few educational results. But everyone had had enormous fun.

Another series of lectures was more sound: "Basics of the Locomotor System" for first semester students, 1992 and 1993. Here, Gunther was extremely knowledgeable and prepared a substantial manuscript with functional illustrations as templates for drawings. The manuscript was a little on the heavy side as far as the illustrations were concerned, but parts of it continued to be used for a long time thereafter. Our instructional templates back then were not labeled. They showed only the outlines of bones, we painted the joint surfaces blue on the overhead transparencies, and labeled all structures by hand. The copying of these labels by hand by the students themselves constituted a didactic dogma for us. Too bad, however, for those who write as illegibly as Gunther. He thought about possible remedies—in those childhood days of computers he already owned a *Macintosh* (a brand he established in our department). He printed all terms in a large font and photocopied them onto a transparency. During the lecture, his helpers would cut out the individual words, hand them over to him, and after placement would paste them in, an incredibly fiddly job. His next attempt was the Advent calendar model. Only the lecturer's copy had the terms printed into it, but they were initially covered. They were then revealed one by one, a predecessor of modern PowerPoint presentations.

Gunther was very involved in the dissection classes, and the students liked him, although he was not equally skilled in all the fields covered. His large-area openings, unusual approaches and ways of dissecting confused some colleagues. "Better to be completely dissected than completely buried," was his creed. He addressed all students by the familiar "Du," and allowed them to address him likewise. Not always very sensitive, he might, for example, say to a student with a malformed pupilla: "You've got a colombola, may I take your picture?" Anatomy practiced on the living, palpating a lot on one's own body, that was what he loved. To this day I show a slide of Gunther's foot in my classes. Over the summer, he wore flip-flops. He had to dig into them with his toes in order for them not to fall off. This caused his extensor digitorum brevis muscles to shorten to a degree that by fall he looked as if he had a tumor on the back of his feet. Every class was a chance for Gunther to try new dissection ideas. In the period of formalin hysteria (1982), he started a major project for the development of a formalin-free injection solution containing an allantoin derivative that eventually did not succeed at the institute.

Gunther von Hagens' foot

The classes for dissection teaching assistants were Gunther's specialty. Dissection TAs are more advanced students with a solid knowledge of anatomy who demonstrate to about ten of the more novice students how to dissect a body. Students suitable for and interested in this job are trained in special classes. Over the course of 20 years, Gunther taught more than 700 of these dissection teaching assistants. "I was a dissection TA with Gunther," every third doctor at the Heidelberg clinics today will tell you when prompted. Gunther created a manuscript for this class that was improved again and again, and which he intended to some day publish as a book. Titled *"Memorandum zum Vorpräparandenkurs 1992,"* this manuscript was subtitled by him "For unofficial use by senior students of anatomy only." A little sample (am I allowed to give one?) demonstrates the jocular attitude that, together with his expertise, lent Gunther the status of a guru among his charges. "Dissection of the ingenious canal. Split the aponeurosis of the external oblique abdominal muscle parallel to the directions of its fibers about one width of a Neckar River duck's bill medial of the spermatic cord." The manuscript contains dissection tips, illustrated with homemade computer graphics that seem a little stiff-jointed in view of today's possibilities. It also contains–and that is what makes it valuable to me–a five page essay on group psychology, strictly geared towards the needs of a dissection class. How do you obtain the alpha-position? Who is your opponent–the material to be studied or the docent? How do you employ the expertise of the betas for your own purposes? How to treat the omega whose destructive attitude weakens the group? For dissection, Gunther postulated four levels: The poke or pluck stage of the beginner; dissection based on basic knowledge and following directions; goal-directed dissection; and the individual, creative dissection transcending from routine to art. Today, dissection guides are commercially available, colorfully illustrated and highly recommended. But they lack the jocular tone ("size of a chicken fist") and especially the psychological introduction. Too bad that Gunther's little jewel will not appear in an updated version. As he often does, he killed several birds with one stone in the classes for the dissection TAs: He fulfilled part of his teaching obligation, practiced his dissection skills, implemented new ideas, and at the same time built a reservoir of motivated students who might work for him at a later time.

Cheaper by the Dozen

Mailing out plastics and plastination supplies was something Gunther did mostly by himself during the early years, on Saturdays. As if he had nothing else to do that day, first thing in the morning he would drive his landlord, with at most 20 pounds of fruit or vegetables to be sold, to the farmer's market in nearby Dossenheim because he could not stand to have the 80-year-old man pull his hand cart there (which took him two hours). Afterward, Gunther shopped for his packaging supplies, always on a grand scale: If he needed two rolls of twine, he quickly discovered that the product was available significantly cheaper if he bought, say, 50 rolls at once. Soon, storage space became scarce; and even cheap items in huge quantities tie up capital. Not everything lasts forever, and it was even worse when there were technological changes and certain items were no longer needed. I am thinking here of sealing tubes, or the black binder clips that were hardly ever needed because very few customers were interested in the sophisticated slice plastination. These items became rustier and rustier in their box that was accidentally wetted in the storage room.

To us at the institute, those bad investments were always cause to once more make fun of Gunther; many of his activities were very entertaining to us. His capability for using department store products in the lab was truly impressive. For example, the grids that were used to separate and support tissue slices during the dehydration process were made from the plastic paint grids used to wipe off paint rollers. Another original use was that of a bowl that Gunther employed to avoid deformation of freshly removed brains which are unnaturally flattened if set down before fixing. The bowl actually was a pudding mold with a kind of snout that yielded hedgehog shaped puddings if used for its original purpose. He also sold this as a plastination aid through his company BIODUR. His attempt to introduce cheap poultry scissors as rib shears, however, was not successful: they were rejected on emotional grounds, were prone to rust, and did not cut cleanly.

Working and Publishing with Gunther

You cannot work with him, only under him, is what I told journalists who wanted to interview me and whom I spontaneously disliked. It would have been better to turn them away without saying anything. This summary statement does not do justice to the topic. Working with extremely gifted and creative people rarely is all fun and games, as every musician knows who has ever worked with a star conductor.

In the early 1990s I once asked Gunther to find a certain technician's phone number for me in his files. After a few days, I pressed him on it. Gunther pulled an organizer from his pocket and announced that when I had first uttered my request I had been 21 on his list of priorities and in the meantime had advanced to 14. In about another five days I could expect my request to be fulfilled. The problem was, as I learned, that he had not noted the number on a piece of paper or, like truly systematic people, in an address book. Instead, he had entrusted it to the only higher being he worshipped, namely to his computer. But–on which of the numerous disks and filed under which key word?

Gunther's relationships with his co-workers followed dynamics similar to that of a marriage. Initially in love and glorifying the partner, followed be a period of peaceful co-existence, until eventually a kind of marital dispute interrupted the idyll or even ended it in divorce. What caused friction often simply was the nature of an inventor, who, overnight, decided on technological changes; no one could adapt that quickly. Where a lot of work is done, many mistakes will be made as well. In such moments, that are also economically critical, it is easier to find a scapegoat than to unemotionally research the causes.

Friction between him and me occurred in the context of negotiations about a joint book project, an atlas with dissection slices that was published in the U.S. in 1991 as "The Visible Human Body," and, almost at the same time in Germany, and backtranslated by me, as *"Farbatlas der Schnitt-anatomie."* This was preceded by our experience (at the institute) with an atlas of plastinated brain slices, for which it had taken years of effort to find a publisher and to fund the project, in spite of the brilliant photographs available. Around 1990 it no longer was common for authors to approach a publisher, offering one's manuscript, but the publishers instead approached individual authors, asking them for manuscripts that would fit exactly into their market segment. Thus, it seemed to be a lucky coincidence that Gunther was approached by the anatomist Michael Ross from Florida, who asked him to publish an atlas of body slices that he, Ross, would enhance by adding computer-tomographic images. We knew Professor Ross as the author of good histology atlases. He had great connections to a publisher, we had plastinated body slices–ideal prerequisites for co-operation. Because Gunther did not have enough time to evaluate our slices in detail, to insert the correct terminology, and to proofread, he generously left the project and the negotiations to me. In doing so, he assumed that the book later would be referred to as "Tiedemann-Ross." He saw himself, very modestly, merely as a supplier of material.

When Ross came to Heidelberg, he was accompanied by a somewhat colorless colleague whom he insisted on having as a co-author. He also had his eyes on being named as first author himself, and he used his connections to the publisher (also to the German office) for leverage. This was, I have to admit, not only a question of honor, but also of money. The book was intended to be "a real kill in the market," it was to be found in any student's backpack. The same morning, I had been instructed by Professor Kriz not to sell out, for only we had the plastinated body slices. Suddenly, it was two to one against us, in addition to the problem of splitting the expected royalties three ways now. Because I felt that I was being taken to the cleaners, I fought the entire day, using various arguments and models of author sequencing and splitting the money. At night, for a change at a good restaurant, Gunther accused me of treating his friends badly and just like that told me I was no longer to lead the negotiations. Eventually, a compromise was worked out that was also agreed to by Kriz, who had thought that Gunther had been underrated. The book now traded as von Hagens, Romrell, Ross, and Tiedemann. Heidelberg once more was entitled to half the royalties, I had the same amount of work, but more fellow authors I did not like, and half the original amount of money. A year later, having been disappointed himself by our co-authors in the meantime, Gunther acknowledged that I had the better insight into human nature.

What a great deal we had made became obvious four years later, when the number of copies sold in the previous year had decreased to less than 50 worldwide. Amounts of less than 50 US dollars were not paid out by the publisher for cost reasons, but instead were added to the payment (if any) for the following year. So there were years in which we did not receive any royalties at all. The idea that a lot of money is to be made by authoring textbooks is superficial. Our calculations were initially based on a market price of just below the psychological threshold of 20 US dollars. To compensate, a huge print run of 40,000 was envisioned. By the time the atlas was finally finished, that relationship had almost been inverted: Only 20,000 copies were printed, but they cost about 38 US dollars each. That was equivalent to a yield of almost four dollars in royalties per copy sold, and that had to be split among four authors. Well, you might say, it is quantity that counts. But if during the first year after publication, when advertising is still effective, not even half of the print run is sold, the prospects are grim. During the first year, we were hardly able to sell 2500 copies, many were returned later as goods on commission by the wholesalers. The German edition had an even sadder fate: its publisher, Schwer-Verlag, went broke shortly after the atlas came out, and later was apparently taken over by another publisher. We did not see a single German mark, and also had lost interest in further following up on this.

Concluding Remarks

I have emptied my shotgun and have not much left to talk about. Because of my previous experiences, I am wary and wonder whether I should give voice to all these thoughts. Is it too intimate (stories about affairs), does it reveal production secrets that might be relevant although patent protection has long since expired, does it give a hint of something illegal, would it be grist for the mill of Gunther's enemies? I have come to avoid–for example, during choir practice–mentioning that I once was closely acquainted with Gunther. For depending on what people have read, heard, or seen about him they already have an unshakable opinion, and lately it often is a negative one. My account will hardly convince them otherwise, so it is not worth the effort. Those who met Gunther during his inventor's period, as I call it (although his inventiveness continues to exist, after all, it is his disposition), thought positively about him, were fascinated by him. One should ask some well-versed participants of his plastination workshops for their comments-they came to Heidelberg from all over the world to study Gunther's methods. What, I wonder, may have become of them. There was the homosexual artist from Paris, France, who wanted to plastinate horses' eyes. There was the attractive female anatomist from Australia. And of course, the big mouth from America, of whom we never did find out for sure whether he was an academically trained forensic pathologist or an undertaker? Did we at the Anatomical Institute only love Gunther so much because, otherwise, there usually is not a lot to laugh about in anatomy? I, for one, would not want to have missed that period of my life.

Wilhelm Kriz, since 1974 Professor of Anatomy at the Heidelberg university and Director of the Institute of Anatomy and Cell Biology, was Gunther von Hagens' superior for many years. Kriz studied medicine at the Gießen university and at Free University, Berlin. In 1963 he obtained his medical doctorate, and in 1971 he achieved Habilitation (formal qualification for professorship in the German university system) at the Münster university, where he worked as lecturer, research associate, and professor, before he was offered a chair in Heidelberg. His publications to date include approximately 150 scientific articles and three medical books. His research interests are the functional structure of the kidneys, the development of these organs, and the loss of renal function in chronic renal failure. In 1990 Kriz was awarded the Jakob Henle Medal by the Göttingen university, and in 1998 the German Society for Dialysis (Deutsche Dialysegesellschaft) awarded him its Bernd Tersteegen Prize.

Wilhelm Kriz

To Gunther von Hagens, on His 60th Birthday

Traditional wisdom has it that old age begins at "sixty." It is the birthday on which the first review of their lives is conducted for VIPs such as Gunther von Hagens. This review often takes the form of a commemorative volume, put together by friends as a surprise, and containing essays that pay tribute to the person's merits as well as anecdotes from his or her life. And so it was my original intention to illustrate Gunther von Hagens' development into a plastinator by means of entertainingly told episodes from the twenty years we spent together at the Anatomical Institute in Heidelberg. These episodes, however, have already been put on paper by my colleague, Professor Tiedemann. His article contains much of what I had intended to write about, but–and I admit this without envy–he has told these anecdotes in a far more witty way than I would ever have managed.

The Puzzling Question: Whence His Motivation?

So I had to think of something else, and soon got stuck on the question that has puzzled me all along: What made Gunther von Hagens what he is today, where did his motivation and his staying power come from that enabled him to work so excessively and exclusively on the production of anatomical specimens? I myself would not have lasted at it, not even had I been promised or even guaranteed more success than Gunther von Hagens has actually attained. He came to me at the Anatomical Institute from the Department of Anesthesiology in the mid-70s. He wanted to go into research, he said, for clinical work was too boring for him. Why did he choose anatomy? At the time, anatomy was not exactly a field known for modern research. Among the basic medical subjects, biochemistry, physiology, and pharmacology were far more popular. Did he actually intend to do research in macroscopic anatomy, on dead bodies? Somewhere, in a short biographical note, I read that as a youngster he had already dissected dead animals. Was this a real connection, or was it–as often happens–construed in retrospect to glorify the master? The latter seems more likely to me. I think that the topic of his professional activity, like so many other things in the lives of all of us, was a matter of coincidence, perhaps of a series of coincidences. It was his first research interest, resulting from the then state of my own research, that led him–certainly via a few switches that could have been set differently as well–onto this track. If I had been interested back then, as I was later, in the size selectivity of the glomerular filter rather than in the medulla of the kidney–who knows, Gunther von Hagens might be managing a company dealing in dialysis machines.

Recently I was again leafing through Robert Musil's great novel "The Man Without Qualities" and came upon the following passage: "He [Ulrich, the man without qualities] could not remember any time in his life during which he had not been inspired by the wish to become an important person; Ulrich seemed to have been born with this wish. It is true that such a longing may be indicative of vanity and stupidity; nevertheless, it is also true that it is a beautiful and proper desire, without which there probably would not be many great people. What was unfortunate about it, however, was simply that neither did he know how to become one, nor what exactly an important person actually was."

Am I correct in assuming that it was similar for Gunther von Hagens? He originally wanted his career to follow an academic path, without knowing exactly in which field–anatomy and pathology both were on his short-list. What was decisive, I am certain, was his first success in research, his first "plastinate." The realization that he had discovered something absolutely novel was intoxicating and gave him more satisfaction than anything else had before. Was it not simply that he wanted to get a taste of this again and again, without paying too much attention to where it would take him, and, especially, without having a definite goal back then?

With his scientific success came recognition by others, and this recognition was greater and more wide-ranging than expected. Anatomists, macroscopic anatomists worldwide, were in a state of turmoil: most of them expressing affirmative enthusiasm, a few–and they were present from the very beginning–fierce disapproval. Even more tumultuous was his reception among laypersons. Among them, too, he was met with overwhelming approval, and by a minority, with strong disapproval. We, i.e., Gunther von Hagens' colleagues at the institute, too, noted the attractiveness of his specimens for laypersons as well, and were surprised by it, but we also saw them as something rather unimportant, something that might be used during Open Houses at the institute to make anatomy more popular.

What it is that constitutes the fascination that a lay audience clearly feels for the specimens has been written about frequently, and we do not need to discuss this again here. What was decisive for the further development of plastination–as I see it today–was the fact that Gunther von Hagens, unlike all his colleagues, clearly and early recognized the potential of his new technology for the education of laypeople, and that he immediately began to plan its implementation. He never made a secret of this, always spoke freely to me about his plans; but I never took these plans seriously and always just attributed them to his bubbling enthusiasm.

Throwing the Decisive Switch–
Instructing Physicians or Educating Laypersons

Originally, Gunther von Hagens certainly strove to achieve both: the instructional specimen to be used in medical studies as well as the attractive specimens for educating laypersons. What we discussed and planned together were the instructional specimens. These plans, certainly not without ambition, related to the establishment of an anatomical collection of instructional specimens that was to be comprehensive and spectacular like

"The Runner"

no other. We talked about the standard specimens used for the instruction of medical students and began good projects such as the "four body project." Specimens created for exhibitions aimed at laypersons, such as the "Chess Player" (on the border of expert and lay education) and the "Runner," came as a surprise to me. I reacted in a rather restrained manner and hesitated to agree to these developments.

There are many reasons why it was not possible to achieve both goals at the same time. The decisive factor was this: One of these aims would make money, and the other one was dependent on subsidies and required a university institute as its base. The balancing act between the two eventually had to fail, and I tried for too long to keep it going. In the end, only one option could be realized, and Gunther von Hagens preferred the education of laypersons. He probably made this decision early on–at the beginning of the 1990s. Possibly as early as the late 1980s Gunther von Hagens ceased to think about and plan for an academic career. He procrastinated when it came to his possible *Habilitation* (the formal qualification necessary for professorship in Germany). For a while, he imagined going to the U.S. and becoming (still embedded in academics) the head and promoter of a large anatomical and pathological collection of specimens, but these plans came to nothing. Instead, he was more and more fascinated by the attractiveness of the specimens for laypersons, and this fascination gave his plans direction. Was this due–to go back to the Musil quote–to the prospect of achieving public recognition and high regard much more quickly this way than by following the slow, hard academic road to the top? Academic recognition is always limited, is the expert recognition from colleagues, and as such is always steeped in qualifying criticism. The recognition offered by laypersons, who, through Gunther von Hagens' exhibitions, find answers to their pressing questions, is more appreciative. Did the latter mean more to him? Whatever it was that eventually decided the issue–his ideas and plans were more and more targeted at a lay audience. And that required a different mindset than the planning of instructional specimens for teaching medical students. For an exhibition specimen, attractiveness is the most important criterion, for instructional specimens, attractiveness is not important. An instructional specimen has to convey systematic knowledge and anatomical facts, which in turn are not really necessary for a specimen used to educate laypersons. Quite to the contrary, too systematic an approach would rather be hindering, as the goal is to make anatomical structures understandable. This is a large and critical contrast, and it was this contrast that ignited the controversies surrounding the BODY WORLDS exhibition and refueled them again and again.

The Dispute over the Exhibtion–Largely Homemade

The controversies began in Mannheim, they continued and became fiercer from one exhibition to the next. In my opinion this was not so much because of the exhibition itself: there was no basic difference between the Mannheim and the Frankfurt exhibitions. The Frankfurt exhibition was, even considering solely technical and educational criteria, better than the Mannheim one. The increasing disapproval of the exhibition, in public and in the media, resulted from the collateral events in "Love Parade" fashion that Gunther von Hagens intended to use to promote the exhibition, but that yielded quite the opposite results–at least among those who spoke to me about them. In the eyes of many supporters of the exhibition (including many colleagues from the medical profession), these populist performances cast doubt on the educational goals of the exhibition. Without actually changing, the exhibition became less credible.

I know from way back that extravagant exaggeration and extroversion are part and parcel of Gunther von Hagens' personality structure. I also understand that one must accept active, creative personalities as a whole–the aspects one does not like and sees as gaffes are not simply superfluous trimmings, they are part of the basis of that which is admirable, of that ability to perform. No ordinary person could have created what Gunther von Hagens has built–no matter how smart, and no matter how beneficial the circumstances. Without a good amount of chutzpa, of cockiness, and without his pleasure in provoking, this exhibition most likely would never have happened.

The Future of the Exhibition–After His 60th Birthday, Once Again Rosy

The exhibition has been shown in Los Angeles, CA, since the middle of 2004. So far, no heated public controversy has occurred, and I hope that this will remain so. My hope is based, not least of all, on this 60th birthday. As Gunther von Hagens enters into his seventh decade, and even though he may feel as if he is at most 50 (as he recently stated), the likelihood that he will "fly off the handle" should have decreased (even for him) and certainly should continue to do so. Considering this, chances are favorable that in the U.S. the BODY WORLDS exhibition will be able to gain and solidify the good reputation it merits. That is what I wish for Gunther and what I wish for the exhibition: it deserves it.

Nevertheless, there will always be controversy regarding the exhibition. For many, it will continue to be a problem to have dead bodies made into exhibits. This fact need not be harmful to the exhibition. As long as this objection provokes a serious discussion of the goals of the exhibition and raises the question of to what extent an individual exhibit meets these goals, it should actually contribute to the continuous improvement of the exhibition. What makes a good exhibit, i.e., a specimen for the education of laypersons? Initially I was not sure how to answer this question. I certainly was focused too strongly on classical anatomical specimens as used in teaching medical students, but I have mastered a learning curve: In the Mannheim exhibition I was still bothered by exhibits, such as the "Runner," that seemed to me to have crossed the line. Not until I had repeatedly watched how laypersons looked at these specimens in the exhibitions did I become more tolerant. Now, the most important criterion for accepting a specimen to me is aesthetics: The specimen must not violate my aesthetic perception, and to me a specimen is perfect if it conveys anatomical realities in a convincing and easily understood manner. Both features should be present: a specimen should be beautiful, understandable, and thought provoking at the same time. In the hopes that Gunther von Hagens will create many, many more of such specimens, I wish him health and creative power for the coming decade.

"The Chess Player"

An Urgent Wish—To Be Taken Literally, If Not Seriously

At the end, I would like to utter another, completely different wish: Should there be a banquet in honor of this birthday (and the "should" here is meant quite seriously, for it would hardly occur to Gunther von Hagens himself to plan such a thing, and neither would he regret not having one), I seriously hope for something tastier than what Gunther served me one time in the late 1970s when he spontaneously invited me for dinner. His family had gone on a trip, the refrigerator was empty, but in the freezer we found an opened, half-full can of corned beef, and another one with peas of the fine variety. With the help of a hammer and a chisel, we chopped off chunks of these delicacies and heated them together in a frying pan. We had milk and tap water to drink. It still tasted great. By the way, our table conversation focused on—guess what?—plastination.

Karine Oostrom, *Gunther von Hagens' first Dutch plastination student in 1982 and today a plastic surgeon, with her husband Bas.*

Happy Birthday, Gunther, here's to you!

Karine Oostrom

For Gunther, With Love

A Dutch Medical Student Gets Introduced to Plastination

Ever since I was eight years old, I wanted to become a doctor. My final aim was to become a plastic surgeon. In 1981 I started my studies in medicine at the University of Utrecht in the Netherlands. The first year of medical school was not as inspiring as I had expected it to be. Most of the courses–especially physics and chemistry–were very basic and did not interest me at all. The highlight of that first year of medical school were the courses in anatomy. That was what I had hoped for and had expected from a medical education. Knowing how our body looked on the inside, knowing the names of all these intriguing anatomical structures, that was exciting. One part of the anatomy curriculum consisted of lectures, but the practical education in the form of dissection courses, naturally, was the best.

One day, Professor Van Doorenmaalen, my Professor of Anatomy, presented a lecture about a totally new concept in the preservation of anatomical specimens. This may not have been very useful to us, first year students, but the professor was so enthusiastic about this new method that, at the end of his lecture, I went down in the theatre to ask him for more information. The subject of his lecture had been plastination. He had been to an international conference of anatomists and had met Gunther von Hagens. At that time, the technique was brand new. Gunther had only started development of plastination in 1977. Professor Van Doorenmaalen was surprised that one of his students showed any interest in an anatomical conservation technique.

One week after this lecture he called me at home and asked whether I would be interested in a course in plastination. Of course I was. Any course in anatomy would be an extra opportunity for me to learn about the human body. Months went by without any news. I didn't dare ask the professor about the status of my application for this course. Finally, in March 1982, I received a letter confirming my registration in a plastination workshop at the Anatomical Institute of the University of Heidelberg in July 1982. Dr Gunther von Hagens himself would lead the course.

I was shocked. I had expected something of a one day course, somewhere in the Netherlands, not a full week as far away as Heidelberg, Germany. The list of participants was even more impressive: they were all professors and researchers from universities all over the world. Being only a first year student, I didn't consider myself to fit into this highly respectable company. I could not distinguish an artery from a vein at that time, so I was determined to learn everything that could be learned about plastination, before starting the course, so that I would not appear too stupid. In 1982, the Internet was not an option, so I went to the medical library, and spent hours searching for publications about plastination. There was not much to find, so I was able to learn and memorize everything that I could get my hands on.

Plastination Workshop in Heidelberg

In the summer of 1982 I attended the one week English language plastination workshop in Heidelberg. The organization was pretty basic. People from all over the world, a total of eight, came to Heidelberg, booked into one of the hotels that Gunther recommended, and showed up at the Anatomical Institute on Monday morning at 08:30. There was a very strict timetable—which turned out to be nothing but an illustration of all the things you could learn about plastination. We met in the laboratory and from the first moment Gunther took off at full speed. He discussed all aspects of plastination in a pretty random order. Everything was demonstrated on the spot. Gunther had five or six students working for him during that week. They were running around all the time to find exactly the specimen that

Gunther wanted to show the participants, to show exactly the technique he was talking about, or to demonstrate immediately what he meant when he was discussing technical problems. It was a very interactive process. Gunther asked questions and we were supposed to answer. I found myself standing out in the crowd: Compared to the other participants I was a nobody, of course, but it turned out that I could beat them easily when it came to knowledge of the plastination processes. I am not bragging when I say that I could answer almost every question that Gunther asked. My preparation paid off well.

It was chaotic and dazzling, very interesting and intriguing. One could not help getting caught up with Gunther's enthusiasm. The other course participants came from Saudi Arabia, Denmark, Japan and England. I was the only female, the youngest, and the first medical student to attend this course. Furthermore, I was the first Dutch person who had taken one of Gunther's workshops. One of his aims with these workshops was to spread plastination around the world like an epidemic. So the more countries, the merrier! All workshop participants were allowed to take a plastinated

At the International Plastination Workshop, photo: Lothar Reinbacher

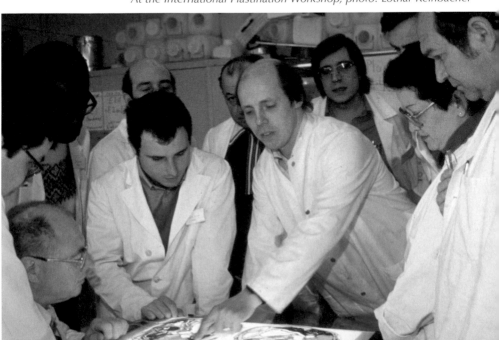

Flastination

The lab was generously equipped...

...the staff was affable...

Technical operations went smoothly...

...chemistry presented its best face...

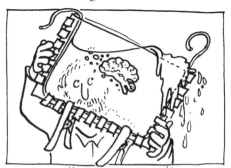

Eventually, we were able to see through things...

...if strenuously.

Workshop VIII/83

...information was comprehensive...

...or in vain.

...and nature was served in an appetizing manner as well.

In short: The work was neatly done!

In the end everyone was able to take something home...

...or not.

specimen home that they had produced themselves during the workshop. We sliced a deep-frozen dog's head in slices of 5 mm and impregnated them with PEM (polymerized emulsion). I'm sure we all took our first plastinated specimen home with pride. To me, the workshop had been a success. I had been to Heidelberg, met Gunther, and had seen his laboratory. I was as enthusiastic as Gunther. The atmosphere at the Anatomical Institute was exciting and vivid. People working for Gunther were young and passionate. I seemed to fit in very well. During the course I took thousands of notes and afterward I wrote a detailed paper, in Dutch, about plastination. This counted as a part of my first year exam in medical school. Gunther had found his first root for plastination in the Netherlands.

Working for Gunther in the Early Days of Plastination

Having seen Gunther's young and ambitious staff in the Plastination Laboratory, I dreamt of becoming one of them, and so it seemed to be a good idea to stay in touch with Gunther. He, for his part, saw me as a potential asset to his team. Accordingly, we discussed the possibility of my working in his laboratory. In February 1983 I sent Gunther a letter outlining my understanding of our discussions. Gunther replied very promptly, within a month, with a very satisfying answer. The letter was warm and welcoming: Just come to Heidelberg, I'll provide you with a place to stay and we will see... In the end, I worked six weeks in the Plastination Laboratory. Gunther saw the first two weeks as an investment on his part. For the second two weeks, I wanted to be paid with a plastinated specimen that I had made myself, and Gunther agreed. And for the last two weeks I earned 400 German marks (about $200 US). In my circumstances, that was a small fortune.

Gunther's staff consisted of students from all fields: Bettina Rinne, a biology student; Renée ("Brainy"), a medical student working on her thesis about plastination of brain slices; Wolli Weber (yes, the same, "Wolfgang" now living in Ames, Iowa); a technician, Rudolph ("Redeye"); a medical student, Klaus Resch, on his way to becoming a neurosurgeon; and several others. In the Plastination Laboratory we worked hard. We always started at eight, only stopped at lunchtime for a quick bite in the Mensa (the student cafeteria), and we seldom finished at five. Weekend work was common as well. Nevertheless, there was always time to have fun. It was an exciting period. We were hardly ever told what to do, for Gunther would pop up time and again with plans and ideas that needed instant execution. The schemes we made in the morning would always differ completely from our real achievements at the end of the day.

It was not always easy to work for a boss like Gunther. He expected his co-workers to be as devoted to plastination as he was himself. For normal, mortal people, that is virtually impossible. The excitement of the processes that we were involved in made it possible for us to work long hours, with enthusiasm most of the time. This did not always lead to the appreciation we expected from Gunther. He could be very proud of us, his co-workers, but he could also throw a fit about the smallest drawback in one of our projects. He was not always a reasonable chief. One Friday evening I was all set to go downtown, including a party dress and glitter spray in my hair, when Gunther asked me to do him a favor. A beautiful body had just arrived at the Anatomical Institute and that body needed to be fixed with formalin right away. He had other obligations, and I was the only one he could turn to. I had never performed the procedure, but according to Gunther it would be a piece of cake. He explained to me briefly what to do, handed me the keys, and off I went to the basement of Neuenheimer

Unusual methods...

Feld 307 of the Anatomical Institute. I found the body and the accessories as Gunther had described. I dissected the inguinal veins, inserted the tubing, and connected the lot to the container filled with formalin. I opened the faucet, and considered my part of the job done. Gunther had been right: it had not been difficult at all.

The next day, Saturday, Gunther knocked on my door early in the morning and asked me whether I wanted to accompany him to the Institute, for he was on his way to inspect the body. Of course, this was an offer I could not refuse. Arriving at Neuenheimer Feld, Gunther first had to go up to the Plastination Lab on the third floor. I went down to the basement to see how my guy was doing. Then I went back upstairs to pick up Gunther at the lab. On our way down, he asked me what the body looked like. I wasn't sure what to say. I thought he looked fine, but due to the infusion with the formalin solution, he seemed somewhat swollen. So that's what I reported.

Gunther got into one of his notorious fits. I was by far the most stupid of all of his co-workers. How could I (literally!) blow a job as easy as this one, messing up a beautiful body? He went on and on, until we reached the basement. He glanced at the fixed body and started all over again. How could I be so stupid as to not know what a perfectly preserved body (like this one) looked like, and thus to upset him without even having a clue? This was one of the moments when I threatened to leave on the spot and to never work for Gunther again. That always worked to calm him down. He did not want me to leave, nor had he intended to be angry or rude. So I kept returning to Heidelberg, where I had lost my heart to plastination.

Gunther considered every healthy young person fit for work in the Plastination Laboratory. Although my husband, Bas, is a lawyer who faints when he sees more than a few drops of blood, there was no way he could avoid working for Gunther when he came to visit me in Heidelberg. Gunther provided him with suitable jobs like organizing his garages, where he kept all kinds of plastination supplies, specimens, and whatever else he could lay his hands on. One day, he asked Bas to jigsaw slices of plastinated tissue out of polymerized E12 sheets. Being a handy man, this, of course, was not a big deal for Bas (the specimens were not too recognizable as human). Then, at the end of the day, Klaus Resch came in and asked Bas: "Could you give me a clean cut on this ragged neck?". He handed him the plastinated head he was carrying by the hair. Without a second's hesitation, Bas took the head and created a smooth, perfect bottom for the head to stand on. He had proven himself to be fit to work in the entire plastination arena!

Staying at Gunther's

Whenever I stayed in Heidelberg, my dwelling was a basement apartment in the Sedlmayer House on Jahnstrasse, next to Gunther's home. The apartment consisted of two rooms and a bathroom. The two rooms were the office that Gunther used for his "brainwork," and a small bedroom, where I could spend the (small) part of the night that remained after exploring the Heidelberg nightlife. For a student like me, it was the perfect place to stay. In the morning I would hop over to Gunther's house where I would have breakfast. That first year I did not meet Cornelia and the children (at that time Rurik and Bera), for they were staying the summer at Cornelia's parents. Their Jahnstrasse apartment was small. It was part of a home for three families and Gunther and his family lived on the ground floor. The apartment consisted of two larger rooms, in use as bedrooms, a small kitchen, a dining room, and a bathroom. There was no living room. One of the two bedrooms was occupied by the children. The second bedroom was Gunther and Cornelia's. Their huge bed, with an integrated audio system, stood in the middle of the room. Around it were a variety of television sets, usually three or more, often all playing different channels at the same time. All the wall space was occupied by bookshelves that were stuffed with books. The kitchen showed signs of intensive use, especially at the height of children's hands. I spent many hours "de-signing" the kitchen. After her return, Cornelia called to thank me for the surprise: a "new" kitchen.

Cornelia was always busy making food for her family and all kinds of guests. She was a great cook. The meals were always a delight. Gunther could hardly ever find the time to participate in the family meals. He had already eaten and had gone to the university again, or would eat later, or not at all. The small dining room was used for these meals, and later it became the lodging for Gunther's father, Herr Liebchen, who came over from East Germany. He was "released" to the free West after his retirement. Cornelia and Gunther had no problem fitting papa Liebchen into their tight apartment.

A Special Wedding Gift

In September 1984 Bas and I got married in the Netherlands. We invited Gunther and Cornelia for the wedding day, and they meant to come. But a few days beforehand, we got a call from Heidelberg. Herr Sedlmayer, their neighbor and the landlord of Gunther's "office" (my former apartment), had just passed away, and his widow had asked Gunther to assist her with the arrangements that had to be made for the funeral. Still, a small delegation from Heidelberg attended our marriage. The group of four consisted of Wolli Weber; Birgit Gross, who was at that time the leading lady in the laboratory; Renée, alias "Brainy", who was working on her thesis on plastination of brain slices; and Sabine, a medical student from Berlin, who worked in the lab together with her husband Arnim. They brought us a special present: Gunther and Cornelia donated a plastinated brain slice, nicely mounted in a wooden frame, all anatomical landmarks engraved, and with a special wish on the reverse side: *"Möge eure Ehe so dauerhaft wie die Plastination sein"* (May your marriage be as durable as plastination). The day after our marriage we drove off to Vienna for our honeymoon. Travelling in our 2CV Citroen (Ugly Duck), we needed a stopover. Of course that was at Gunther and Cornelia's, in Heidelberg.

Tona's Baptism

On July 27, 1985, the third child of Gunther and Cornelia was born. She was named Tona Gerrit. Since my second name is Antonia, I flatter myself with the thought that she was (inconsiderately) named after me. I was asked to be her Godmother. I still consider this a great honor. Cornelia and Gunther explained to me that they wanted to transmit a part of my "way of life" to their youngest daughter. We all got together with Cornelia's family in Verden, Germany, for the christening ceremony. Early Sunday morning, Gunther knocked on my door. He had to speak to me urgently. He needed my advice: was it absolutely necessary for him to be present at the christening? I told him that I considered the father to be one of the key persons in a ceremony like this, and that I saw no way for him to escape this social obligation. He replied that he considered himself like Lucifer, a devil in disguise, who had no business even entering a church. He thought this might be considered blasphemy. Furthermore, he really needed the time to finish the leaflet on plastination that he was working on... I told him I thought that even a complete atheist would have a better chance that God would strike him by lightning when he was sitting behind his computer, than if he were attending the christening of his daughter. And I told him to stop searching for excuses and instead to be a man. He attended the ceremony with the enthusiasm of a fish on a hook.

Third International Conference on Plastination, San Antonio, Texas

During my stay at the Plastination Headquarters in Heidelberg in 1985, Gunther came up with the idea that I would be one of his speakers at the upcoming Plastination Conference to be held in San Antonio, Texas, from April 21 to 25 of the following year. There was no way that I could afford to fly to the U.S., and attend a conference, by my own means. Therefore, advised by Gunther, I made special arrangements with Professor Harmon Bickley, the organizer of the Conference. We made a deal that I would come and work for him in San Antonio for a total of four weeks before and during the conference. In return, he would pay for my plane ticket and conference registration.

I was to present two papers, one on the general principles of fixation in plastination and one on plastination of the heart. It took a lot of preparation.

Gunther helped me wherever he could by providing slides that showed the different aspects of the process in detail and, of course, with all his technical knowledge. For the preparation of the hearts, I spent some weekends with Professor Tiedemann in the Plastination Laboratory, because, at that time, Klaus Johann Tiedemann was the plastination heart specialist. "Tiede" was a formal guy and wished to be addressed as "Professor." He had a habit of continuously telling corny jokes. Gunther warned him that such jokes were only appropriate among friends, and that friends address each other on a first name basis. After the next joke, Gunther refused to address him as "Professor" any longer, but was not so bold as to call him by his first name. The middle name, Johann, seemed a safe alternative. Gunther actively encouraged us plastination people to address Professor Tiedemann as Johann.

Harmon Bickley was a well-established pathology professor. He had founded the first plastination lab in the US. He was gifted with charm, sharp intellect, and very good writing and teaching styles. He was one of the first to publish an outstanding article on plastination: "An Improved Method for the Preservation of Teaching Specimens," in 1981. Of course, Gunther was one of the co-authors of this article. Harmon was also co-founder of the International Society for Plastination. I had met him in Heidelberg once before I saw him again in San Antonio.

With Johann and the calf's heart

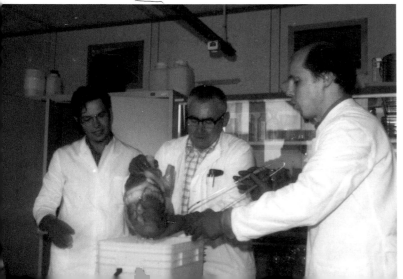

My trip to the U.S. and participation in the preparation and execution of the conference were great successes. We had about two hundred participants from all over the world. All speakers were in some way pupils of Gunther. Gunther, as I remember, was glowing in the dark during the conference. He was radiant with enthusiasm that so many people were meeting with only one goal: to learn (more) about plastination. The conference must have been one of the highlights of Gunther's first decade in plastination.

The Letter of Recommendation

In 1987, the end of my medical school education came into sight. I was about to write letters of application to professors of surgery and plastic surgery in order to acquire an education in the field of plastic surgery. It seemed totally logical, after all these years of labor in the Plastination Laboratory, to ask Gunther for a letter of recommendation. This led to probably our biggest argument. He refused to write me such a letter because I wanted to use it to obtain a position in plastic surgery. According to Gunther, all surgeons were brain-dead and I, in his eyes, was too talented to end up in such a stupid career. This time I really packed my bags. If it had not been for Cornelia, who interfered successfully, this would have been my last encounter with Gunther. She finally persuaded him to let me have my way. Under immense pressure from the two of us, Gunther had to give in.

The Slide (No) Show

The Fourth International Conference on Plastination was held at the Mercer University School of Medicine, Macon, Georgia, in March 1988. As in 1986, the conference was hosted by Harmon Bickley, who had moved from San Antonio to Macon. The format was the same as in San Antonio. Quoting Harmon Bickley: "Judging from both attendance and comments it was a resounding success." What I remember particularly from this conference was that Gunther had a lot of presentations to do and that that turned out to be a hell of a job. The problem was that one of Gunther's cases, in particular the one containing all his slides, had gone missing during the trip to Macon. Gunther had to beg for slides from all of the other participants and had to improvise a lot with borrowed materials to illustrate his presentations. Of course, his knowledge and charisma compensated for this inconvenience. I'm sure he learnt his lesson well: ever since that conference he carries his slides and presentations on his body or in his hand luggage.

Heidelberg, the Scene of Plastination

The Fifth International Conference was the first European one. Of course, it took place in Heidelberg, in July 1990. The organization was firmly guided by Andrea (later changed to Angelina) Whalley. As with the previous two conferences, I was also caught up in the conference organization. The conference was a success even before it started. Anybody who had anything to do with plastination wanted to be there. It was the perfect opportunity to see the species "Gunther" in its natural habitat.

For Gunther, it was the optimal environment to show off his most ambitious projects. An enormous staff worked around the clock to demonstrate to the participants literally everything that Gunther had achieved. The most beautiful specimens, the largest pieces of equipment, the extended scale of his territory in the "Anatomisches Institut," everything was displayed with grandeur. The week went by as if we were all on a pink cloud. It was an impressive meeting, and it was well documented by the poster announcing the conference. I am sure everybody remembers the transparent slide of the plastinated man pictured in front of the scenery of Heidelberg.

Plastination Expands Beyond Limits

The Sixth International Conference on Plastination, at Kingston, Ontario, Canada, was organized in 1992 by Blake Gubbins at the Queen's University. With 120 delegates from 26 countries, it was a very successful assembly again. It was the fourth time that I was involved in the organization of a plastination conference. As a consequence, I was acquainted with everybody who was working in the field. Gunther seemed to rely on me, as one of the Heidelberg ambassadors, to bring plastination and its possibilities in anatomical teaching to the attention of a broad audience. At this conference the topic Gunther emphasized most was the preparation of whole-body slices. Many plastinators considered this still to be a bridge too far. Gunther's procedures, at this time, evolved with such speed that it became difficult for plastinators elsewhere to keep up with all of the new techniques. Gunther's presence therefore was invaluable.

Background of the poster announcing the Heidelberg Plastination Conference in 1990

The Story of the Two Plastinated Hands

In 1993 I worked as a resident in plastic surgery at the Academic Medical Center in Rotterdam. During the previous years I had kept in contact with Cees Entius, the dissector of the Anatomical Department of the Erasmus Medical Center in Rotterdam. He was one of the pupils that I trained in Plastination during a workshop in 1984 in Utrecht.

The next plastination conference was to take place in Graz, Austria, in 1994. I was eager to participate again and wanted to combine my skills in plastic surgery with my experience in plastination. Through Cees and his department, I got hold of two fresh arms that were to be dissected. I called Gunther and, as usual, we were able to work out a profitable deal. I would dissect the arms with the focus of a hand-surgeon. Gunther, for his part, would then plastinate the arms using his current state-of-the-art techniques. One of the arms would be donated to the Anatomical Department in Rotterdam, the other one would stay in Heidelberg.

It was a race against the clock. It took me almost 24 hours non-stop to dissect each arm. I tried to highlight anatomical details in such a way that every finger showed a different element of the anatomy: the nervous system, the vessels, the joints and capsules, the relationship of the flexor tendons with their sheaths and pulleys. With the help of Cees Entius, the fresh specimens were fixed with formalin. We then transported them, probably against the law, to Heidelberg, in a fish container filled with ice. As usual, Gunther did not disappoint me. He plastinated them according to the highest standards. Also, as usual, he managed to keep his promise only just in time: the arms were still being kept in their curing cases with gas hardener when they arrived in Graz.

Gunther had always been a dreamer with a strong drive to pursue his dreams and get them realized. When he started the art and science of plastination, most of the people around him did not believe that he would succeed in even establishing the technique. Time after time he has proven all of those skeptics to be wrong. This happened again when he wanted to organize an exhibition of plastinated specimens. I believed in

BODY WORLDS from the beginning, as did Gunther. Although I knew Gunther's work very well, even I was surprised by the impact of this magnificent exhibition. And the first specimen that the visitors would see at the entrance of the museum was a welcoming plastinated hand–one of the two that Gunther and I had prepared in our fruitful collaboration. I was flattered.

Gunther Goes Social

Andreas Weiglein was the host of the Seventh International Conference on Plastination at Graz, Austria, July 24–29, 1994. It was a very well organized conference. The Institute of Anatomy in Graz provided us with excellent facilities, gracious hospitality, and beautiful weather. With 150 participants from 30 countries, it was a sound conference. During this conference there was, as usual, a meeting of the International Society for Plastination. For Gunther, it must have been a special meeting, for both he and Harmon Bickley were elected "distinguished members" of the ISP.

Gunther is always somewhat uncomfortable when he needs to participate in social gatherings. In Graz, however, he seemed to fit in very well, even with the abundance of very well organized social programs. It was the first time I had seen him in high spirits while he had to interact with a lot of people and was unable to work. Maybe credit for the socialization of Gunther should be attributed to Angelina Whalley, for she even managed to get him to the dance floor one evening. It was a weird and wonderful sight: Gunther, including his black hat, waltzing around with his beautiful wife.

Gunther Needs a Spokesperson for Belgian TV

For nine years now, I have been very busy in my fulfilling and rewarding job as a plastic surgeon in the Netherlands. I am not actively involved in plastination anymore, although I have never lost contact with Gunther and his family. The last time that I was of service to Gunther was in 2001, when he had an exhibition in Cureghem-Anderlecht in Belgium. There was much ado about the ethical aspects of this exhibition. The Cellars of Cureghem, the former slaughterhouse, were specially equipped for the BODY WORLDS exhibition.

People were filled with indignation about the choice of this special location. One of the neighbors even initiated a lawsuit against the BODY WORLDS organization because he feared that the exhibition was a threat to his unborn child. His pregnant wife had seen boxes being unloaded from a truck and had (nearly) fainted when she realized that the boxes probably contained human remains. Some people suggested that Gunther had abused those who had donated their bodies to anatomical departments for scientific purposes by exposing them in a "horror show". Others questioned the origin of the bodies that were plastinated. A well-respected professor of anatomy, Jan Pieter Clarijs, declared that the exhibition was

BODY WORLDS in Belgium, in 2001

a "violation of human dignity." The Belgian television network, VTM, asked Gunther to refute all this criticism by participating in their discussion show *Recht van Antwoord* (Right to Answer), hosted by Goedele Liekens. This show starts as a discussion between two opponents, followed by the "verdict" of a panel of experts. The panel consisted of a judge, a journalist/newspaper columnist, and a professor in media law. Gunther's opponent would be Professor Clarijs. There was one small problem: the show is in Dutch, and even the multilingual Gunther does not speak that language.

This problem was solved within a week. Gunther called me on Tuesday, arrived at Enschede, where I lived, on Wednesday, discussed the matter with me on Thursday, and I went to Brussels for the broadcast of the program on Friday, September 21, 2001. Gunther had never found the time to visit me before, in all those years, so that in itself was a zenith experience. He was so determined to explain his opinion on the controversy that he considered it worthwhile to undertake a trip of two days to the Netherlands in order to personally discuss the subject matter thoroughly with me. I was pleased that Gunther turned to me for help on this issue. It revealed that he still regarded me as his "Dutch base" after all these years...

Bernd Hillebrands was one of Gunther von Hagens' colleagues while attending university from 1987 to 1995, initially at the Anatomical Institute of Heidelberg university and in management support at BIODUR, later as product manager, and eventually as CEO of BIODUR. Today, Bernd Hillebrands lives and works as an international independent management trainer and personality coach in Heidelberg.

Bernd Hillebrands

Pushing the Limits through Plastination

My Perspective

This contribution is from one of Gunther von Hagens' colleagues from his consolidated Heidelberg anatomical period of the late 1980s to the mid-1990s: The technologies for slice plastination (epoxy) and gestalt plastination (silicone) had been patented and were already in use on all continents by narrow circles of scientists and educators. Having just become an ex-theologist who was then embarking on a second course of study of political science and philosophy, I simply was in need of extra money to pay for my psychoanalysis and was grateful for the motivating welcome to "Gunther's colorful troops."

The following reflection represents a look back, from today's point of view, to my time spent with Gunther von Hagens ten years ago. This article, for me, certainly is a daring experiment, full of apparent contradictions, pushing some limits–accompanied by a wink. Together with my best wishes for Gunther, this text contains the resonance that is generated today as my memories are reconstructed, prompted by the request (about which I was pleased) to write for this occasion.

The Drive Behind It

Looking at Gunther von Hagens' plastination work with a consciously out-of-focus, wide-ranging view that is possible only from a distance, I recognize in his person and in his work self-similar, returning patterns that have something to do with limits. What opportunities are there at the limit, and which dynamic do they create? We humans are drawn to limits in order to overcome them. And so we behave in basically two different ways: On the one hand there are cultures intending to teach us humans, during the process of maturation, to accept the forces that limit us. This attitude is not to be misunderstood as one of resigned weakness or fatalism. Instead, what is meant is the extreme strength inherent in the calmness that results from accepting life and death, beauty and ugliness, light and dark, as forming a whole in our daily lives. When they accept reality in its entirety for what it is, humans gradually will let go of their combative desire to push even the most extreme limit of finite existence. That which is limiting loses its power through the daily practice of attentiveness. Eventually, limits and limitlessness become one. That is the Eastern way of avoiding suffering, through equanimity towards happiness and suffering: "He who is without desires will be able to discover the miracle of the path; he who has desires will only discover the apparent." (Lao Tse) I think it interesting that, for years now, Gunther has been spending a lot of time in the Eastern hemisphere.

This is contrasted by the occidental, involved position of the pursuit of happiness and the fight against suffering. A fight against limits with the visionary bundled strength of limit-breaking goals. The practical striving for relative victory by moving limits to benefit oneself. The I-sayer Martin Luther, with his "Here I stand, I can do no other," stands as an ancestor at the beginning of our Western modern age. I see Gunther and his plastination as children of this age. In him, I see much of this protesting energy.

Similarly, medicine in our hemisphere obtains its developmental strength mainly from the intentional "forever young." It opposes the natural aging processes of the body and attempts to at least extend, if not remove altogether, our biological limits. But even the bodies of our Western medicine men and women require occasional rest. Recurring acts of lying low in a horizontal position, that in a certain way constitute getting used to dealing with the brother of sleep, cannot be avoided completely if one wants to be refreshed for rising up, strengthened for "insurrection." I am talking about the mentally disliked, for paradoxically assessed, period of sleep. I have noticed that lifesaving work, for example in German hospitals, often is done under especially unhealthy conditions that are beyond the human measure of time. Gunther, at least, has, in my eyes, always sought to gain new victories on the battlefield of tirelessness.

Looking back to the beginnings of Gunther's plastination work, one may recognize in the idea the Faustian longing giving it its impetus: "Oh, moment, stay, thou art so fair!" The idea originated in the fleeting daily business of instructional dissection. What is stopped here is the naturally accelerated degradation process of the body from which life's energy has withdrawn–to cause a degradation of the second order. A typical dissection in anatomy class moves from tissue layer to tissue layer and from organ to organ. It exposes insights for the students, thus creating instructional situations, for example regarding rare disease-related changes in the organs. As the dissection progresses, these instructional situations have to be destroyed again. This is in contrast to the teacher's knowledge of *repetitio* as *mater studiorum*: according to this saying, repetition is the mother of all learning.

The second impulse for the development of plastination came from the haptic orientation of the crafts-like disciplines of medicine. The surgeon seeks to grasp something with his or her hands in order to be able to grasp it mentally. The traditional art of medical dissection had to confine its desire for repetition, as we know, largely to the visual experience of specimens that were stored behind separating glass, lasting only for the medium term, and the price for this repeatability was "ungraspability."

The Controversy About "Hic"

Written across the open ceiling of the main staircase of the Anatomical Institute of the Heidelberg university, confronting all those who enter, is its motto: *Hic gaudet mors succurrere vitae* ("Here, death gladly serves life.") This motto, in suggestively large letters, may be interpreted as either comfort or as a claim. Gunther von Hagens, in his work, went further than others in opposing the validity of the claim for "Here," for "only here, at the Anatomical Institute," i.e., in opposing the exclusivity of this claim to the buildings and staff of scientific medicine. His intentional provocation of limits of taboos made him a publicly and politically noticed and much debated person–and moved the focus of his work out of the country, to Asia.

It does not seem to be an accident that, much earlier, the first large public exhibition of plastinated human bodies that attracted huge crowds was in the Far East. There, the desire for insight into the governing (body) structures still seems to be more active in the background. The mental traditions are more likely to call for finding one's own place by integrating oneself into society.

Institute of Anatomy and Cell Biology at Heidelberg University, photo: Henri Wagner

The way I see it, in our Western world, the plastic-based presentation of the final defeat of the body is causing ambivalence. In viewing the plastinates we oscillate between the fascinated staring of our dominant analytical understanding, and our personal shock in the face of the suggestive borderline experience of the deceased body, which makes it clear that a true and fulfilled life can be achieved only if death is included in it. What can plastination contribute to the path of significant insight and development in the West and in the East, and in the North and in the South? And how can it do so?

Human Nature

Experience teaches us that people who have had a hard life often become especially strong. I have an image of Gunther von Hagens growing up under narrowly confined conditions. He tried to cross the state border: almost two years behind bars due to the authoritarian state power of the German Democratic Republic; then his freedom bought by the Federal German Republic from the other side of the Iron Curtain. For Gunther, loss of his homeland was the price of freedom. Enthusiasm for the Western/American model of possibility. Modest new beginnings.

Then, Gunther's idea that was expressed in the slogan he coined: "Fascination through Plastination–BIODUR maintains the Structure." Another experience of limits/limitations: His vision is rejected within the academic framework of the university as unrealistic. Painstaking private-enterprise beginnings in a garage in Heidelberg; as time went on, more garages were added. Later, the move into a small, old, confined house south of Heidelberg, whose limitations were soon completely removed by painstaking remodeling and state-of-the-art information technology.

Gunther was drawn to the subjective annulment of the rules on speed. As a passenger, I often had the frightening experience of him applying maximum acceleration to his car in order to make a traffic light that was not completely red yet. Nights spent with a *Macintosh* computer. Gunther exhibited the special talent of frequently loading another more impressive clock as a screen saver, or some other little utility, onto his computer. Unfortunately, this talent did not warn him of his other talent of crashing the system altogether due to incompatibilities. But no problem, in the early or later morning Gunther usually had the boxes back up and running, thanks to his skills of improvisation and his intuition.

Persevering success in discovery and invention. Gunther pursued his developmental work very intuitively and according to the principle of trial and error most of the time. He would, for example, listen closely to one of the great experts of the plastics industry, and then arrive at his own solutions by combining and applying, in novel ways, the information received. Resilient problems, inadequate hardening of plastics here, yellowing effects there, often gave cause to a single-mindedly dogged series of experiments leading to small or big innovations in plastination technology.

Academic provocation: the person pretending to be unscientific as scientist. How much unorthodox creativity in looks, behavior, working style and methods can a German university stand? What degree of humbleness, in the face of the academic code with its rules and its desire for adaptation and acceptance of limits, is Gunther von Hagens willing to display? Often, I felt the air in the Plastination Laboratory was heavy with these questions. Eventually–and it really was not to be expected otherwise–they were answered in the direction of the breaking of limits, to the disadvantage of the university.

Premature combination of still different cultures: *Science/Business* and *Business/Science*. To put it simplistically, in the German academy the acquisition of external funds has increasingly lost its somewhat disreputable taste and, compared with one's publication list, has gained in importance for personal performance assessment. Gunther may well be seen as an early and radical exponent of this new time.

Multifaceted wonder: *plastination goes world*. International plastination conferences got talked about. Important university deans from far away countries traveled to see the Heidelberg scientific assistant. A misunderstanding?

Pragmatic decision against the projected academic path: visiting professorships in other countries. Gunther's zest for action and his enormous intuitive creativity perceived the German academic career path to professorship as confining and inconvenient for his own work.

Crossing Jordan: the scandalon of plastinated body experience for everyone. A German museum (the technology museum in Mannheim) was set into the oscillation of the 24 hour tact. One evening I attended the exhibition. As a visitor, I was impressed; as a person, I was touched. Entrance into the exhibition had required a short phone call—it had been years since our last contact—and Gunther himself had opened a back door for me, saving several hours of waiting in the cold that would likely have ensued. Thanks!—From Gunther's look, it seemed that several cameras had been pointed at him during the day in order to record interviews.

Anatomical Museum, Heidelberg University, photo: Henri Wagner

Vesalius redivivus: the great predecessor of the Middle Ages demanded the right to insight into the human body that until then had been refused on religious grounds. On the threshold of the third millenium, there is the public dissection, transmitted by the electronic media. The plastinator as headline.

And where to, now? It seems the answer can only be foreseen by yet more limits.

Andreas Vesal (1514–1564)

Gratitude

to Gunther von Hagens for numerous important experiences in the seven years of our intense collaboration: for experiencing a tandem of contrasts, productive in the long run. Here, something like a crocodile, sitting motionless in front of the computer whenever writing an important article, waiting for the inner answer for a good sentence. There, a virtuoso of the keys, mercilessly hammering combinations of letters into the keyboard with unbelievably fast fingers, only to make them victims of the Delete button moments later. This, of course–from the point of view of the crocodile–in never ending repetition.

As a professionally trained thinker and re-thinker, in my work with Gunther I was confronted with the clenched willpower of the deliberately pure type of man of chance who refuses to recognize seemingly insurmountable barriers as such, much less to accept them. This dynamic has inspired me on my own path and helped me to see my own challenges more clearly.

For an inventor and discoverer it must be an extraordinary challenge to appropriately reconcile his vital interest in the protection of his intellectual property with the required trust in his surroundings and his co-workers. One solution often chosen by Gunther, however, was to become silent so loudly, that people who had previously been completely indifferent paid attention exactly when that was what he wanted to avoid. For example, he would achieve this effect by gesturing in a way that made it very obvious that he was about to convey an important news item–which he subsequently "whispered" out loud.

Gunther made basic and far-reaching decisions most often only after having discussed them. The discussion often was started by a typical question of his: "Say, what would you do in this situation?" If I were the one asked, I would always feel very much appreciated, taken seriously. In addition, Gunther often touched me on a human level, with his personal trust, when he sought me out to discuss his own inner concerns and questions. Lastly, he endured, without exerting any pressure, the fact that I, as his CEO, intuitively, i.e., without being able to give a rational reason, was not ready to donate my body for plastination in the event of my death.

Rurik von Hagens was born in 1980 in Heidelberg, where he was also raised. When he was nine years old, his parents separated, and he continued to live with his two younger sisters, his mother, and his father's father. He graduated from the upper level of a German high school in 1999, and afterwards fulfilled his mandatory military service. Since the fall of 2000 he has studied business administration in Bamberg, Germany, and Birmingham, UK. In addition to his studies, he often works—as he did during his high school years—at the Institute for Plastination, where he is especially involved in organizing the exhibitions. His relationship with his father is very good, even though for many years he saw him only irregularly and often only for very short periods of time.

Rurik von Hagens

About my Father

The "Workaholic"

I always find it very hard to describe my father very briefly, in just a few sentences, or even with only a handful of characteristic key words, as journalist often ask me to do. That is mainly because my father has many characteristics, and some of them are even self-contradictory. For example, he is extremely generous both towards others and himself, but at the same time he is very unassuming. He is organized, just as he is chaotic. He is a calm and quite person, but he also can become very heated and agitated. These contrasting characteristics are part of him, and after naming one, one simply has to list many others in order to adequately portray him. My father is a distinctly multifaceted person but–another contrast–his work always is his absolute focus.

My characterization of him will begin with his central quality, the one that most stands out, one that is undisputed: He is a true "workaholic." This is how I remember him, even from my pre-school days. My father usually was at home for breakfast, and then again briefly for dinner. The time in-between and afterwards he spent at the "institute," or, to be more precise, at the Anatomical Institute of the Heidelberg university; or in one of his numerous rented garages-turned-laboratories, where he was, in his own words, "taking care of plastination." Very rarely had he time–back then as well as today–for anything besides plastination. I remember well how special an event it was when, on the occasion of one of my birthdays, he took a few hours off to spend some time with me setting up my present, a model train set. Today, too, I hardly ever see him for more than a few hours at a time–unless I am visiting him in China–and the better part of those hours usually is spent taking him to the train station or the airport.

When I was still very little (my sister had just learned to walk), we drove to France in our Volkswagen van to spend two weeks of vacation at the Mediterranean Sea. At least that had been the plan as discussed with my mother. After we had spent exactly one day at the beach, my father suggested that we should drive back early, so that we could have a leisurely trip and would not have to rush. But what actually happened was that we

Father and son

drove the entire distance in one night while we kids slept in the car. We did not realize, until our arrival in Heidelberg, that our vacation was over–after about half a week. An important order had been received at the institute, and to fill it numerous plastinates had to be produced. That, of course, was more important than our vacation.

To my father, vacation really is something useless, a plain waste of time. Whenever he takes any time off, he does so in order to be polite to his fellow human beings (who, of course, will sense this). After this one failed attempt at a family vacation, the next time I and my two sisters spent a holiday with him was after my parents had already been divorced. We had a few short vacations together, and they constituted the only times during that period when we children got to be with him for more than a few hours.

In general, my father hates spending even one minute not doing something useful. He always carries index cards with Chinese words. So, whenever he has to wait at a red light, or for his food at a restaurant, he takes them out and memorizes a few new characters. If he is not carrying his index cards, he has a portable cassette player and earphones with him. And in situations like the ones mentioned, he almost never fails to ask me, unbelievingly, where my word cards are, and how I could possibly waste those minutes just waiting for the traffic light to change.

Whenever I spend an extended amount of time with him–as I've already mentioned that usually happens only when I visit him at his Chinese home–his diligence usually ends up making me feel guilty. But no matter how hard I try, I hardly ever succeed at working as much as he does, let alone more than he does. One of the reasons that I fail is that I need more sleep than he does. When I go to bed at 1 a.m., my father usually is still at his desk, and when I get up at seven, he usually greets me with a cheerful report of the things he has already accomplished that morning. If I ever stay in bed until eight, I can be pretty sure to be woken with the question of whether I really intend to sleep the entire day away. To him, sleep is another waste of time. Once he even told me that he was sorry every night when he finally had to go to bed.

The Imaginative One

Whenever I tell these stories to my friends, and especially when I add that my father remembers my birthday only when reminded by others, I encounter mostly pity: "What a terribly strenuous father," is what I hear, or, even more often: "Doesn't it bother you that he never takes care of you, that he never has any time for you, and that you hardly ever get to see him?" No, it does not bother me. As I said at the beginning: hardly a single one of his characteristics can be viewed in isolation. In order to gain a comprehensive idea of him, one always has to know several characteristics at the same time. As a father, for example, he manages–at least the way I see it–to be intensely involved with me, in spite of his limited time, and probably in a way very different from that of other fathers. Explaining this is not easy, but I would like to try.

When I was little, I was mostly impressed by his enormous inventiveness and his habit of not conforming to any rules, at least the rules whose breaking would cause no harm. My sisters and I loved, for example, the "wobbly van." That was our aforementioned VW van–which, by the way, still is my father's preferred type of car (obviously because it allows one to easily transport several barrels from point A to point B). When driving with us kids in the van from one of his garages to the next to look after his plastics experiments, he would suddenly drive the "wobbly van" in zigzag lines, braking abruptly, or going in circles in empty parking lots. We kids back then actually believed that it was the van, not the driver, conducting this "wobbly" business. In doing this, my father was still working while having fun with us. The wild driving maneuvers cost him only a few minutes of his precious work time, and we kids were extremely happy about these fun experiences, and also loved being with him.

At the lab as well, my father knew how to keep us busy so he would be able to work himself. When I had not yet learned to talk but already was accompanying him to the lab, he would simply give me two boxes: one empty and one filled with numerous vials. Then he showed me how to put the vials into the empty box. I was busy, and once done was presented with a new box into which the vials should be transferred next. The only purpose of this exercise was to give my father some quiet time for his own work.

Sometimes he also purely took care of us, i.e., without him working at the same time. Usually, however, this would happen only when his inventiveness was required. Back then, I owned a toy cable railway set. Just as my father, I am interested in everything technical, and so, when I was a child, I was not at all happy with the fact that this cable railway had to be operated manual-

Occupational therapy at the lab

ly, not automatically by a motor. My father was ready to help as soon as I voiced my complaint. Somewhere at the institute he found the motor of an old pump. It was a giant unit that made a terrible racket, and my mother dreaded its setup in our apartment. With the help of some rubber rings, it was possible to hook up the motor to the manual crank of the cable railway, and then I had a motorized toy. That was all that I had wanted. And none of my friends owned such a huge and noisy machine, that was for sure.

Something else that we enjoyed tremendously when we were little was, of course, our birthday parties. A paper chase was usually organized on these occasions, just as at other children's parties. But unlike the others, our chases would not end at some hut in the woods, but in the mile-long corridors of the basement of the Anatomical Institute of the Heidelberg university—at that age, nothing seemed more exciting to us than that. And no one other than my father was able to come up with these crazy ideas.

The Modest and the Generous One

Another unusual characteristic of my father is his aforementioned mixture of modesty and occasional thrift, combined with generosity, often accompanied by wastefulness. I cherish all of these qualities in him–in their, again, very contradictory combination. He never begrudges me, his son, any comfort, and is always glad if he can do something good for me. At the same time, he enjoys teaching me the importance of both modesty and generosity in life.

His own modesty shows, for example, in the fact that he always (and proudly so) flies in economy class. Given that he spends practically one entire month of each year in the air, I find this quite unusual. But to him it is more important to spend his money on "useful" things rather than on a few hours of comfort. Useful, in his eyes, is any expenditure that will save him time. If he wants to grab a quick bite to eat, he will go into the next restaurant at hand, not paying much attention to whether this is a simple or a rather exclusive and expensive place. Neither does he care much about

During a „wobbly van" excursion

what he eats. Should he have happened onto a fancy restaurant, his first question for the much-surprised waiter or waitress, approaching to offer him an aperitif, will be "What is the quickest dish you can serve me?" Social rules simply are not important to him.

Other useful investments to him are expenditures for electronics, books, suitcases, and in general anything that could possibly be used for plastination purposes. When buying things such as these, my father is regularly overcome by buying crazes. Anything that can be used in any way is to be bought, no matter the price. Also, only the very best product in the store must be bought. Occasionally, however, I will buy a product for him (or for myself) and, driven by a student's thriftiness, will settle for one that I deem to be fit for the intended purpose, without blindly choosing the most expensive one. Such a purchase will usually be followed by a short lecture on the subject, and afterward the better product will be acquired as well. On these occasions it does not matter whether the purchase was made for him or for me, once more demonstrating my father's basic and great generosity towards others. He will not begrudge anyone—least of all his children—any expenditure, and he is happy when others are doing well.

Spending money freely, on himself and on others, is something I have seen him do ever since I have known him. It never mattered much to him whether there was a lot, a little, or even no money, in his bank account when he was doing it. When I was a child, I was not directly affected by this behavior, but it must have been a burden on my mother. Any money my father earned was immediately spent—and almost exclusively on plastination. After our failed attempt at a vacation, described above, we never again went on a leisure trip together. We ate mostly potatoes (that happened to be my father's favorite dish, anyway), and all of us, my parents, my two sisters, and later even my grandfather, lived together in a two-bedroom apartment. My father never seemed to be bothered by any of that.

I think that my father's attitude towards money is very unusual. Back then, and also today, he has always viewed it as a mere means to an end. Those who—possibly driven by envy—accuse him of being greedy for money apparently do not realize this. Whatever he buys has to be useful; he never purchases anything with the intention of enhancing his prestige. I still remember the one time when he returned from shopping and I informed him that he had just bought a number of luxury items of clothing made by several well-known manufacturers. He himself had not noticed, and had never even heard of those brand names.

The Teaching One and the Knowledgeable One

Status symbols are not important to my father. He cares about entirely different aspects of life. First and foremost, of course, come knowledge and education: his own, sure, but especially that of his fellow human beings. I, his son, naturally have been subjected to this attitude especially strongly. When I was only four years old, he had already taught me English while giving me baths. I quickly was able to say my name and where I was from, and whenever we had English speaking guests I had to demonstrate this knowledge. When he was not teaching me English, my father instructed me in anatomy. I have read again and again that I supposedly knew about 50 anatomical terms back then. I can still recall a few of them, but most of them I forgot quickly.

When I just had mastered writing in the second grade, my father asked me whether I would be interested in learning to touch-type. Of course I was, especially because he had promised me an electric typewriter as a reward. To me, back then, when the entire operating system for a personal computer still fit onto a single floppy disk, a typewriter was as valuable as perhaps a computer would be today. As with the anatomical terms, he introduced typing to me quite early, and it was very hard for me, especially because the computer program that I used to practice was available only in English. Thus, I did not understand a single word of what I was typing, and I sometimes practiced for several hours a day. Occasionally, I even cried when the program introduced new letters. But the reward was effective. Today, I touch-type faster than I write longhand, and I am very grateful for having learned to do so. Whenever I see someone typing at a computer using the hunt and peck system, I get—just like my father—very anxious. This

Studying Chinese at every opportunity

unnecessary slowness, indeed, is a waste of time, and the few weeks it takes to learn how to type quickly are made up for later. Have you noticed? My father has simply convinced me of this (just like many other things)–a result of another one of his talents.

Even today, my father still encourages me to study whenever he gets the chance to. Ever since I was in high school he has wanted me to buy every single textbook that might have any value to me, and without prompting has always given me enormous amounts of cash for this purpose. A few weeks later he would ask which books I had purchased. And, of course, I am not allowed to sell even a single book after having used it, not even now that I am a university student. But again: My father is completely right about this. His drive for efficiency in education goes even further: He will regularly give me extra cash, instructing me to go and eat at a restaurant so I will not waste precious time on useless cooking activities, but instead will be able to use that time for studying.

The Unusual and The Multifaceted One

By now you will have come to realize that my father is unusual in many ways, and that having him as a father is a very pleasant experience. At the time of this writing, he has been studying Chinese for more than ten years, often spending several hours a day on it. He is, however, not satisfied by simply deciding on a textbook, studying it and complementing this with some classes. Instead, he probably owns by now every single textbook for studying Chinese that has ever been published. He worked with each of them for a while, only to declare the method and theory of instruction of the particular book insufficient. He then went on to the next one. After a while–unhappy with the textbooks–he began creating his own computer file that now contains more than 5000 signs, together with numerous mnemonic phrases, structures, and study aids. Whether this enormous expenditure of time makes him study more efficiently is another question.

Rurik, Tona, Gunther, and Bera von Hagens, 2004

As I said in the beginning: he is at the same time very organized and very chaotic. When he searches for a certain piece of information in a book (or even for the book itself), it usually takes very long until he finds it.

My father is interested in many, many things. In addition to anatomy and chemistry, he is a true expert in several other fields, for instance, in photography and in psychology (he even knows how to hypnotize people). His latest interest is in playing the violin, and for about a year now he has practiced as much as two hours every day. He loves to travel, is very interested in other cultures, and everywhere in the world appears as someone of great intercultural expertise. It is very pleasant to be his son since he has all these multifaceted characteristics. In spite of his sometimes vehemently uttered convictions, he is a very tolerant person (yet another contradiction). He is very understanding when I see things differently, and so gives me a lot of paternal freedom.

By now you will certainly know: I would not want to have any other father. And perhaps by now you will also understand why it is not important to me to have a father who remembers my birthday every year. For the coming years I wish for him to eventually find a little more time for all his many interests and hobbies, and that he may remain as young as he has been until now.

Dear Papa, happy birthday!

Dr. med. Angelina Whalley met Gunther von Hagens at the Anatomical Institute of Heidelberg University in 1987. She has been his partner ever since and they married in 1992. Since 1988, they have been working together in plastination, first at the Plastination Laboratory, and later with her running the business side of their plastination enterprises. This period of joint work was interrupted by her two year position as scientific assistant at the Institute of Pathology of Heidelberg University (1989–1991). Since 1993, Angelina Whalley has managed BIODUR Products, a company that sells the plastics and ancillary devices required for plastination. In 1997, she also took over the position of managing director of the Institute for Plastination in Heidelberg. A plastination artist, Angelina Whalley has been responsible for the concept of all plastination exhibitions held until now, and also was the organizer of the BODY WORLDS exhibition in Germany.

Angelina Whalley

CARPE DIEM–Seize the Day!

Love at Second Sight

He was not exactly a handsome man. His pale complexion and deep-seated eyes, frequently with dark rings caused by many nighttime hours spent working, made him look rather sickly. Sleeping, as well as socializing, going out, dancing, visits to the theater, and other leisure time activities so eagerly pursued by most members of our society were, to him, a waste of time, that only kept him from doing something useful, from pursuing his goals and ideas. He was equally indifferent to his appearance and clothing. The worn-out jeans, faded shirts, and the Birkenstock sandals, even back then his favorites, gave him an unkempt look. In addition, most of his clothing was covered with plastic stains, just as durable, of course, as his plastinates. In short, at first sight he did not seem to have many qualities that would make him attractive to a young, ambitious woman with a zest for life. But one thing he did have–charisma! He bubbled over with humor and natural charm, and was distinguished mainly by his unconventional ways of thinking and acting that created unlimited riches of ideas. He stood out in a refreshing manner from all his, mostly conservative, colleagues at the university. He was like a colorful crazy bird, who at the same time seemed to have incredible strength and unlimited energy. In spite of this, he was not really taken seriously within the university community. He was thought of as an endearing, always ready to help, and extremely committed colleague. But at the same time he was seen as a pitiable screwball who had gotten stuck on an idea—an idea which was considered not without merits, but which eventually would not lead anywhere and which certainly did not warrant the attention of "real" scientists.

We met in 1987 in the dissection room of the Anatomical Institute of the Heidelberg university. I had just finished my medical studies and had applied there for a scientific position for a limited term in order to prepare for my dream profession of surgeon. I immediately was given a job that involved isolating certain proteins from body fluids and also included teaching responsibilities in the dissection classes. However, my own knowledge of anatomy had become a little rusty, and the dissection techniques that I was supposed to teach were all but forgotten. So I was glad to learn that it was customary at the Heidelberg Anatomical Institute to hold a so- called "Class for Dissection Teaching Assistants" before the start of the semester, in which students of higher semesters were intensively trained as dissection table assistants, so that they would be able to teach groups of ten to twelve beginning students during the dissection classes. This class seemed to be just right for me and I signed up. And that was where I would meet the man who soon after would be my lover and later my husband and business partner, and who would give my life, both personal and professional, a direction that I could never have dreamed of back then when I was a newly graduated physician.

From the early days

Gunther had taught this class for many years and was, among the students, one of the most popular teachers at the Anatomical Institute. In addition to his unconventional behavior—for example, he would always address the students with the informal *"Du"* instead of the customary formal *"Sie"*, and allowed them to address him likewise—he was also known for his didactic talent and his unusual teaching methods. He was able to win students over and motivate them in ingenious ways. He would encourage his students with made-up rhymes such as:

> *Scratch it, scrape it, cut it, look now,*
> *deeper dig, and look again now,*
> *off with fasciae, leave the tendons,*
> *Friends, let's sharpen our scalpels!*

As a result, the students actually had fun in his classes, which generally could not be said of the very study-intensive anatomy curriculum. The students were enthusiastic about him—and so, of course, was I! And after only two or three days of the preparatory course I was hopelessly in love with him.

At that time, Gunther was still married to his first wife, gynecologist Cornelia von Hagens. Their children Rurik, Bera, and Tona were seven, five, and three years old, respectively. The relationship between Gunther and his wife apparently had suffered from increasingly divergent personal goals in life. Her idea of a "normal" life, appropriate to their social standing, in which they would "settle down," was contrasted to Gunther's unrestrained ambition, his restlessness, and his uncompromising determination to invest everything into the development of plastination and to always subordinate everything private to this goal.

We hardly spent any personal time, or what is generally meant by that, together. But because we both worked at the same institute, we were able to see each other quite often. In the evening hours I enjoyed helping him at the lab, because I, too, was enthusiastic about his invention, plastination, which I first learned about in the course.

I was even more impressed, however, with his unshakable belief in it. In spite of the circumstances, Gunther and I had a wonderful, carefree, and also very passionate time together. Soon we agreed

Rare twosomeness

that we wanted to continue our lives together. His unconventional ways, his passion for swimming against the stream, and his inventiveness meant, to me, that life with him would never be boring.

After nine months my work agreement with the Anatomical Institute expired, and initially it was not clear whether there would be funds available to allow me to continue. So Gunther offered me a position at his laboratory: a proposition that, under our personal circumstances, seemed very attractive, at least for a limited time. Thus, I accepted.

Big Business?

Back then, plastination was not what it is today, not by a long shot. The main inventions had been made, and several patents had been filed, but the specimens did not have the perfection they have today. Whole-body plastinates were unthinkable, not in the least owing to the high cost of preparing them that a university laboratory simply could not afford.

Unlike his colleagues, Gunther did not have any research funding— except for his initial lab equipment provided by the German Research Council (DFG), but always raised the monies for the upkeep of his lab and the further development of his technology himself. He would accept orders for the production of anatomical teaching specimens from other universities. The process of making those plastinates was always tied to research relating to plastination methods. He would, for example, use novel plastics mixtures on those specimens, or try out new fixation and preparation techniques. The proceeds were used to pay for the cost of production, including the salaries of the required assistants, and they also facilitated an occasional modest investment in new technologies or equipment.

He often created entire collections of educational specimens for other universities, jobs that occasionally paid 200,000 or even 300,000 German marks each. Initially, that seemed like a lot of money to us, but jobs of that magnitude were rare, perhaps only one or two per year, sometimes none. Considering that in order to fill such an order, a number of assistants had to work for several months, and that the annual salary for a scientific assistant even back than was more than 60,000 German marks, not much was left for further research. There often were financial bottlenecks that Gunther bridged with personal loans or with money that he made in his business. He had already founded BIODUR, a small company selling plastics and ancillary devices for plastination purposes to other universities, and thus was spreading the techniques of plastination.

When I first heard of this risky financial commitment on his part, I was completely surprised. Taking out a personal loan in order to fund the salaries of university employees seemed so ludicrous to me that I could not believe any "rational person" would do it. Gunther also was venturesome when it came to purchasing equipment. He loved spending the money he expected to earn later, and he always assumed, optimistically, that the interest and compound interest would be more than paid for by the benefits gained from the investment. This attitude, that he continues to display today, often led to further financial bottlenecks, and also continues to do so, except that the order of magnitude of these investments has changed in the meantime.

One of Gunther's character traits always has been and continues to be concern about the bottom-line. However, that does not at all mean that in implementing his ideas he would follow economic laws. In business, investments need to be amortized before they are replaced by other innovations. Additionally, investments are made in order to raise profits. Not so with Gunther. He often had a new and much better idea before the previous one had had a chance of establishing itself. Whether or not an idea eventually yields a profit is secondary to him–his primary concern is the realization of possibilities. And he can always find good arguments for why a certain purchase should be made right now. Thus, quite a few investment skeletons have accumulated over the years. From a business standpoint, this does not look good. However, it seems that it is just this wasteful spending, combined with personal selflessness, that significantly contributes to Gunther's continued successes in advancing the technology. After all, occasionally he hits pay dirt with an idea.

Gunther makes his decisions mostly based on intuition, in a seemingly chaotic or random fashion, both in business and in the lab when developing new plastination methods. The strictly scientific development process involving controlled experiments and theoretical preparation is rather foreign to him. Yet, he is extremely capable of strategic thinking and goal-oriented acting. There are many examples of this seemingly contradictory characteristic. As chaotic as the running of his business often seems, he had, for example, very early on, created an extensive office handbook prescribing in detail how his workers were to respond to certain requests, including which form to use, how to file documents, and even how to place a stamp on an envelope (upper right hand corner, and straight!).

The university lab itself, with its many spilled plastics residues, always looked a little unkempt: as if it had been hit by a bomb. The devices found there also were highly unusual. They often were items from everyday life that Gunther had gotten his hands on and had thought perfectly suited for

Love at the band saw

plastination work: Soup ladles (for transferring liquid plastics), spatulas (for handling the extremely fragile brain slices during processing) and pantyhose (because of its narrow mesh size it is great for filtering tissue debris and blood clots from the plastics impregnation baths)–

Lab equipment

nothing at home was safe from him. And although one could not help but think of this lab as chaotic, closer inspection revealed that each and every item actually made sense.

It is as if Gunther is constantly living in organized chaos. This chaos facilitates the creativity he needs, but the organized structure prevents him from getting lost inside his own inventiveness. In his private life, he applies a different strategy for maneuvering his personal chaos, namely the conscious acquisition of all items of daily life in large numbers. I have no idea how many pairs of glasses, hats, violin stands, metronomes, etc. Gunther owns, but this "consciousness of the pack," as Gunther likes to call it, helps, at least occasionally, to find one of these items when needed.

In some areas, on the other hand, Gunther is extremely disciplined. If it will help his goals, he is quite able to dedicate time and energy to even the most annoying and unpleasant task, be it mastering a computer program that will be helpful in organizing the office, or studying the Chinese language. The latter he has been doing for several years now, for at least two hours a day, if possible, but only before 6 a.m., because that is when the mind is at its clearest.

Once we even took an accounting class at the local adult school together. As the business grew slowly but steadily, it simply became necessary to learn more about keeping the books, for BIODUR unfortunately was much too small a company to hire expert help. One thing can be said for certain: Gunther really tried. But the art of accounting simply would not yield to him. The world of numbers clearly is not his thing.

Money has never meant anything to him, other than that it was necessary in order to make his ideas reality. Even thinking about his outward appearance, such as clothes, cars or other things, is tiresome to him. In his opinion, such only serve to broadcast one's higher standard of living. So, for example, if he has to buy new shirts, he will buy ten of the same, saving himself the need to ponder which one to actually wear. Cars, too, for Gunther have only practical meaning. He had acquired our VW van, orange like the city's service cars, before we met. After thirteen years of use and with 300,000 kilometers, it was finally retired in 1999 and replaced by a new van. However, it did not go to the junk-yard—equipped with a new motor and a new transmission, it continues to serve plastination, with its own chauffeur, in the capital of Kyrgyzstan.

Gas mask for handling solvents

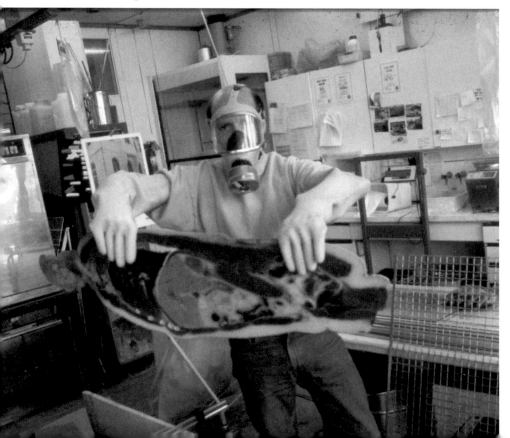

A Bit of Horse-Trading
and a Wedding with Unexpected Consequences

Organizing money matters is another aspect of life that Gunther tries to avoid–he prefers leaving that to others. Thus, it is not surprising that the managing of the business became more and more my task, first as his partner and later as his wife. On the one hand, we complemented each other in this way. On the other hand, given Gunther's nature and his relationship with money, it was a difficult job for me. Many times I needed to slow him down, and often I had to put limits on the realization of his plans. As the "killer of ideas" I was not exactly popular! And, as I gained more experience, I also developed a different idea of how to run a business.

I had assumed a role that I had not at all sought, and because I was not really interested in it, and had no prior knowledge nor experience in it, I initially felt that I was not up to it; and in fact, I was not. In addition, I had had completely different plans of what I would be doing after graduating from medical school. The reason that I did assume this role, in spite of these objections, was Gunther's desire to live in the U.S. that went back to his days as a refugee from East Germany. America! Even back when he had been a political prisoner in Cottbus, the country of unlimited possibilities had been Gunther's dream, unlikely as it was that he would ever set foot on American soil. With the help of a dictionary smuggled into the prison by his father and sewed into his mattress by Gunther himself, he secretly studied English. His approach was to tear out one page of the dictionary at a time and to memorize it word for word, until he knew it by heart without any errors. Subsequently, he would destroy that page and take on the next. Thus, after his release from the secret police prison, he knew a large number of words without actually knowing the language.

Later, in the mid 1980s, he and his first wife rekindled these old plans of emigrating to the U.S. His wish to realize them was only made stronger by the fact that plastination was recognized much more in America than in Germany as an important process. Back then he had been offered a position at the Armed Forces Institute of Pathology (AFIP) in Washington, D.C., the largest pathology institute in the world. His job would have been to manage the institute's own museum and to establish a plastination laboratory. Obtaining the security clearance necessary for working in a military institution, however, turned out to be so difficult and time-consuming–in spite of his conflicts with the GDR regime–that, after two years of waiting and no decision forthcoming, Gunther finally declined the job offer.

In 1989, about a year and a half after we had met, he was offered a second chance in the form of a position as scientific assistant at the Institute of Anatomy of the University of Florida in Gainsville. However, as much as I loved him, I was not ready to follow him to the U.S. After long, almost desperate debates, Gunther eventually had one of his convincing ideas: I would not, as I had planned, become a surgeon, but would continue to work with him in plastination–and in return he would remain in Germany. It was not an easy decision for me. After my long years in medical school,

Black hat at the Golden Gate

the idea of spending my career in a plastics lab, with an uncertain outlook for the future, while being completely dependent on Gunther's professional fate, did not seem appealing. Relieved to have found a solution for continuing our lives together, however, I eventually accepted this horse-trade, even though my heart was not really in it.

Looking back, this decision has turned out to have been a lucky one for both of us. Lucky for Gunther, because when the Iron Curtain fell, the East opened up to him. Lucky for me, significantly later, because when we started the BODY WORLDS work in the mid 1990s, I was once more able to actually identify with my professional tasks. From the beginning, I was in charge of the didactic concept and the design of the exhibition, and I also authored the medical texts accompanying it. A new field of activity had been opened up for me, one that led me closer to my professional roots once again. In addition, I suddenly faced completely new challenges that could not have been more colorful and varied, especially because of the international scope of the exhibitions and the resulting intercultural implications. Today, I would not want to trade my job for that of a classical physician for anything.

Before then, however, I worked for two more years with Gunther at the Plastination Laboratory of Heidelberg University—until it became clear that university funds were drawing to a close and that soon there would not be enough money left to pay for the employees' salaries. Gunther's line of credit had been exhausted once again, and third-party research jobs that would have remedied the situation were not in sight. Thus, we decided that I would, at least temporarily, move over to the Department of Pathology to relieve the burden on the plastination budget of Heidelberg University. The field of pathology is one of morphology, thus closely related to anatomy, and so this move seemed like an obvious choice. It was not exactly my dream subject, but at least it had some clinical relevance and came closer to my idea of a medical job. I actually ended up enjoying my work there so much that I seriously considered continuing on in pathology and even specializing in this field. But after two years I returned to anatomy and Gunther's lab, as we had agreed.

On September 17, 1992, Gunther and I were married at our friends' place in Vermont, at the end of a business trip. We were married by a very unconventional (she was wearing shorts) and thus very much to Gunther's liking justice of the peace, in the garden of our friends' house, underneath giant sunflowers. There had been hardly any preparation for the wedding, for it was a rather spontaneous decision. We sent a fax to our colleagues at the Anatomical Institute stating "Just married, because of sex and money." Our rather conservative colleagues were not amused.

Our wedding caused Professor Kriz, who back then was the boss of both of us at the Anatomical Institute, to no longer extend my work contract. He did not want to appear to support nepotism at his Institute and expose himself to criticism. His decision was unexpected and painful for us, but from a neutral point of view he was absolutely right. Thus, I left the university at the end of 1992 and took over BIODUR in 1993.

Just married because of...

This happened at a time when the technology of plastination had long since reached the limit of what was possible within the realm of a university setting. Although Gunther had been able to annex more and more rooms in the basement because no one else wanted to work there, and although he even had rented a few garage spaces outside the university campus, the laboratory was bursting at its seams. After much consideration, we decided to try to found our own plastination business. After all, Gunther had been managing plastination at the university just like a business anyway, so there would be no major changes. Plus, entrepreneurship promised more flexibility and freedom, because in our own business we would no longer be subject to the internal policy-based restraints of the university. Therefore, at the beginning of 1993, Gunther cut back on his university hours to half time and founded the Institute for Plastination. This reduction of his university hours came with the added benefit of fewer teaching obligations, so he would have more time to spend on the further development of the technology of plastination.

Initially, we set up a dissection room in the basement of our home, but this never was a sufficient solution and only lasted for a very short time. With the help of some bank loans, we soon bought an old car repair shop situated in a small industrial zone of Heidelberg. The shop seemed to be beautifully suited for our purpose, especially since it had an attached spraybooth. That meant that the explosion-proof equipment for handling solvents, which are essential for the plastination process, had already been installed. With the limited funds available to us, we little by little turned the workshop into a plastination laboratory and filled our first orders. Business was slow and difficult and—as always—associated with major risk. We always existed on the very border of liquidity and with both our credit limits stretched to the fullest. The proceeds did not allow us to do much, but we were happy about any little bit of progress.

Idea for an Exhibition

The major breakthrough came with the BODY WORLDS exhibition, which generated revenues that in turn spurred the explosive growth of our institute. The idea for an exhibition had actually first come up in 1989, elicited by the inquiry of a physician working for a local health insurance provider (AOK Pforzheim) who asked to borrow a few plastinates for his educational classes in preventative medicine aimed at lay people. We liked the idea so much that we created a small exhibition of all the functional systems of the human body. Since we did not yet have plastinates for all the individual topics, we had to substitute with specimens from the university's collection that were stored in formalin, as well as with some plastic models. Although the pieces on display were not as perfect as current plastinates, the concept already was similar to that of the later exhibitions. The most spectacular specimen consisted of a series of transparent head to toe body slices, which I had, on this occasion, assembled into an 18-foot-long single exhibit for

The „Transparent Human Being" in Pforzheim, Germany, 1989

the first time. This piece lent its name to the exhibition: The Transparent Human Being. Back then, there were no whole-body plastinates. The largest solid exhibit in the show was a lower extremity. The setting of this first exhibition was rather unspectacular: a few tables in a community room in Pforzheim, Germany, on which the plastinates were displayed and explained. And yet, the public's response was resounding: in only two weeks, more than 14,000 lay people poured in to see the show.

Awed Japanese exhibition visitors

After this unexpected success, Gunther often asked me why I did not follow up on the idea of exhibitions. But I thought that we would not be able to afford it–after all, what museum pays for itself? And aside from the enthusiastic visitors, we had not managed to find any supporters. Local pathologists had publicly voiced their indignation at the "marketing" of real human specimens which the exhibition constituted, in their opinion. At the Heidelberg university as well we had been watched skeptically. And we still were dependent on the university; going it alone back then was still completely out of the question.

Thus, the idea of exhibitions was shelved until, in 1995, the Japanese Anatomical Society invited us to participate in an exhibition that was being prepared in honor of its 100th anniversary and that was to take place at the National Science Museum in Tokyo, Japan. We jumped at the invitation, since it meant re-opening an old opportunity. With the help of an established, well-known museum, we would be able, we thought, to overcome the reservations against such an exhibition in Germany as well. We produced a number of new plastinates especially for this exhibition, so that in the end about 70 percent of the displayed specimens came from our laboratory. Among them were four whole body plastinates, along with the "Transparent Human Being" in slices, as well as some organs of a sperm whale that had been stranded in Northern Germany in 1994. For more than 250 years, it had been prohibited to publicly display dead human bodies in Japan. Thus, the exhibition constituted the breaking of a major taboo of Japanese society. Still, there was no public criticism at all. Quite to the contrary, the exhibition was characterized by a high degree of acceptance, and within four months it attracted not the 150,000 visitors that had been predicted, but instead approximately 450,000 fascinated people. The order of magnitude of this success was astonishing, even to us. We were simply overwhelmed when we saw the masses of clearly amazed Japanese people—usually extremely reserved in their public display of emotion—pushing past the exhibits, while long queues formed outside, occasionally resulting in waiting times of up to four hours. That was the final confirmation we needed to continue exhibiting our work. The first exhibition completely

furnished by us, and more comprehensive than the Tokyo one, was held the following year in Osaka and was organized by a Japanese business partner of ours. It was just as successful. There were other Japanese locations in Hamamatsu, Nagoya, Urawa, and Yokohama before we finally took the exhibition to Germany for the first time in the fall of 1997.

In spite of the major successes in Japan, it was not easy for us to find a museum or other suitable site for the exhibition. The administration of the Heidelberg castle, for example, informed us that "an exhibition such as the one suggested does not fit the traditions of the Ottheinrich Building." At that time, the ongoing exhibition in the building was one of instruments of torture. We finally found an interested party in the Mannheim State Museum of Technology *(Landesmuseum für Technik und Arbeit)*. But even there, the administrators were not impressed with our Japanese successes. The Japanese were different, in the museum's experts' opinion, and had a different attitude towards the body. Their most optimistic estimates for the total number of visitors was, therefore, somewhere between 50,000 and

Waiting time: up to four hours

90,000. The actual number turned out to be 780,000—more even than the world-famous exhibition of modern art, *documenta*, in Cassel, as Gunther liked to frequently emphasize later.

Shortly before the opening of the exhibition, serious voices of concern were heard for the first time. This led to changes in the contract we had with the museum—only four weeks before the opening. The museum no longer was ready to accept responsibility for the exhibition, so we, or rather I as managing director of the Institute for Plastination, had to assume that role. Indepently of these events, the museum surprisingly was unable to come up with sufficient funds for the advance financing of the exhibition. Gunther and I took a major risk and arranged for advance financing through huge personal loans. The situation became critical when, only a few days prior to opening, both the Mannheim dean of the Catholic Church and the Mannheim superintendent of the Lutheran Church turned to Baden-Württemberg Prime Minister Erwin Teufel "seeking remedy" in order to prevent the exhibition from happening. Quickly, a committee was formed to inspect the exhibits on the day before the scheduled opening. In a secret vote, the committee approved of the exhibition by a majority of one vote. Luckily, I must say, because cancellation of the event would have meant bankruptcy for us.

Unlike in Japan, a steady stream of public criticism accompanied the Mannheim exhibition. Supporters and opponents fought tooth and nail about whether or not the public display of human specimens, and the inherent commercialization, was ethically justifiable. This was a debate we had expected, but its intensity came as a surprise. What we had not been prepared for at all, however, was the claim that human bodies in our work were "degraded to works of art." More than 1.7 million people had seen the exhibition previously in Japan, and the thought that the exhibits might be works of art apparently had not occurred to a single one of them. Gunther, facing all accusations publicly as best he could, simply could not cope with this particular point. Why were these bodies all of sudden considered art? And if so, why did this constitute a "degradation?" Was art not highly esteemed in our culture? What, after all, is art?

The reaction of Germany's anatomists could hardly have been more different from that of their Japanese colleagues: In Japan, anatomists were actually grateful to Gunther and held a festive ceremony honoring his work for the exhibition. His German colleagues, on the other hand, noted in a "Statement on the Commercialization of Body Donations" issued on the occasion of a board meeting during the 93rd annual meeting of the German Anatomical Society on March 28, 1998: "The board of the Anatomical Society regrets the Mannheim exhibit as it is a presentation of the field of anatomy, which actually deals with problems of functional-structural research, inappropriate to modern times, with partially distorted body specimens that in some cases simply cannot be justified by any didactic principle."

The Chinese Adventure

The dispute over the exhibition eventually caused quite a stir everywhere in Germany, and in all segments of the population there seemed to be supporters and opponents. The Anatomical Institute of the Heidelberg university was split into two camps as well. Under the circumstances, Gunther no longer found it possible to continue his work there and thus left the university at the end of 1997. Just before that we had tried to obtain recognition as a scientific institute for the Institute of Plastination from the Baden-Württemberg authorities. Such recognition would have allowed us to invite foreign visiting scientists, just as a university is able to do. Those contacts had always been important to Gunther during the development and dissemination of plastination. Initially, the proceedings seemed to be going well, but suddenly, as if by suggestion or directive from "higher up," everything came to a standstill and our application was denied. It was obvious that the dispute over the exhibition once again had worked against us.

During subsequent exhibitions, the dispute would break out again and again, always with the same arguments on both sides. This lasted until the end of 2003, when, in Germany, the tone of the criticism shifted and began to focus more strongly on Gunther von Hagens as a person, eventually leading to nasty disparagement of his character. Criticism in other European countries always was much more moderate, and nowhere in Asia or in the U.S. did the exhibitions provoke any public criticism at all. Was this reaction, therefore, a "typically German" one?

When he left the Anatomical Institute of the Heidelberg university at the end of 1997, Gunther decided to leave Germany altogether. He had at that time already been offered a visiting professorship at Dalian Medical University–Dalian is a harbor city on the Yellow Sea in Northeast China, with more than 4 million inhabitants–where he was also told that he would be able to use an entire building on the university campus for plastination purposes. There were many reasons to get involved in this particular adventure. One was the uncommon challenge. Also, in China as in almost all of the countries of the Far East, macroscopic anatomy still plays a much more important role in medicine than in the West. The Eastern countries often lacked the money to implement all the developments in the areas of electron microscopy and later cellular biology that had, by then, been well established in all Western anatomical institutes. Consequently, Gunther's chances of finding qualified technicians with superior fine motor skills to work on his plastination projects were especially good in China.

„Plastination City" under construction

Chinese dissectors at work

Thus, he agreed to the Dalian offer, and the Chinese adventure began—much to my chagrin, because it meant not only absences of several weeks at a time for Gunther, but also that I would have to bear the responsibility for our Heidelberg enterprise all by myself from then on. I also was the organizer of all the German exhibitions and so had additional important tasks involving exhibition coordination.

Later, in 2000, Gunther founded, in addition to his institute at Dalian Medical University, a private institute in the "High Tech Zone" of Dalian, the "Von Hagens Dalian Plastination Company, Ltd." This was to grow into a mega-institute of plastination, comprising several groups of buildings with a few hundred employees. Gunther dubbed this project Plastination City, and it incurred astronomical costs which were covered by exhibition revenues.

Initially, this step into the Far East triggered another immense thrust forward for plastination and Gunther's work. There seemed to be new, and apparently unlimited, possibilities for him. In real life, however, the cultural differences, on several levels, turned out to be a factor that could not be neglected. For instance, a Chinese "Yes" may mean nothing more than confirmation that a certain message has been received–not necessarily implying that an agreement will be kept or even that the message itself has been properly understood. This problem is also prevalent in the fields of contracts and negotiations with the authorities. Not only did one disloyal employee build, during the period of his employment, a competing business with the help of Gunther's know-how and at Gunther's expense, but he also did not exhibit any consciousness of wrong-doing by Western standards. Quite to the contrary, he made a significant effort to not "lose face" and to cause more damage to Gunther. Such developments show there was a difficult and costly learning curve that eventually somewhat mellowed Gunther's enthusiasm.

Crucial Experiences

I have often wondered where Gunther gets the strength to constantly come up with new developments entirely from within, and to again and again push the envelope, in spite of all the criticism and objections that cross his path. And where does he get the self-assurance that allows him to question and even to defy established structures and authorities, and how does he manage to remain completely unperturbed by public criticism and even name calling (that he sometimes even seems to provoke on purpose)? Gunther is, no doubt, an exceptional personality. From what he has told me and from what I have observed myself, I have made out three major events in his early life, that, in my opinion, were formative in the development of these aspects of his personality.

Gunther suffers from the bleeding disorder "hemophilia." His body produces too little of a certain clotting factor, so that even tiny injuries lead to massive hemorrhages that are difficult to stop. This syndrome was especially hard on him in his childhood years, when even minor injuries meant hospitalizations of several weeks. He became an outsider and eccentric, for he rarely had the opportunity to measure his strength against that of his peers. As the alleged weakling that he was, he became the scapegoat for his classmates. The introspection forced on him by his disease taught him to find esteem and satisfaction mostly in himself and his actions, and not to primarily strive for recognition by others. He increasingly managed to successfully defend himself against his peers, and those circumstances were formative for his self-esteem from an early age on. They became an integral part of his personality structure, and even today he is mostly immune to peer pressure and does not attribute any importance to what others may think of him.

Another crucial experience was that of his thwarted illegal emigration from the German Democratic Republic and his arrest in the Czechoslovakian Republic. One of the border patrol officers left Gunther alone in the interview room with the window open to give him a chance to escape. But Gunther stayed. He was absolutely sure that he would be able to convince the authorities in the GDR that he had merely planned a trip of a few days and simply had not known about the paperwork he would need, and therefore had not applied for the appropriate permits. Not taking this chance to escape eventually cost him almost two years of his life, which were spent in a prison of the state police. The image of that open window would haunt him for many years to come, reminding him that life not only punishes those who are late, but also those who do not take the chances that they are given. According to Gunther, this image was especially vivid for him when he held his first plastinate in his hand. Completely shrunken and darkened, most others would have tossed it into the garbage. But Gunther knew, thanks to his good knowledge of chemistry, acquired back in the GDR, that the shrinking could be attributed only to the too quick impregnation process, and that the staining had to be a result of the obviously inappropriate refractive index of the particular plastic he had used. He would only have to find plastics that would allow longer processing and that, at the same time, had different optical properties. He understood that that tiny piece of plastinated kidney was another window that fate had opened for him, and that he must not leave it unused.

The third formative experience is rooted in his time spent in the state police prison. Gunther had been raised, mainly by his mother, to be a loyal communist, absolutely true to the party line. When he was only 17 years old, he had joined the party "in order to be even more active for socialism and to help eradicate the faults of the system," as he phrased it in his letter of application. The older he got, however, and the more he learned to think critically, the more he began to have basic doubts. For example, when he asked senior party officials inconvenient questions, he received answers that really were not answers: "Comrade," he was severely admonished, "those are not your own questions, but those of the class enemy. Where did you get these questions?" Another such experience, taken from daily life, happened when he visited his uncle's farm and saw that the cows were kept in so-called "open stables", unthinkingly copied from the Soviet "socialist cousins", that necessitated the amputation of the tails of the emaciated cows because they had frozen to the ground. He became more and more disappointed with the system. He was also irritated by the constant contradictions between Western news reporting and reports from *Neues Deutschland*, the main official organ of the ruling Socialist Unity Party. Gunther tried to leave the party but learned that such a step would cost him his university place and was, therefore, not an option.

When, in 1968, the troops of the Warsaw Pact states invaded Czechoslovakia, he saw only two options for himself: to work against the system or to leave. He initially tried his hand at the former. Together with some like-minded people he began printing flyers intended to "denounce the untruthful representations of the newspaper *Neues Deutschland*." The printing blocks they used were homemade plates of gypsum into which they scratched their messages in mirror image. Using the dyed plates, they were able to produce print runs of about 200 sheets, black with white writing, that they distributed by motorcycle during the night. The secret police reacted by bringing the regular police out in intimating numbers in order to catch those responsible. It was enough so that Gunther and his friends were suspicious of any car equipped with an antenna. The pressure increased until it became unbearable and Gunther realized: "I have to get out of here!"

Once in prison, Gunther was, in his own words, "cured of communism once and for all." The number of people that had been unfairly treated and punished by the system was enormous. There were examples like that of a student of history who had been sentenced to five years in prison because he had pointed out discrepancies by referring to arguments from old SED (i.e., party-owned) newspapers. Or that of a 24 year old who had to spend seven years of his life incarcerated because of three attempts at escape. Educational measures that bordered on brain-washing were employed to bring the disloyal back in line. Eventually, they had to apply for "reintegration." Gunther wrote in his form: "I ask that I may remain imprisoned until the authorities have convinced themselves of my unworthiness of reintegration into the socialist community of the people." That sentence cost him two weeks in the "tiger cage", i.e., solitary confinement, in a cell that was so small that he could touch both walls when stretching his arms, and that was furnished with nothing but a plank-bed that was locked in an upright position during the day.

The „tiger cage," photos: Florian Falcke

I first realized the impact that Gunther's GDR past, and especially his imprisonment by the secret police, had left on him, when we visited a building formerly owned by the state police in Leipzig, shortly after the wall had come down. There was a cell there that was exactly the same, down to the last detail, as the one that Gunther had been imprisoned in. Gunther laughed loudly and began to tell me anecdotes from his jail time. He slapped his thighs and especially joked about how they had constantly tried, every single day, to convince him that one day he would be on his knees, begging to be re-admitted to the GDR. All of a sudden he broke out in tears. This weeping was tantamount to a cathartic liberation from all the suppression and degradation that he had had to suffer. It represented his relief that, in spite of everything, he had made it. He had proven to himself that he had not been wrong.

These decisive life experiences taught him that established structures and authorities are not necessarily right, even though they may be in power, and that it is not only quite legitimate, but even necessary, to occasionally challenge them and question their behavior. Thus, his extreme tendency today, to be a total nonconformist and to not accept common social standards, is rooted in those experiences of the past, just as is his pronounced pleasure in fighting secular or church authorities. The more he had been told that he would fail in the West and would return, full of remorse, to his hated socialist homeland, the more he wanted to prove himself to "those up there." Even after he had come to the free West, this attitude remained the principle by which he lived. Whenever someone tries to put obstacles in his path, it only serves to release more energy in Gunther. He actually feels the need to defy whoever tries to tell him what to do.

Concluding Remarks

Journalists these days often ask me what it is like to be married to Gunther. Well, I would like to know, too, for he is never around! Plastination is his life, and he is following this path, uncompromisingly and single-mindedly. That does not mean that he does not care about our relationship, or that he expects me to conform to his goals. Quite to the contrary, his idea of partnership requires a wife who knows what she wants and takes what she needs.

From the very beginning, I have been fascinated by his single-mindedness and his strength to move things that seems to come from within himself. But creative people like Gunther are also difficult and tiring. One always has to expect that from one day to the next very basic assumptions may be questioned or even upset. What had been right and important until a minute ago now may be considered wrong and inappropriate, and therefore may now be discarded. But no matter how often this behavior has tested the limits of my ability to cope, I would not want to miss a single moment of our common experience. I wish for him—and, implicitly, for myself—that his tremendous, youthful strength will remain his for many years to come.

Dr. Wolfgang Heindl is an independent tax and financial consultant living in Heidelberg. His first contact with Gunther von Hagens in the early 1990s was of a professional nature. Their cooperation evolved into close contact and eventually friendship. This friendship has survived Gunther von Hagens' leaving Germany: He still consults with Wolfgang Heindl on his international activities.

Wolfgang Heindl

Traveling with Gunther

Approximation

"You absolutely have to come to Dalian," I had heard him say many times. And, of course, I was curious, finally wanted to see what had been created over there in China. I did not have a concrete idea of what Gunther von Hagens had built over there. All I knew was that he had invested a lot of money, that he had made with his exhibitions, in his institute for plastination. "You have to see it so you will understand why I am doing it just there!" Ever since I've known Gunther von Hagens, the question of how to address him has never been a problem. He does not want to be seen as boss, but rather as a co-worker, and so the use of the familiar *"Du"* was a basic principle of his way of dealing with his co-workers and employees. Over the course of time, I came to understand that he manages his various institutes more like academic institutions than commercial enterprises. This attitude derives from his history, and he gladly accepts the disadvantages that the more business-oriented onlooker might perceive. Critics are met with leniency.

One gray fall evening the time finally had come. My suitcase was stuffed, for I did not know what climate to expect. I had my passport with my visa in my pocket, and I was happily excited about my imminent trip into the unknown. Gunther picked me up by car for our trip to the airport. An employee of the Heidelberg institute was driving. Gunther's first sentence was: "Hello, my dear, is there any room in your suitcase?" There was a little room, and so something happened that I was to witness again and again when traveling with Gunther–the distribution of a large number of packages, smaller packages, books, and catalogs to his co-travelers. When Gunther travels, one cannot help but be reminded of a caravan.

After the redistribution of luggage we took off for the airport. Silently, I wondered why we had not used a shuttle bus rather than the expensive employee, because, from my point of view, that would have been more cost-effective. My question was answered in a surprising manner once we got to the airport, where the employee had an important role to play. Once we arrived, one piece of luggage after another almost burst out of the trunk. Pushing three heavily loaded luggage carts we headed for the check-in counter. But stop! Just before we reached the counter, Gunther pointed out something to the employee, and, as if practiced many times before, the employee left our caravan, positioned his luggage cart at some distance from the counter, and waited. Gunther probably had noticed my clueless and questioning look. Amazed, I listened to his explanation that he was planning on carrying on all the items of luggage on the employee's cart. My amazement will become understandable to the gentle reader once I mention that among all of these pieces of "carryon" luggage there was a photocopier intended for the university institute at Dalian.

The ground staff at the check-in counter would never have accepted this "carryon" luggage as such, had they ever seen it. On his many travels, however, Gunther had learned that the cabin crew never gives him any trouble because of the number or size of his carryon items. All he had to do, therefore, was to get his "carryon" luggage past the check-in counter, and that was his employee's job.

Everything went as planned, and there was only a minor glitch on board, for the photocopier simply would not fit into any of the overhead luggage bins. However, thanks to Gunther's fame, a flight-attendant took loving care of it and returned it to us after our arrival in Dalian.

Dalian

At the Beijing airport we were met by an employee of the Dalian institute who took care of our carryon luggage. Because the photocopier was a gift for the Dalian university institute, there were no problems with customs' formalities. From the baggage claim hall we moved into the arrival hall-a bustling crowd, an ocean of voices. Before our trip I had not looked at a map, and because I only had a plane ticket to Beijing, I had assumed that Dalian was some kind of a suburb of Beijing. Now, however, Gunther informed me that Beijing was merely a stopover for us, and that we would have to fly another hour to Dalian. Dragging along our luggage, we pushed and shoved our way from the arrival hall to the departure hall. Gunther was on the lookout for a ticket booth. In China, domestic flights are government subsidized so that less affluent Chinese also have the means to cross the huge distances in the country. Therefore, a ticket to Dalian was significantly cheaper when bought at the ticket counter in Beijing than if booked from Germany. And flying within China is as simple as train travel in Germany. There are large display boards showing the departure times–fortunately they are displayed in English as well as Chinese–where one looks up when the next plane for one's destination is scheduled to leave. Then one buys a ticket for the next available seat at the counter, and off one goes.

Flights from Beijing to Dalian depart almost every hour, so we had no problem obtaining tickets for a plane that was soon to depart. Naturally, Gunther was happy, obviously to not only to be saving money, but also to be making use of his knowledge of the Chinese language. I had noticed that Gunther, at all times–in the car, while waiting at the airport, while standing in line–was busily studying a Chinese textbook. On another occasion I was able to witness the success of his diligent efforts.

That was during a taxi ride from the Beijing airport to the city center. We got into the cab and asked the driver for a flat rate, and were quoted 100 Yuan. Gunther was sure that it should be 70 Yuan at most and began an animated discussion with the driver. From their gestures I inferred that Gunther asked the driver to turn on the meter, which the driver in turn declined, insisting on his flat rate. This debate, held in Chinese, was heated, but I was under the impression that both Gunther and the driver had a really good time and a lot of fun. After a while, the driver caved-in to Gunther's insistence and turned on the meter. When we reached our destination, the fare actually was only 70 Yuan. Gunther gave the driver 100 Yuan, 70 Yuan for the trip and a tip of 30 Yuan. The great exercise in speaking Chinese had been well worth 30 Yuan, he said.

For the flight from Beijing to Dalian we took a rather new Boeing, and there were even chickens on board. Dalian is a large port city, nestled into a wide bay. Only a few dozen miles away is a famous navy base–its English name is Port Arthur–which played a sad military role in Japanese-Russian history. Thanks to Gunther's pull, I was able to visit this place, which continues to be a prohibited military area. Traces of the battlefields of the Japanese-Russian war are still very visible, similar to the area around Verdun, France, and they serve as an eloquent memorial to the pointlessness of armed conflict. My visit to this theater of war preoccupied me for a long time.

Our descent to Dalian, over the bay and towards the low sun, was breathtakingly beautiful. Above the bay there is a skyline of high-rises that could compete with that of New York. After having overcome the arrival formalities, we were picked up by a minivan belonging to the institute–my first experience with Chinese road traffic. Could it possibly be due to the large population that a human life does not seem to be worth much in China? Or is it that in Europe, 2000 years of Christian philosophy, oriented towards charity and compassion, has furthered the development of a different kind of respect for life, for the individual? Seemingly without rules and regulations, the cars fight their way along the roads and streets. The right of the stronger, the faster, the more reckless seems to have become the standard. Pedestrians, the weakest element, do not receive any consideration. The good news: there are cross walks. The bad news: no one pays any attention to them. I saw a child in the middle of an eight lane road, surrounded by fast traffic in both directions. The child had already crossed four lanes, jumping from one to the next. Cars were honking angrily: how dare a child get in their way. The automobilization of China will become a major problem.

Having survived the automobile war all across this city with its close to four million inhabitants, we safely reached Gunther's apartment. As expected, Gunther lives among the natives. In a Chinese apartment house, only a few years old, his dwelling is on the top floor. Seven floors, no elevator! Climbing up is a test of endurance for the entire body. The weight of our luggage challenges muscles and lungs. Passing his Chinese neighbors' doors is an endurance test for our noses. Whatever is being cooked behind those neighborly doors, I do not want to know, and probably would want to eat even less.

Finally, at the top, I luckily find that in spite of Gunther's preference for everything Chinese, his apartment has been furnished to suit my rather European wants. Only the central heating–a gravity cycle without a pump–seems like an antique, but works very well! Stretched out on a comfortable chair, I reflect on the events of the day, while in the room next door, Gunther is already at his desk, checking his e-mail. Secret hands have provided bread, cheese, and fruit, and for me even a bottle of red wine, "The Great Wall," not a revelation but better than expected.

The Institute

The next morning we are picked up at eight. Gunther wants to show me his institute and introduce me to his employees and students. He has been given a rather large building, situated in the area belonging to the medical school of Dalian university. Here, at the Institute of Plastination of Dalian university, co-workers and students are developing, under his guidance, the technology for the preparation of corrosion specimens. Proudly, they present to him what has been achieved over the past few days. Their faces reflect the enthusiasm that Gunther, via his personality, has kindled in them. I watch from afar and, for the first time clearly see how Gunther, in this milieu, becomes completely and passionately wrapped up his work and forgets about everything else. I am met with extreme politeness, but I feel that I am an outsider. Then I wander through the rooms of the institute, admiring the corrosion specimens. The employees practice this technique with rabbits and chickens, and I can tell that they are enjoying it from the poses they have given to those fine blood vessel structures. Time is short, we have to continue my tour, and Gunther pulls himself from his co-workers and students. The employees at the second part of his institute, situated further out of town, also are eagerly expecting their mentor.

The institute's bus takes us to the institute's lot in the outskirts of Dalian. This is where the so-called "High Tech Zone" is, a large and only recently created technology park in which the city of Dalian maintains a settlement program for certain technology companies. Innovative enterprises from all

Dalian Medical University

over the world are given the opportunity to set up their operations and research institutions under favorable conditions. The administration of the technology park is proud to have Gunther and his institute on site, among big name companies from all around the world.

Set atop a hill, the building complex of Gunther's institute greeted us from afar. Extensive underground facilities connect a two story square building which houses teaching theaters, dissection rooms, and technical equipment with a multi-story administrative and residential building. During my visit, about 180 employees and students were working there. A majority of them lived in the residential part of that building. I learned that in China living quarters are commonly part of the employment package. While Gunther once again dived into the environment of his co-workers, I was interested in the furnishings of the living quarters. I was given a tour and saw with surprise that the apartments offered to employees and students, equipped with cooking niches, showers, and toilets, could easily compete with the student apartments in German dorms. Gunther takes good care of his employees.

The manager of the accounting department, whom I visited afterwards, invited me to lunch at the institute cafeteria. Providing a cafeteria for employees is another practice of Chinese companies. The dishes offered were very strange to my European taste, and so I was glad to have the accounting manager by my side as a consultant. Competent in the English language—Gunther has made English the working language across the entire institute—she explained to me the contents of the various pots. And that was truly necessary, for the rice was the only item I was able to identify. The food had nothing in common with what is served in Chinese restaurants in Germany—it looked a little strange, but it tasted better than anything I had previously sampled of Chinese cuisine.

After lunch the friendly manager of the accounting department again took me under her wing and gave me a tour of the institute. I will never forget the view from the roof terrace of the building. From the rolling hills in the background over the Dalian skyline to the silvery China Sea glit-

View from the roof of the institute building towards the Yellow Sea

tering in the distance, the entire view reminded me of a painting. The institute's complex fit harmonically into this image and impressively illustrated Gunther's achievement. I understand why Gunther is revered by his employees and students, and respected by the administration.

Musings

The following day found me sitting on a tiny balcony that is attached to Gunther's seventh floor apartment like a swallow's nest. I was deeply engrossed by the view of the China Sea when the sound of hammering called me back to reality. On a neighboring lot, the construction of what looked like a large apartment complex was underway. A large number of workers were busy laying the foundations for the buildings. Dalian's geology it is such that beneath a shallow layer of soil, solid rock exists. In order to create the desired foundations, this rock had to be removed.

Instead of machines, I saw about 100 workers in the lot, working away at the rock with nothing but hammers and chisels. Three workers form a team, in which one of them held a chisel about the size of his own body, while the other two took turns hammering away at the chisel. Seemingly incessantly, ant-like, the many teams of three workers dug their way into the rock, from 6 a.m. to 8 p.m. The workers lived in temporary huts erected on the border of the area, cooked their food on open fires and hung their clothes to dry between the huts. The only machine I ever saw was an ancient wheel loader removing the resulting rocky debris. Later I learned that it took about three months to finish the foundations. I was told that the hourly wage of these workers was about 25 euro cents. Estimating about 120,000 man hours for the completion of the foundation, it should not have cost more than 30,000 euros.

I have seen similar geological conditions in other parts of the world. On the island of Mallorca, Spain, for example, the construction of building foundations involves similar obstacles. As far as I have seen, however, machines are used there to complete such tasks. Excavators with chiseling attachments, operated by a single worker, dig down into the rock. Rough estimates have convinced me, however, that in spite of the use of machinery, the construction of foundations there has to cost at least twice as much as in China.

Because of the seemingly inexhaustible reservoir of cheap labor available in China, it is more efficient from an economic point of view to replace the production factor "capital" with the production factor "labor", at least for simple production processes. This early capitalist way of production demonstrates that the Chinese economy, in many areas, still is at the very beginning of industrialization. This is just one of many contradictions in this contradiction-rich country. The construction of the tracks for the super fast train Transrapid in Shanghai–a product of state-of-the-art technology–was

Von Hagens Dalian Plastination Company Ltd.

achieved utilizing a huge number of cheap laborers. And it was completed at a speed that our Western capital-intensive construction companies no longer seem to be capable of.

This method of production certainly is not only favored by the price of labor, but also by the patience, persistence, and capability for suffering of the Chinese workers. I can only assume that this attitude has its roots in Confucian principles. And it is precisely two of these characteristics that cause Gunther to be so enthusiastic about the precision of his Chinese dissectors. He cannot imagine finding another place in the world where his ideas could be realized with so much dedication and with such fine motor skills producing such quality. But, of course, Gunther's skilled employees are paid an appropriately higher salary.

My conviction that the patience and persistence of the Chinese people have to have their roots in a Confucian system of thought was hardened during a walk around Gunther's residential neighborhood. Except for Gunther, no foreigners live there, and I thus had ample opportunity to study authentic Chinese life. I was strolling down a street when I noticed an old man to the side of the street. He was sitting on a bench, a big bucket of water next to him, and a huge paintbrush in his hand. From time to time he took the paintbrush, dipped it into the water and painted huge calligraphic signs on the black asphalt of the street. The signs were transient, for they were exposed to the hot sun which made the water evaporate very quikkly. Again and again he painted new signs onto the asphalt and seemed satisfied whenever one of them turned out exceptionally well. He did not

Kyrgyz employees

EAI08080
12:00
X 7

GA2

303

CASH
AEE508
8-AUG-09
ADULT
14.00
4-59669

3 6517239 7011

ADMIT ONE : 12:00 TIME SLOT

ENTER BETWEEN 12:00 - 12:30

3 6517239 7011

BODY WORLDS
& THE MIRROR OF TIME
THE BUBBLE AT THE O2
VALID SPECIFIED TIME ONLY
SAT 08-AUG-09

PRICE 14.00 S/C
ADULT 4-59669   AEE508   TOTAL 14.00
ADULT   8-AUG-09   8-AUG-09 12:14

The O2

TERMS & CONDITIONS

The O₂ for either The O₂ **arena**, Indigo or The Bubble (each a "Venue") is authorised to sell tickets to events as an agent on behalf of the promoter of the event (the "Event Promoter"). All tickets sold by or on behalf of The O₂ (the "Tickets") are sold subject to the Terms and Conditions of the Event Promoter and The O₂ (a full set of which are available at **www.theo2.co.uk** and in writing from The O₂ T & C's, PO Box 02, London SE10 0UZ).The general Terms and Condition relating to admission have been extracted and reprinted here for your convenience.

1. You must produce a valid Ticket to gain entry to each Venue and upon request for inspection at any time. Failure to produce your Ticket when requested may result in you being ejected from the Venue. 2. All children must have a Ticket. Under 14's must be accompanied by an adult. Standing areas are not suitable for under 16's. Events may be age restricted and it is the responsibility of the Ticket holder to check before purchasing. Please visit **www.theo2.co.uk** for further information. 3. Removing the Ticket stub invalidates the Ticket. 4. Tickets cannot be cancelled or exchanged after purchase unless the event is cancelled, rescheduled or subject to a material alteration (see full Terms and Conditions for details). 5. The Ticket holder has a right only to a seat of a value corresponding to that stated on the Ticket holder's Ticket and management reserves the right to provide alternative seats to those specified on the Ticket. 6. Tickets are not transferable. Reselling a Ticket for profit or commercial gain or use for competitions, promotions or hospitality packages without the express permission of the artiste's management or promoter will void the Ticket. Failure to adhere to these conditions may result in the Ticket holder being refused entry to or removed from the event. 7. Tickets bought from unauthorised agents are not valid and admission to the event will not be permitted. 8. The Venue is not liable for any Tickets that are lost or stolen. Standing tickets cannot be duplicated under any circumstances. 9. In order to facilitate the security, safety and comfort of all patrons, the Venue reserves the right at its reasonable discretion to refuse admission and refund the Ticket value. 10. Customers may be ejected from the Venue if, in the reasonable opinion of the Venue, the Ticket holder is a risk to the safety of any patron; affecting the enjoyment of other patrons; and/or the running of the event. Examples include but are not limited to being (or appearing to be); drunk or incapable or intoxicated, under age (where relevant), abusive, threatening, behaving anti-socially, carrying offensive weapons or illegal substances, declining to be searched or in breach of the Terms and Conditions. 11. To ensure safety we will conduct security searches of persons, clothing, bags and all other items on entry and exit and reserve the right to confiscate items which may cause danger or disruption to the event or other patrons or are in breach of the Terms and Conditions. 12. No food or drink is permitted to be brought into a Venue. A variety of food and beverages will be available for purchase inside each Venue. 13. There is no re-admission once you have left the Venue. 14. Latecomers may not be admitted until a suitable break in the performance of the event. 15. CCTV and film cameras may be present at the Venue. Purchase of a Ticket means you consent to filming and sound recording which may include you as a member of the audience and its use in commercial distribution without payment or copyright. 16. The use of unauthorised cameras, video or sound recording equipment is prohibited and such items may be confiscated. 17. In seated areas other members of the audience may stand up during the event. 18. Crowd surfing and moshing are strictly prohibited. 19. Animals, with the exception of assistance dogs, are not permitted in The O₂. 20. Customers are requested to address any special needs requirements in advance of their visit by contacting **ticketing@theo2.co.uk** or by calling Ticketmaster on 0870 4000 750. 21. If you experience any problems please contact a steward or duty manager as it may not be possible to resolve issues after the event. 22. In case of emergency please follow instructions and directions from stewards, staff and/or other officials. 23. Loud music can damage hearing. 24. All events are subject to licence. 25. The O₂ is a no smoking venue. 26. When purchasing alcohol if you appear to be under the age of 21 you may be asked for proof of age. 27. Official Merchandise is only available from outlets within The O₂. Please be aware of unofficial traders offering inferior goods. 28. It is the responsibility of the Ticket holder to ascertain the date and the time of any rearranged event. 29. Please consider our neighbours and leave The O₂ site quietly. Please note that seats located on Level 4 are not recommended for those with a fear of heights.

For further information about Events, Facilities and Travel or to book Tickets for The O₂, visit **www.theo2.co.uk**

create anything persistent, but still his satisfaction from this activity was evident. How quickly would we, who are used to different ways of thinking, call this activity useless. After about an hour we nodded a friendly good-bye to each other without having exchanged a single word.

On to Bishkek, Kyrgyzstan

The next day Gunther asked me whether I wanted to come with him to Bishkek. Gunther manages another plastination institute, founded by him, at the medical school of the Bishkek university. That institute is very dear to him, and not only because he has been named honorary professor there. His employees had contacted him and had urged him to come and see them soon. Gunther quickly decided to do so and booked a flight from Beijing to Bishkek, and I was happy to accept his invitation to this country that was completely foreign to me. Naturally, I had mixed feelings, for I remembered from my high-school geography class that Kyrgyzstan is a neighbor of Afghanistan, certainly not one of the safest regions in the world.

From Beijing we were to take a direct flight to Bishkek aboard a plane operated by the Kyrgyz state airline. Our trip to Beijing the next morning was without any problems. In Beijing, we checked in for our flight to Bishkek and were assigned the first-class seats 1A and 1B, and thus our adventure began. The boarding time passed, minute after minute ticked by. At some point I asked Gunther whether the flight would be cancelled. Gunther calmly explained to me that he had experienced this several times before when flying the Kyrgyz state airline. Either the plane still needed to be fueled and the pilot was busy rounding up the money for the kerosene bill, or something needed to be fixed on the plane. Gunther's calmness did not really pacify me. I later learned that the Kyrgyz state airline owns only two or three able airplanes that are used for travel to and from Western countries. Only those machines are in a technical state that allows them take off again after the obligatory technical inspections at Western airports. For inner-Asian travel, on the other hand, old Russian planes are used. Their technical state is something I dare not imagine!

Six hours after our scheduled boarding time, we were finally asked to board. Apparently the kerosene bill had been paid. After stepping onto the plane, I immediately understood why Gunther, who usually flies economy class, had reserved first class seats for this trip. The "first class" encompassed three rows of seats, separated from economy class further back on the plane by a curtain. It was remarkable: None of the seat covers matched and the floor coverings were threadbare with many holes. Still, I refused to believe what I saw behind the curtain. Could those actually have been wooden seats, or did my eyes fool me?

We were just about to sit down in our seats 1A and 1B when the co-pilot rushed over, explaining in broken English that those seats were reserved and we would have to sit in the back of the plane. Of course the seats were reserved, we explained, namely by us! He waved this objection away, tried to push us towards the back, and fell more and more into Russian. Then came Gunther's moment of glory. He drew himself up to his full height, which, including his black hat, is pretty impressive, and let out a torrent of Russian words–Gunther has been pretty fluent in Russian since his GDR high school days–directed at the perplexed copilot. I do not know what Gunther said to him, but the effect of his words become immediately visible. The copilot fell silent and quickly disappeared back into the cockpit. Afterwards, Gunther explained that he had had similar experiences before: The pilots try on every flight to save the front (i.e., the best) seats for themselves and their accompanying concubines. And indeed, just before

En route to Bishkek, photo: Henri Wagner

takeoff, a few ladies who clearly did not belong to high society appeared on board. Sulking, they had to sit further back in the plane.

During takeoff the plane shook mightily, the flight was bumpy, and the sandwiches served later tasted horrible. My stomach and my nerves craved some calming substance. On a rattling dinette cart the flight attendant pushed a few chocolate bars and a bottle of vodka back and forth across the hole-ridden floor covering. I asked her for a glass of vodka, and she demanded five US dollars, which would also include a chocolate bar. I agreed and received, much to my surprise, the entire bottle of vodka in addition to my chocolate bar. The bottle, not significantly depleted, then accompanied me for the remainder of our trip.

Curious Events at Immigration

After we had landed in Bishkek we had to take care of immigration formalities. The baggage claim hall, where there were no luggage carts, served simultaneously as the customs and immigration checkpoints. The obligatory immigration forms were available in Russian only. But the hall was teeming with young men wearing track suits, offering their services in obtaining a luggage cart or filling in the forms. Obviously, they had previously removed both luggage carts and English language forms in order to swindle the arriving foreigners out of their first dollars. The income from this business, I am sure, they shared with the immigration officers—how else could they have gained access to this international part of the airport?

With us, they were out of luck. We did not need any luggage carts, for our suitcases had wheels, and Gunther, thanks to his knowledge of Russian, was able to direct me in completing the forms. Still, I was surprised at the normality governing the attitude towards corruption that I had been able to observe ever since we had set foot on Kyrgyz soil. At the customs counter, in line ahead of me, there was a Kyrgyz man heavily loaded with suitcases and boxes. He openly handed his passport containing a number of bills to the customs officers. The bills changed ownership, and his luggage passed through customs without any problems.

At the airport exit, an employee of the institute was already waiting for us and took us to Gunther's apartment. Overtired as I was, I quickly lay down on the bed I had been offered and registered only subconsciously the low rattling noise coming from the kitchen.

The Exhibition

The following day at the institute I met Gunther's co-workers. The professors of the medical school had prepared a small reception for Gunther and me on the occasion of the recently completed BODY WORLDS museum of the university. They proudly showed the museum to Gunther and eagerly awaited his comments. It really was impressive what had been created with the simple means available. A tour of the museum was followed by a small lunch, and I was overwhelmed by the warmth with which I was welcomed into this circle. The day passed quickly with tours of the various facilities that Gunther either directed or cooperated with. At night, in the apartment, I wanted to find out what had caused the rattling noise in the kitchen which I remembered from the previous night. Gunther's well-meaning advice on this issue was: "Well, turn on the light before you walk into the kitchen. That way, there will not be any surprises!" I decided to leave well enough alone and went to sit on the balcony of the apartment. In the distance, the Himalayan mountains were glowing in the evening sun. The beauty of this sight was a true conversation stopper.

Nomad in front of traditional round tent, photo: Henri Wagner

The Yurt

The following day turned out to be the highlight of my trip with Gunther. The day had been exciting even before the afternoon came around. Visits to several academic institutions were followed by a tour of the Bishkek city center and a visit to the local GUM department store. The hustle and bustle surrounding me, the typical local dress of the passers-by, the food offered at small booths, the yelling of the merchants in the market halls all seemed very foreign to me. During our tour I was, I thought, observed with some curiosity, but not with hostility.

In the afternoon, one of the leading professors of the university had prepared a surprise for Gunther and me. She and some other colleagues invited us on a trip to the mountains. Late in the afternoon we left the city in a minivan and drove towards the nearby mountains. The road ran alongside a river flowing from the high mountains down to the plains. Kyrgyzstan is a dry country, large parts of it are covered by desert. Only alongside the rivers fed by the glacial melt high up in the mountains is there a rich flora.

We drove higher and higher up, alongside the river in its valley. With the last rays of sunlight we reached a small, fertile high plateau. In the middle of a lush meadow we suddenly saw a large yurt in front of us, the traditional round tent used by the nomads in this part of Asia. Its construction has remained the same since the time of Genghis Khan or even before. Only the design of the outlet hole for the smoke in the middle of the top of the yurt differs from tribe to tribe.

We were cordially invited inside the yurt and welcomed with bread and salt. At the center of the yurt was a table a little less than a foot high, and we sat down around it, cross-legged, on soft rugs. Gunther was assigned the seat of honor. The table was covered with an overabundance of food and drink. There was mutton baked in bread, meatballs, deep-fried foods, cheese, fruits, vegetables—a feast! The evening in this friendly circle lasted for a long time, and at the center was Gunther, upright, his black hat on his head, glowing with satisfaction, almost brighter than the candles.

Nyschanbek Kotschkorov was born on March 12, 1958, and is a national of Kyrgyzstan. A trained journalist, he spent the beginning of his career in the newspaper business, and since 1981 has been working as a TV journalist specializing in legal topics. He has been awarded the title of "Outstanding Artist" by the Republic of Kyrgyzstan and has won international awards for his work on "The Propaganda of the Law" in the U.S. in 1998 and in Germany in 2003. As of this writing he works for Kyrgyz State TV and Radio as producer of the news magazine "Adilet" (Justice) that, in addition to other topics, deals with questions of the law.

Nyschanbek Kotschkorov

The Avicenna of the 21st Century

I have known the man who always wears a black hat since November 2002. During the fall of that year, Doctor Gunther von Hagens was frequently a topic of the Kyrgyz mass media. The newspapers *Agym* and *Alam*, especially, reported that he was "doing business with dead bodies, which has nothing to do with science." The newspapers, understanding nothing of plastination, began calling von Hagens a "robber of the dead." This was the reason that I, as a journalist, decided to look more closely into Gunther von Hagens' activities in Kyrgyzstan. My research, however, was not limited to this one country, but also involved learning about his history and his activities in Germany, in China, and in Russia. In addition, I made about 100 video recordings of the doctor with the black hat. This work forms the basis of a two-part documentary, the making of which I initiated and which is ongoing at the time of this writing. The documentary on the plastinator, the world famous scientist and anatomist, will be called "The Avicenna of the 21st Century." This article is a brief summary of my activities and research results regarding Doctor Gunther von Hagens, written on the occasion of his birthday.

Life is not easy. We know that those who are unable to give their lives proper direction are not numbered in the thousands, but in the millions. These people like to insist on the validity of their own judgment (whether they admire or criticize someone). They believe that they are always right and they try to spread their opinions as widely as possible, and often we do not know what to do about them. I believe that this is the reason that the great anatomist and scientist von Hagens meets with such lack of appreciation and such a negative attitude. What angers me most is that it is not only lay people who refuse to understand him, the inventor of plastination, but also scientists, elected politicians, and especially journalists. This was reason enough for me to take a closer look at von Hagens.

While still in high school I read some books on the world-famous physician Avicenna. What was especially interesting about him was that he had wanted early on to become a physician, and that he would dig up dead bodies during the night in order to study their anatomy. His father always scolded him: "You smell like dead bodies!" Again and again Avicenna, who lived from 980 to 1037, ran into obstacles, but he eventually became one of the founding fathers of modern medicine. And Gunther von Hagens? His merits resemble those of Avicenna. What is different is the age in which they live and lived, respectively. If Avicenna, who was one of the first scientists to study human anatomy, deserves to be called a physician, then Gunther von Hagens deserves to be called an educator and informer, one who has brought the mysterious world of anatomy and the human body closer not only to physicians, but also to lay people, the general public, and to society. And that is why, to my mind, Gunther von Hagens is the Avicenna of the 21st century.

My journalistic research began with the questions: How and when had Gunther von Hagens come to Kyrgyzstan? The first bilateral arrangement between Gunther von Hagens and the Kyrgyz State Medical Academy (KSMA) was made on May 14, 1996; and on February 20, 1997, an agreement "on the founding of a center for plastination at the KSMA" was signed. This agreement on the founding named Professor Valerij Gabitov as the coordinator of the center of plastination, and he was given full power of attorney for the Kyrgyz institute by Gunther von Hagens. When reviewing these documents, I also discovered a letter that had been written on December 1, 1996, by the then president of the KSMA, Muraliev. In this letter, Muraliev asks Gunther von Hagens to establish a center for plastination at the KSMA and for scientific cooperation. The letter is indisputable proof that the great German anatomist and plastinator was invited to come to Kyrgyzstan as a scientist.

In 1997 a new KSMA president, Professor Iskender Akylbekov, took office, and it was between him and von Hagens that the scientific and operational cooperation began. With the help of von Hagens, the educational facilities of the KSMA were completely remodeled. The work of the German scientist and investor was very much appreciated, and in 1998 Gunther von Hagens was ceremoniously awarded an honorary title of Professor in the presence of the then prime minister, A. Muraliev; the Minister of Health, N. Kassiev; as well as many scientists of the Medical Academy. During those years, von Hagens handed over more than 1600 plastinates to the museum of plastination in Kyrgysztan, more than 30 scientists became motivated to work in the field of plastination, and 20 researchers received additional training in Germany. And the director of the center for plastination was very proud of "the only museum of its kind worldwide." In this way, the plastinator von Hagens had brought significant innovation to science and to the lives of scientists in Kyrgysztan. The then president, Akylbekov, declared that the center of plastination was making good progress, making more than 300 bodies a year available to the students of the Medical Academy.

Museum of Plastination in Bishkek, photo: Henri Wagner

Anatomists from neighboring states, including Uzbekistan and Kazakhstan, envied Kyrgyz science, according to the local newspapers and magazines. From 1998 to 2000 the center for plastination in Kyrgyzstan appeared to be progressing nicely. Thanks to von Hagens' initiative, a dream of Kyrgyz physicians seemed to be coming true.

Reality, however, was different. The general manager of the center of plastination, Gabitov, began to use the funds von Hagens had invested for his own purposes and not in keeping with von Hagens' instructions. None of the employees bothered to keep records of their work; salary payments were handled in a haphazard manner; and the center of plastination did not pay any taxes to the state. According to the agreement, the KSMA was responsible for the center for plastination and was legally obliged to financially audit Gabitov's work. The KSMA, however, was unable to detect any wrongdoing, as Gabitov's reports were forged.

Gunther von Hagens wearing the Kyrgyz kalpak

Why am I investigating and reporting this story? Because my fellow countrymen defrauded and tried to disparage the scientist and investor von Hagens, who always had been so helpful to us. That is what my research yielded, and as a Kyrgyz I personally feel responsible for this as well. On October 22, 2003, von Hagens held a press conference at the Kyrgyskabar news agency, in front of journalists, and informed us of Gabitov's financial crimes and his unauthorized and illegal handling of the budget. During this press conference, von Hagens, for the first time, released detailed figures to the Kyrgyz public. He let us know that, until that day, he had invested one million euros (55 million Kyrgyz som) in Kyrgyzstan, a sum that is easily spoken, but not easily handled. Fortunately, Gabitov's crimes did not go undetected, for Gabitov had had help from a member of the chamber of delegates of the Supreme Soviet of Kyrgyzstan, Akbökön Tashtanbekov. This delegate was not even ashamed to publicly demand "a considerable amount of money" from Gunther von Hagens to enable him, von Hagens, to avert criminal proceedings.

I know von Hagens as a kind person who always wears a black hat. He had no part in what happened at the center for plastination, and together with his colleague Eduard Borsiak, he has proven this to be true in front of the delegates. The speaker of the chamber of delegates, A. Erkebaev, initially tried to insist that von Hagens take off his hat, but he refused: "I am not going to take off my hat. Michelangelo came to see the Pope in Rome wearing a hat." Gunther von Hagens refuted all charges extensively and proved his innocence before the Superior Soviet. Four months later, in December 2003, von Hagens appeared before the Kyrgyz public wearing a *kalpak*, the traditional Kyrgyz hat, and addressed his audience warmly in Russian. It is a matter of my personal concern that this event be remembered.

In 2004 I met the chair of the Kyrgyz-German Friendship Association, Valerij Dill, in Heidelberg. Because of the accusations issued by his delegate colleague Tashtanbekov, he had visited Gunther von Hagens' Institute for Plastination. In an interview, he made it clear that "all rumors surrounding von Hagens turned out, to my surprise, to be untrue. His institute has been defamed as a mere "garage." Instead, it is a respectable institution with several buildings. Von Hagens is an honorable scientist and plastinator." I made this interview with Dill part of the aforementioned documentary, citing it as another irrefutable piece of evidence of Gunther von Hagens' innocence.

November 2004. It is not cold in Bishkek. Von Hagens' name has been cleared in Kyrgyzstan, even though the mass media had reported on him solely in negative terms. Only the TV magazine *Adilet* of the state TV station supported von Hagens–and today I am proud to be the producer of this magazine. A goal of *Adilet* is to broadcast, in 2005, the documentary on the work of the world famous scientist and plastinator that I have made in my position as investigative journalist. Once that has happened, I believe, the name von Hagens will be completely rehabilitated. By the way, criminal proceedings have been initiated against Gabitov in keeping with article 4 of the penal code, and the documents are now before the court. Kyrgyzstan will not forget to support the great scientist and plastinator in this trial. From 2005 on, Gunther von Hagens will continue to develop the science of plastination in Kyrgyzstan. I hope that everyone will learn from the "Gabitov affair."

I cannot conclude this article without mentioning that I intend to dedicate the rest of my life to joining Gunther von Hagens in furthering the development and dissemination of the science of plastination. Why, you might ask, because, after all, I am a journalist? When I saw the long lines of people waiting for admittance to the BODY WORLDS exhibitions in Hamburg and Frankfurt in Germany, I realized that Gunther von Hagens is giving people all over the world a chance to get to know their own bodies. I then decided to study anatomy and plastination science and to teach them to others. For when man knows his body, he can live a modern and healthy life.

And we, the people of Kyrgyzstan, have suffered a setback of about three to four years regarding von Hagens' teachings. The prosecution of those responsible for the "Gabitov affair," and the process of finally clearing it up, have created major chaos in this country. Meanwhile, von

Hagens has invested twelve million euros in China. Many lay people and scientists recognize and regret this great loss for Kyrgyzstan. Now Gunther von Hagens turns 60. But I see him as a young man who loves his profession and never tires. Whoever does not know him, and does not want to get to know him, may continue to call him "Doctor Death," but I will always call him the "Avicenna of the 21st century." That is my personal view of him, and I think that I have substantiated it with many arguments and facts.

Harald Biskup, *born in 1951, studied history, political science, and English studies. He has been senior correspondent for the Cologne newspaper "Kölner Stadtanzeiger" since 1995. Previously, he had been the GDR correspondent for this newspaper and after German reunification had reported from Berlin and the newly formed (eastern) federal states. He met Gunther von Hagens during the BODY WORLDS exhibit in Basle, Switzerland, and later visited him in Kyrgyzstan and China.*

Harald Biskup

The Cosmopolitan from the East

Out and About in Beijing

Everything in this huge area is larger than life, even the rattling loudspeakers from which shrill revolutionary songs are played. The area measures an unbelievable 100 acres. Gigantic. The Great Hall of the People is aptly named as far as its size is concerned. The people, however, do not really have a say here. It is a Sunday morning in Tiananmen Square. In the middle of Beijing, Gunther von Hagens suddenly is reminded of his choir practice with the Thuringian Thälmann Pioneers. When a guard of honor of the People's Liberation Army goosesteps past, the man who went to jail for attempting to illegally emigrate from the German Democratic Republic experiences mixed feelings. Because he had wanted to leave his country without permission and for good, he spent almost two years in the Cottbus penal institution.

The Chinese state power is unobtrusively present, but one cannot miss it. The trauma of 1989 is still in effect. Half a year before the fall of the Berlin wall, police and soldiers bloodily stomped out the peaceful protests of demonstrating students here. In Leipzig, as everywhere else in the GDR, when hundreds of thousands of people took to the streets and shouted in an ever repeating chorus *"Wir sind das Volk!"* (The people, that's us!), the East Berlin writer Stefan Heym worried that the square outside the restaurant "Auerbachs Keller" might turn into a German Tiananmen Square if the state officials lost their heads and started shooting at their own people. As we know, history took a different turn, and Gunther von Hagens is convinced that he, too, contributed a tiny little bit to the crumbling and eventual fall of the world's ugliest and most superfluous structure when the Federal German Government bought his freedom at the then going rate from East Berlin.

Outside the Mao mausoleum a long queue of people waits patiently. Constantly, whole busloads of tourists from every province of this enormous country arrive. The faces of the passengers are devoid of any signs revealing whether the visit constitutes an irksome duty or an eagerly awaited event. The Great Chairman's mortal remains rest in a glass coffin. As time goes by, a renowned tour guide remarks, slightly mockingly, that they do seem "a little waxen." The opening hours may vary, depending on the current state of preservation, and sometimes the heavy gates remain closed altogether. At certain intervals the embalmed body is removed from its formalin bath and given a complete overhaul.

Goosestepping across Tiananmen Square, photo: Harald Biskup

He who dies too soon will be punished by life. The Great Chairman stepped off the stage of life in 1976, two years before von Hagens made his, literally, cutting invention. Thus, the Chairman is fated to remain a mummy forever. What would Mao have looked like as a gestalt plastinate? Or as a glowing slice plastinate, slightly reminiscent of a stained-glass church window, sawed in slices 1/12 to 1/3 of an inch thick, framed between sheets of glass? When his time comes one day, von Hagens sees it as a matter of honor to "do his duty as a didactic plastinate." The plastinator wants to immortalize himself for posterity. As tempting as it doubtlessly would be to "take a peek under Mao's skin," he probably would have declined such a job: "I do not want to create icons." This in spite of the fact that he once plastinated one of the heel bones of the saint Hildegard von Bingen, as von Hagens remembers, "but that had been an anatomical specimen before that."

This special place not only recalls his own history for a brief moment, but it also prompts the ex-dissident to unexpectedly tell old jokes about Walter Ulbricht, the first head of state of the German Democratic Republic. Once the uniformed troops are out of sight, von Hagens stands at attention and shows himself as a talented mimic of the goateed politician from Leipzig. A sample: "Comrade, aren't there any pots available here?" an annoyed customer asks the sales clerk at the "Consumer" department store. "Pots are not available one floor up. This is where underwear is not available," is the answer. Von Hagens had already proven his parodistic talent on the long trip from Bishkek, Kyrgyzstan, to Beijing, during an involuntary 16-hour stopover in the not exactly welcoming transit lounge of Moscow's Sheremetyevo II airport. He made it a lot more bearable through his performances.

It has to do with his life story—and it is a small, but symbolically not to be underestimated, sign that he managed to win over Professor Chang Bao Lin, a scientist who had been imprisoned in a re-education camp during Mao's cultural revolution, as a coworker for his Chinese branch. The former opponent of the regime still is a shy person, but he no longer breaks out in perspiration whenever someone enters his office.

Outside the Gate of Heavenly Peace, photo: Harald Biskup

„Plastination City"

In Tiananmen Square, which is so huge that we take a taxi to get from one end to the other, a student recognizes Gunther von Hagens among the Europeans (referred to by the Chinese in a rather endearing, non-derogatory manner as "long noses"), and asks for his autograph. He has heard about the exhibitions in Seoul, Korea, and Taipei, Taiwan. So, he muses, it should be Beijing's turn soon. "There certainly would be enormous interest." Spontaneous encouragement from people, such as this, is well liked by the master, and he provides the aspiring computer scientist with material, that he always has at hand, on BODY WORLDS. The 2008 Olympic Games would be a great opportunity for a Chinese premiere, the student suggests and then politely says goodbye. "Good idea," agrees the German anatomist, winking at him, clearly touched by this chance encounter.

Von Hagens is now off at a fast pace to what is likely Beijing's largest bookstore, where he intends to acquire an encyclopedia in five languages, several computer programs to perfect his already quite respectable command of the Chinese language, and a few picture books. "Those are just right for practicing everyday conversation," he grins. And it would be surprising indeed if he did not use unconventional methods for studying Chinese as well. He is a perfectionist and does not like doing anything halfway, which is certainly true for his plastinates. Inside the bookstore, which provides a huge selection suggestive of the great leap that China currently is making towards becoming a knowledge society, on a mezzanine floor, Mao Zedong, Zhou Enlai, and Deng Xiaoping look down on us from large portrait photos.

Most Chinese are still unaware of the other cultural revolution that has been triggered by the man restlessly waiting with his stack of books at the check-out stand. They do not know that with his inventions, his crossing of limits, and breaking of taboos, Gunther von Hagens is turning the world of anatomy upside down. And they are even less aware that at his branch at Dalian he is utilizing the centuries-old dissection skills of their compatriots, and that his corpse company in the far Northeast of the People's Republic produces instructional specimens sent to anatomical collections all across the globe. "The class enemy approaches on tip-toe," von Hagens mocks his own mutation with apparent joy, returning his notebook to his back-pack. "The locked up inhabitant of the Soviet zone as cosmopolitan," he continues. The accommodation of socialism and capitalism, as has been successfully practiced by the Beijing post-communists for quite some time now, is a late victory for the theory of convergence, so to speak. Pragmatically, von Hagens benefits from the opportunities inherent in doing business in China. Anything goes–there are virtually no barriers.

Gallery of ancestors in a bookstore,
photo: Harald Biskup

The booming port city of Dalian on the Yellow Sea, east of the capital, a little more than an hour by plane and geographically closer to Pyongyang, North Korea, than to Beijing, offers practically ideal conditions for the future of project plastination. The rapidly growing city, that will likely be home to four million people in the very near future, has been one of 30 "special economic zones" in the People's Republic since 1984, and its impressive skyline represents the lightning-fast upturn of a former provincial town. The city, which after the Russian-Japanese war 100 years ago, was ruled for some time by the emperors from Tokyo, and whose harbor today is home to an important navy base, first experienced prosperity when the Trans-Manchurian railroad was built.

Thus, let us make tabernacles here, said the heathen von Hagens when he chose Dalian as the site of his company in 1996, and so it was done. Plastination City was born. The local authorities, who hold back the tides of immigrants from other parts of the country by requiring them to have a master's degree, are said to be especially open towards innovative fields of science such as genetic engineering and biotechnology, and so they were also prepared to listen to the German anatomist's ambitious plans. Situated in an industrial park filled with software and pharmaceutical companies, von Hagens acquired a 7.5-acre lot and built an institute, including an administration building and a dissection hall. Future plans call for 500 to 800 employees to produce high quality specimens here, following all the rules of preservation. In spite of these large production figures, the boss avoids the term "body factory," having been sensitized by the hostility expressed towards him in faraway Europe. He prefers the more neutral terms "enterprise," or "company." "Factory," in von Hagens' opinion, "triggers the wrong images. It sounds too much like conveyor belts."

On our way to the bookstore we happen to pass a few bronze sculptures that are supposed to promote the Olympic games. To von Hagens' critical eye, however, most of these works, on temporary display in a modern shopping street, do not pass the test—not from an anatomical point of view, and most certainly not from a didactic one. In some, the locomotor system has not been carved out accurately, and in others the extremities have the wrong proportions. For a brief moment he tries to politely ignore those errors, but then he can no longer contain his pedagogical impetus, and von Hagens positions himself first next to a sprinter and then beside a discus thrower, demonstrating in skillfully imitated poses the weaknesses of the sculptures. These figures do not serve any educational purpose and are, at best, aesthetically pleasing and

Bronze sculptures for the Olympic Games

intended to build bridges from the arts to sports. The passers-by do not really know how to react to the spontaneous anatomy class presented by the man with the felt hat. Some young girls in a group giggle abashedly.

Art? Anatomy? Anatomical Art?

As with most Chinese, the inhabitants of Beijing have no idea of the controversy surrounding BODY WORLDS in Europe, the controversy that has always focused, from the beginning, on the same questions: Happening or education? Serious transmission of knowledge or cheap showmanship? Respect for the transient body or irreverent flaunting? Awe at the perfection of the body? Death as a spectacle in a voyeuristic fun-oriented society eager for new, ultimate kicks? Longing for immortality (if only post-mortem)? Involuntary degradation of the dead by sensationalist showpeople? "When will there be," asks Rolf Verres, Professor of Medical Psychology at Heidelberg university and years ago a declared opponent of his anatomy colleague, "when will we see the plastinated grandmother for use as umbrella stand?" And again and again von Hagens' traveling circus prompts heated debates over the question of whether his pleasure in dissecting and defamiliarizing dead bodies was not going too far, serving only provocative, publicity seeking purposes, rather than educational ones.

I still remember the amazed faces of BODY WORLDS' visitors in Basle, who, impressed by the unusual insights into the body's interior, by the "fascination beneath the surface", seemed surprised that the "artist" and producer of the exhibition actually was a physician. On the one hand von Hagens was flattered by this wonder, but on the other hand this image has been causing him more and more problems with his scientific seriousness. When his opponents disparaged him as "Dead Body Beuys," von Hagens would smilingly interpret it as hidden praise. They mainly call him that because he always wears a hat and a leather vest. I still remember precisely what von Hagens once told me, inside one of these tiny fair booths into which he liked to withdraw when the bustle in the halls got too much for him, about his hat. Namely, that the hat had already been his trademark many years back, when a much younger von Hagens worked at the dissecting tables of the Anatomical Institute of the Heidelberg university, and that he takes it off "basically only when showering."

How important to him are his hats, of which there are four or five variants? "Oh, well, that is a costume I use so I can have some freedom from conventions." And then he says that he never met Beuys, but felt connected to him in some ways. "For example, we share a dislike of intellectual arrogance: Beuys courted the layperson and not the intellectuals. I courted the favor of my peers and found the approval of normal people." He strives only for one thing: "democratizing" anatomy. Knowledge about the human body should no longer remain the "secret of a privileged caste. Nothing is as close to us as our body. But there is nothing else that is close to us and about which we know so little." What drives people to see his show in droves? I ask him when the board displaying the number of daily visitors approaches a new record. "The longing for the authentic in a time of practically unlimited reproducibility," he replies. This conviction, to this day, may be the strongest impetus for him to again and again come up with new specimens and to strive for more perfect ones when it seems that the limit has already been reached.

After our walk through the exhibition we sit down together–meaning, of course, that Gunther von Hagens keeps jumping up, for example to show me his refurbished sausage slicing machine: "One of our first investments. Initially, all the experts piously wrinkled their noses, and today anatomists all over the world use it." More than 400 institutes worldwide are working with products von Hagens has developed; new plastinates are continuously being created for BODY WORLDS, which has been seen, as of this writing, by more than 15 million people from Seoul, Korea, to Los Angeles, California. Wherever it is shown, the exhibition is a magnet for the public, and sales of specimens are thriving, facilitating additional investments and expansion of the enterprise in China. "Primarily," says von Hagens with a smile, "I am a physician and an inventor, but somewhere there also must be a few genes of entrepreneur in me."

Inspiration

He is a holder of patents worth millions, but he can be as pleased as a three year old with a new toy when he suddenly develops a simple, ingenious solution to a problem that has been bothering him for some time. And when he then follows through with it, with all its consequences, the joy increases. Dozens of times Gunther von Hagens has walked over to the Institute of Alpine Pathology on the outskirts of Bishkek, Kyrgyzstan. The institute is a gray pile of a building, its plaster crumbling everywhere. Now, in the middle of the Kyrgyz high summer, when all of the grooves from the winter's snowmelt have run dry, he suddenly has a realization: A pond is needed, a small artificial pond, not much larger than a kiddy pool! And he already has a name for the object he has just completed plans for: the Pool of Corrosion! Perhaps not a seminal concept, but another one of those moments marking a focal point in the development of his unconventional anatomical education project. It takes a moment before the group of physicians and other coworkers, following the master as during specialist's rounds at a hospital, understands that they have just witnessed an instance of inspiration, an act of creation, so to speak.

There is plenty of water available. Clear, cold snowmelt comes directly from the glaciers of one of the twelve thousand foot high mountains that are always covered by snow, whose contours are barely visible in the shimmering heat. Soon, in the corrosion pond that has just been invented, water fleas and all kinds of microbes will splash about and pursue targeted activities. Their job will be to destroy hollow organs–blood vessels and bronchi–floating in the water. Step by step, so that eventually only finely chased vessels remain. A natural bacterial flora and fauna, breaking down the remaining tissue until the finest branches become visible: arteries, veins, coronary vessels. Tiny fish exposing bones and cartilage skeletons. Visitors to the "Tour of the Dead," of course, will not suspect any of this when admiring the odorless and perfectly styled sculptures.

Gunther von Hagens pulls a heart from the corrosion bath, dries it, and inspects it from all sides. A truly magnificent heart. "Humans are just as individual and singular beneath their skin as they are above it. Every plastinate," the visiting and honorary professor of the universities of Dalian and Bishkek lectures, "is an anatomical treasure." During his entire anatomical career he has not seen two hearts that were identical regarding their vessel shapes. Everything is unique.

In moments such as these, the plastinator's awe of the life that has been becomes tangible, an awe that he never looses amidst all his zest and zeal for action and his insatiable joy for experimenting. Whatever von Hagens has been given to preserve for eternity is holy to the man who does not believe in either heaven or hell. However eccentric his public appearance may be, especially when the cameras are rolling, and even though some of his ideas certainly are extreme and occasionally feed the doubt that his intentions are purely educational: He is no clown, no friend of macabre jokes who enjoys having fun with dead bodies, as some of his opponents like to insinuate. Even though there is no denying that Gunther von Hagens appreciates unconventional promotional activities, in retrospect he does sometimes wonder whether he should have done without some of the promotional gags that did generate media attention, and that he had been practically urged to embrace by the media. An example from this category was the "Dance of the Dead," his appearance as a living plastinate atop float 11 at the Berlin "Love Parade." Von Hagens actually feels like an alien element in a fun-oriented society. He has never allowed himself to engage in cheap gags. Unlike certain British body art protagonists, he disapproves of turning a penis into a revolver or a bladder into a vase. Making parts of brains look like heads of cabbage seems just as tasteless to the Heidelberg agent provocateur, as does turning stomach walls and bone marrow into carnival masks. But where the aim is to use aesthetic and dynamic means for educational purposes, he knows (almost) no limits.

There was no doubt about this even back on that gray December afternoon in 1999 when I met Gunther von Hagens in his narrow, winding Heidelberg house (which is actually more like a hut with an attached tract of shacks) for the first time. Seeing the slightly anarchic chaos–in every conceivable place you encounter the tools of a restless inventor and come upon traces of a scientist of apparently insatiable curiosity: books, CDs, anatomical atlases, dozens of vials and test tubes-one gets an idea of what Gunther von Hagens means when he says: "I live for anatomy." He led me into his laboratory in a former wine cellar and gave me a lump of dissected placenta to hold, a treated cube of tissue. "Wonderfully soft, is it not? You have to be able to squeeze a specimen." Perhaps even the specimen as your current squeeze? He needs these small evolutionary steps just as he needs air for breathing. Awed, he stepped up to a table on which he had spread out his latest creation and said that he "really liked it very much." If you were ill-disposed towards von Hagens, you could easily use statements such as this, that he blurts out quite frequently in numerous variations during one of his 16 to 18 hour days, to show that "Death's Make-up Artist" actually is who his opponents have made him out to be from afar: an artist-craftsman who cynically lives out his megalomaniac fantasies, and whose toys are dead bodies. Because, through plastination, he assigns a body a new identity, he sets himself up as some kind of creator, they say. And did not von Hagens himself supply his critics again and again with new ammunition, for example, when in an essay he enthused that his specimens are "like figures from cyberspace, figures of a new time" who have overcome the limits of our existence? "They are the modern, the real-fantastic resurrection of our bodies." Death in von Hagens' eyes is "the greatest insult to human existence."

Now, years later, while looking over his shoulder in Dalian, I remember how on that gray winter day in Heidelberg he had slipped on his working gloves and picked up a file. "Dissector's caress" is what von Hagens, in one of his inimitable spontaneous coinages, calls the finishing touches to a whole-body plastinate. Back then, when the debate about the ethical permissibility of his work had reached a first peak, critics in white coats and black cassocks, in a rare case of unity, accused him of necrophilia, and of creating grotesque faces of horror for his artificial figures. Quite the opposite is true, according to von Hagens' creed back then and today; it is classical anatomy, which he likes to refer to as the "anatomy of remainders," which tears apart and chops into pieces, while he is always focused on the entire body. "What is so human about a liver in a canning jar?" The organs pickled in formalin cause shuddering and feelings of disgust and eventually fade. His counter concept is the creation of the beautiful dead body. If not for eternity, then with a predicted shelf life of at least 1000 years. "Memories of Heidelberg are Memories of Happiness" could be heard from jukeboxes everywhere in the 1960s.

Restless Liveliness

His "event anatomy" made the breaking of taboos into a downright stylistic device. He had been fascinated by skeletons as a child, and he was only 17 when he first attended an autopsy. In his little student's room in Jena he copied, in clay, figures from his textbooks. He talks about how his fellow students in anatomy class, "driven by this almost compulsive desire to give life to specimens," had put pointed caps on the dead, had wrapped scarves around them, and had put cigarettes between their teeth. Even as a medical student he had been certain: "There was a motive behind these actions. They want to somehow make the object of their studies more alive, and thus they adorn it with some accessory from life. This was not because they lacked piety, but rather because they wanted to increase the didactic benefit. From then on he never stopped thinking about how the "aesthetically-instructively designed interior of the body, the functional pattern of a human being," could be displayed in a manner different from what had been practiced for the previous 500 years.

He does not at all, in his opinion, follow a timeless cult of beauty, as his opponents also have accused him of doing, especially those who have merely heard about the exhibition. That is not to say, as the master freely admits–and this just as we are climbing down the Great Wall of China, perspiring–that his decision to have himself artfully defamiliarized and displayed in the BODY WORLDS exhibition was completely free from a "certain narcissistic vanity." From a scientific point of view and for the purposes of education, he does not think a diseased heart and a shrunken liver are less attractive than healthy organs. "Pathologists," he says on the final, especially steep part of the stone steps, "are downright enthused about wonderful metastases."

Quickly he heads back to our minivan with our personal guide. Let's not loose any time and let's get away from this place before the masses take over. Organized bus tours are a horror to von Hagens, who, in spite of all his popularity, often seems as shy as a confirmand. However, we cannot get away from a shared meal with local wall climbers, even though we are on our own individual tour, and von Hagens succumbs to this fate. He is the personified opposite of a pleasure-seeker; eating to him is nothing but food intake, and he has no sense for culinary delights. And this in spite of the interesting fish specialties served in Dalian that are really, as stated, "freshly caught," if only from giant aquariums from which the diners may choose.

This anti-gourmet has no reservations about asking for a glass of fresh milk, anywhere, and on any occasion, even though this wish may trigger slight confusion at first. Would not a dry white wine be better with the chicken breast? But since when does Gunther von Hagens care anything about convention? When he actually agrees to eat with a larger group, you can be certain that he will find his most recent e-mail message containing a progress report by the Bishkek corrosion group far more interesting than the menu. Or he may suddenly be completely transfixed by the server's locomotor system–just as he was during our check-in in Moscow when the physiognomy of an Aeroflot ground staff member commanded his undivided attention: "Her nasal cartilage is extremely interesting."

It takes a lot of persuasive talent to coax this bustling anatomist into such unproductive activities as dinners and excursions. His motive, if he decides to participate, is never diversion, distraction, or even relaxation. No, he is motivated instead by the promise of stimulating conversation, especially if controversial and slightly outside his areas of expertise. Then von Hagens reveals himself as one who does not have a ready-made answer for every question, not by a long shot. He does not try to avoid the problematic issue of the dead bodies of executed Chinese prisoners: "Right now, I do not know what we would do if we were approached by their loved ones who often cannot afford burial services about this." Ethics aside, the bodies of executed persons are hardly suitable for plastination because, in China, executions are carried out via shooting. It may sound like a captivating (and sales enhancing) idea to portray him as someone who will stop at nothing, but this is a verdict that can only be reached by those who have never made a serious attempt to grapple with this agent provocateur beyond the common clichés.

During our nighttime rounds and long flights, I experienced von Hagens as a pronouncedly interested and very thoughtful listener who loves being inspired by thoughts that would normally not fit inside his own coordinate system. When a confessed agnostic and a critical Catholic talk about God and the universe, they sometimes will reach unexpected spheres. I no longer remember exactly what it was that prompted von Hagens to say that he "never had thought about that"–an astonishing admission, one that I will always remember.

Visionary Fanatical Zeal

Leisure for its own sake seems suspicious to him, relaxing is not in his vocabulary, and doing nothing constitutes an unknown dimension. Imagining Gunther von Hagens on one of the long beaches of Dalian bay, possibly dozing in a reclining chair–what an absurd idea! Actually, such an idea would not be that absurd, for the maritime climate attracts tens of thousands of people during the summer months. But that image alone would keep him away from such pleasures–the individualist von Hagens is easily sickened by the masses. One exception to this rule may be the hordes of exhibition visitors trekking past his sculptures, to whom he occasionally grants the opportunity of a personal encounter. Rare chances.

Even rarer appearances by the master are the norm when tours of the countryside surrounding Plastination City, by co-workers or guests, are scheduled. Only when participation is unavoidable and his absences could be construed as impoliteness does he allow himself an excursion, for example into the Chinese past, to Lushun, formerly Port Arthur, situated on the southern tip of Liaoning peninsula. A museum documents everyday life during the Japanese occupation, and one may admire a brick grave with preserved wall paintings from the Han dynasty. On this day, as is often the case in summer, there is a blanket of smog over the rocky coast, which, underneath this veil, casts itself in a mild light, as if it were an object of a Caspar David Friedrich painting. Korean and Japanese weekend tourists compete in taking pictures, and Chinese brides and grooms like the lovely landscape as backdrop for their most beautiful day. Von Hagens urges us to hurry, he wants to get back to his realm. It will be another long night. Or a short one, depending on how you look at it.

Breaks, imposed on him for example by flight schedules, are viewed as irksome interruptions. Wide awake at three in the morning, he turns on his notebook while riding on the bumpy road to the airport of the Kyrgyz capital in order to read the more than 100 e-mail messages that he has received, and to take care of his electronic correspondence. This includes letters to body donors, or urgent questions from Heidelberg or Dalian. With almost monk-like frugality he focuses on what is important to him. Six hours of sleep are the most he allows himself, usually he sleeps only four and a half to five hours per day. Nature has equipped this frequent and long-distance flyer with the enviable gift of being able to fall into a restful, deep sleep anywhere and anytime, from one minute to the next. But even then, it seems, his educator's brain does not really rest but instead develops creative fantasies in his sleep, so to speak.

Of course, von Hagens is fanatically zealous, obsessed by a vision of no longer cultivating anatomy as a secret science, but instead making it available, free from horror and disgust, to large sectors of society. On his computer he virtually resurrects his modern mummies, and thanks to his pronounced capability of three-dimensional thinking, he plans new figures in his mind. Restlessly and without breaks he tinkers with ideas, venturing into new dimensions. Inside his Kyrgyz laboratory of immortality, he wants to create "what no man's eyes have seen before:" an entire body, bright red blood vessels, white skeleton. Spectacular insights into the finest inner structures of the vessels, intended to give a yet more awe-inspiring idea of the uniqueness of the human body. "I am," von Hagens admits, "driven by gigantomania." In concrete terms, however, this means more quality instead of quantity. And sometimes he even diagnoses himself with signs of monomania, the obsession to realize his ideas, driven by the practically uncontainable passion for fascinating people who had already forgotten how to be fascinated.

Revolutionizing anatomy to him means continuing with the tradition of the "holistic approach" that has been forgotten in the West. In the Far East it has survived because there is no money or know-how to do, for example, electronmicroscope-based cell biological research. And in general the Far East has stayed closer to its roots. Western anatomy, says von Hagens angrily, "has been degraded to mere chopping up. As they revealingly say, they 'dissect down.'" In China he has discovered the most talented and most patient dissectors under the stars, "far superior to us Europeans in terms of their fine motor skills. They can work with a precision of 1/250 of an inch." They work eagerly and with precision, and with an extraordinary respect for the anonymous body. And they work completely without guidelines issued by ethics committees. There is a downright reverent quiet at the dissection tables.

A Pose for Eternity

Elvis!? Elvis Presley!! No reaction from his young dissectors. Gunther von Hagens throws off his blue lab coat, turns on his own axis with a perfect swing of his hips, and lists a dozen of Elvis' songs. He then picks up an imaginary guitar and brilliantly performs a boogie, as if practicing for the Gold Dance Medal of the Free German Youth, FDJ. The young people in their lab coats, blue as well, who have lined up in front of one of the almost finished specimens, giggle abashedly as their boss quickly draws a spit-curl on a pad of paper. They cannot make any connection of this with the still wrapped, whole-body plastinate that is about to be finalized.

A tiny culture shock early in the morning. The master, with his sparkling imagination and his pronounced tendency to seek out reference points relating to real life, could not help making the comparison. The entire pose, the extremities, the bone structure—a resurrected Elvis. His apprentices show awed admiration, but they simply do not get it. For once, his didactics fail. But that is an issue of mentalities. He was not immediately able to convey to them what is important to him in his productions.

Memento mori

Normally, von Hagens picks images with right-on instincts, but this time his antenna for them failed. Even though the high-rises in downtown Dalian seem to touch the sky, and although the city center makes it feel like Houston, Texas, or Atlanta, Georgia, the West still is very far away, and cultural barriers may last a long time. While high-school student Gunther Liebchen surreptitiously tuned his GDR portable radio to the Western station RIAS Berlin in order to listen to Elvis songs, the music of the former G.I. turned pop-icon of an entire generation still seemed like the model of capitalist decadence to the Chinese officials for cultural affairs.

A great leap forward, to the present. In the large dissection hall there is a hustle and bustle as happens immediately before the opening of an exhibition. The works are still carefully covered by plastic tarps. Here, the "largest mental challenge of the entire plastination process" is about to take place—the posing. Dress rehearsal in the beauty parlor of death. "Every pose has its instructional potential, and every instructional need requires its own optimum pose." I cannot help but remember a little incident in von Hagens' living room when, in front of a pleasantly crackling fire in the fire-place, we talked for the first time about the fact that a pose is able to make typical moments of movement more dense, to even exaggerate them. And that every plastinate "is an anatomical treasure, individual down to the

Gunther von Hagens, "modeling", photo: Harald Biskup

microscopic, even to the genetic, and thus the molecular level." Having said that, Gunther von Hagens had turned on the TV set and switched channels until he came across one of the ubiquitous soccer games: "The best instructional material for the locomotor system." That said, he jumped from his chair and positioned himself like a teacher of pantomime, ready to kick from the imagined 10 yard line.

Self-critically, this perfectionist concedes that the early poses he created now seem either rigid, like lifeless dolls, or unnaturally twisted, even grotesque. "Here I still miss some spirit," says the boss, pointing to a half-completed plastinate that looks rather conventional, lifeless, without a "face," more like a skeleton. "Good dissection," the creator of plastination remarks offhandedly while we are touring the hall, "actually is nothing but the skillful removal of connective tissue at the right places." At least 30 different poses are moving around in von Hagens' brain simultaneously, urging him to assign them to one of the bodies awaiting further processing in one of the large silver containers in "Bunker 1." And sometimes he is so fascinated by one of these bodies "overcoming the limitations of our existence" when he looks at it again, that all of those images want out at the same time. Gunther von Hagens has already saved many, many more to the hard disk in his brain, which has a significant capacity. The bike rider, perhaps even a twosome on a tandem, the ice-skating couple, "in general more people interacting with each other." In awed silence, a group of dissectors watches as he bends flexibly from the hips and suddenly holds his position in a split, as if petrified. The scene is captured by a digital camera—instructions for the final corrections to the plastinate. "We need lifelike poses, down to the position of the pinky." The lifelikeness of his figures irritates only "notorious intellectual skeptics; laypersons are not at all offended."

Like a male mermaid he is squatting in position, the "Thinker," arms resting on his knees. Should von Hagens place him on an acrylic stool, or would some steps of a suggested staircase be the better base? These questions are not at all unimportant. "Accessories stimulate the imagination of the viewers significantly." When inspecting one of his creations again and

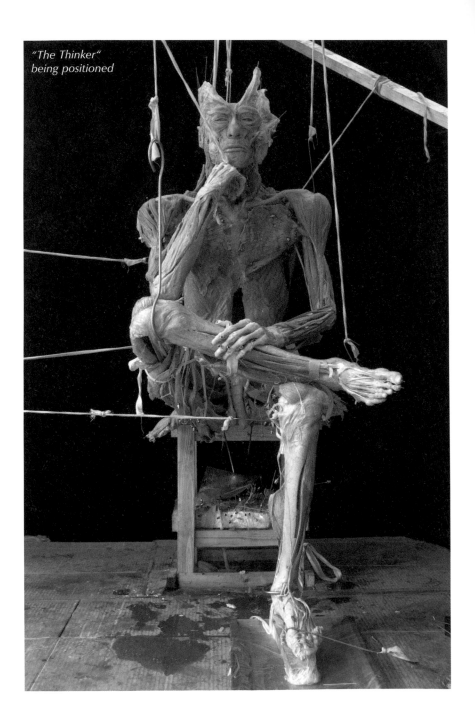

again, the plastinator forgets about space and time—and that requires a lot of patience from his co-workers. They are used to this man, with his zest for action, suddenly imagining new ways of perfecting them during each inspection. And they are used to the sudden dismissal of yesterday's final inspection because a new idea has made his previous judgment worthless. He will not be satisfied until one day it will be possible to expose the origin of a lymphatic vessel by means of corrosion. But that is today's perspective. Who knows what will be true tomorrow or even the day after, which self-made measures Gunther von Hagens will subject himself to then? "It will be a while" until the next level of perfection of his high-tech vision of the "modern approach to our finite being" has been reached, until everything has matured so that he is no longer plagued by the common anatomist's nightmare of having to answer for specimens not done to ultimate perfection. It may even be long enough so that he is not around to witness that final quantum leap, "at least not in his current aggregate state."

Mao in his formalin bath will not, as we know, last forever in his mausoleum built for eternity. Gunther von Hagens' beautiful bodies, on the other hand, do not carry an expiration date. In a certain way they are immortal. A comforting idea, finds von Hagens. And for once, this is a truly egoistic notion.

Stephan Rathgeb, born in 1978, is a journalist and lives in Switzerland. He is CEO of "fast forward film GmbH" (www.fastforwardfilm.ch) and writes for "Das Magazin" of the Zurich daily newspaper "Tages-Anzeiger", for "Frankfurter Rundschau MAGAZIN," for the radio station "Deutschlandfunk" and for several others. From 2000 to 2002 he was head of communications and spokesperson for the BODY WORLDS exhibition at several locations including Cologne, Oberhausen, and Berlin in Germany, Brussels, Belgium, and London, UK. Additionally, he accompanied Gunther von Hagens, as part of a documentary project, on many of his travels to China and Kyrgyzstan. Before that, he had been editor-in-chief of the largest independent youth newspaper in Switzerland for two years.

Stephan Rathgeb

The Journalistic and the Personal Approach–Which One is "More True"?

Preliminary Remark

Those trained in constructivist thinking know: Reality depends on perception. And perception is always subjective. Always depends on which lens one is looking through. On the point of perspective of the beholder. And on the purpose of the analysis. That is why I have written two articles on Gunther von Hagens: a journalistic one, and a personal one. Now, which one is "more true?"

I think the question is not phrased well, because truth, like reality, does not exist independently, in an absolute form. And thus, both perceptions, both sets of notes on Gunther von Hagens, are true. They even are indispensable to each other. The journalistic approach describes from the outside, looks at the production and ties it to fact, narrates in quick steps–as is my way of approaching the world as a journalist, switching back and forth between the global and the local.

The personal text was a much bigger challenge for me, since in German journalism the use of the narrative "I" is frowned upon–unlike in Anglo-Saxon journalism. Also, making a completely subjective perception the object of one's writing is something that simply is not done in German journalism. But that is exactly what is covered in the personal article. It answers the question how I, Stephan Rathgeb, have experienced Gunther von Hagens?

When writing such an article, one always runs the risk of being dismissed as a sycophantic flatterer, especially in professional circles, and more so if one happens to be a former spokesperson. It seems to be a matter of good taste, especially when dealing with a controversial topic enveloping a strong taboo, such as the processing of dead bodies, to hold one's own by uttering the harshest possible criticism. The motto seems to be: "Whatever you do, do not fall for his line!" After all, he is a devil, as I was recently told, in all earnestness, by the producer of a major news show. He added that this was the reason to not use any original sound bites of his that would cast a positive light on him. Always choose a clip in which he seems pale and speaks haltingly over one in which he is seen laughing heartily.

Do not get me wrong: I, too, think it false, even irresponsible, to make one's personal feelings one's journalistic maxim. But as important as it is in journalism to be as comprehensive as possible, objective and reserved–more and more I think it is just as important to tell personal stories as well, for they are just as true.

In this sense I hope you will enjoy reading the two "truths" about Gunther von Hagens–for one is not thinkable without the other.

Dead Bodies On The Conveyor Belt

A Visit to "Plastination City,"
Gunther von Hagens' Chinese Factory for Human Bodies

His BODY WORLDS exhibition made him the most famous, but also the most infamous, anatomist of our time. In his adoptive country China, the German doctor Gunther von Hagens is already working on his true great vision: He wants to industrialize the processing of dead bodies. Eleven Britons were allowed to look around in his factory for human bodies–for some day they themselves will end up there.

"If you have never seen a dead body before, beware," the doctor with the large black felt hat and the obligatory leather vest warns. He is standing atop a forklift, so he can be more easily seen, and looks down on his crowd of visitors. This is an important day for him. It is the first time he has opened his Chinese factory to the public. Its specialty: the processing of dead bodies.

The warning, however, is unnecessary. For the visitors who accepted his invitation to take a look at the dead bodies are handpicked VIPs. They are, so to speak, the suppliers of his raw materials: Eleven Britons between the ages of 18 and 77, determined to leave their bodies to him after their deaths. They call themselves "body donors."

For the German physician Gunther von Hagens prides himself on being able to preserve bodies better than anyone else of his profession. He calls himself "plastinator" and his works "palatinates:" anatomically dissected human bodies, preserved for eternity with the help of plastics developed for this particular purpose. He sells them to universities worldwide and puts them on display for audiences numbering in the millions in his traveling exhibition BODY WORLDS–"Fascination beneath the Surface."

Von Hagens' dead body donors are now predominantly processed in the low-wage country China. In ever growing laboratories in Dalian, a city of four million inhabitants, one hour by plane north of Beijing. On this unknown piece of earth, away from the public view, Gunther von Hagens has settled down in order to pursue his vision.

The two-person operation of the von Hagens family has long since grown into a small empire. The doctor, who started his body business in 1993 with only his wife, is now the boss of 300 employees worldwide. More than half of them work here in China. "Plastination City" is what he calls this 7.5 acre lot on which he erected the buildings for his factory. It is situated a little outside the city center, in the so-called "High Tech Zone." It is an area where certain companies within certain industries are allowed to settle and invest in promising technologies: companies in the pharmaceutical industry, the packaging industry, electronics multinationals. And: Gunther von Hagens.

To promote the body donor program in the United Kingdom, where he showed his exhibition in 2003, von Hagens invited the first round of donors on an "all inclusive" PR trip–for the eleven Britons a trip like none before. When they come to Dalian the next time, they all know, they will travel in special refrigerated containers. Via cargo ship. Ready for dissection.

Welcoming the British body donors

"Because I Love My Body"

"Feel free to look into every box," von Hagens encourages his visitors. "I have nothing to hide." And he takes them to an underground warehouse that he introduces as "Bunker 1:" a garage-like room, filled from bottom to top with large metal boxes. "Bringing the dusty cellar of anatomy," the doctor announces like a fiery prophet, "into bright daylight!" That is his goal, that is why they are here today. One of his employees interprets in Chinese, because the doctor also invited a few local body donors on the factory tour. The visitors nod.

Jane, the blond reporter of the English sensationalist rag Daily Mirror, does not need a second invitation. She grabs body donor Sophie, 21, the one with the great bust, and places her in front of a dissection table. Behind her, covered by a white cloth, there is something resembling a human shape. The reporter helplessly fumbles with her compact camera, her newspaper not having sent along a photographer, and scribbles quotes onto her notepad. "I donated myself," Sophie says, "because I love my body." One day, when she is displayed in the exhibition, the young woman hopes it will help visitors respect their own bodies more from that day on.

"Come to the back!" von Hagens calls and directs his visitors to one of many boxes. He removes the lid and pulls something from ice-cold water. "An organ package," he explains and holds up the innards. Holding them by the esophagus; lungs, heart, and bowels hanging down. The tongue rises over the top of his hand. Pit, the short bald journalist of the London free paper Metro, watches with interest, pushing a piece of chewing gum around in his mouth. "Now, that seems a little disrespectful to me,", one of the body donors says. "He is presenting those organs to us like a shot duck," says Phil, parking garage manager by profession. However, the 45-year-old is not easily rattled. "After all, I accepted this invitation in order to get to know the people who will dissect me." And so he had prepared himself for a shocking experience. The initial shock quickly faded. "I was a paramedic in the army, so I am used to quite a bit," says Phil. Also, he has a rather "healthy relationship" with death: "If I dropped dead tomorrow–I could live with that." He tries to enjoy his life as much as he can while he is alive. "To avoid altogether the feeling of having missed something." In addition to other things, he has traveled a lot, he says.

Before Phil discovered plastination, he had willed his body to a university. That was until he visited von Hagens' exhibition in London–which was, as in any city where it is shown, at the center of a heated debate: The question always is whether it is science or art. Whether it would not suffice to display wax models rather than real humans. Whether von Hagens, who often stylizes himself with his Beuys hat as artistic creator, abuses the dead bodies he is entrusted with to live out his morbid character traits. An academically trained expert anatomist with an entrepreneurial spirit, making money by perfectly embalming dead bodies: For some critics, that was pushing the limits of conventional medical ethos.

Not for Phil. The parking garage manager was so impressed by the novel presentation of human anatomy that he donated himself to von Hagens' institute shortly after his visit to the exhibition. For free. Just as more than 6000 people have done worldwide. Phil is even ready to pay for the transportation of his body from England to von Hagens' institute in Heidelberg, Germany.

"Guess what this is!?" Von Hagens has moved on to the next box. It contains a giant piece of flesh, ribbed and about three feet wide. The lump turns out to be the tongue of a whale that died off the Dalian coast. The doctor identifies the yellow pile floating next to it as human skin, detached and in one piece. Both will serve as raw material that one day may be used in one of his exhibitions. Tiny puzzle pieces on his way to the realization of his life vision that he is relentlessly pursuing. For the doctor has great plans. The fact that his BODY WORLDS exhibition already has made him the most popular anatomist of our time is not enough for him.

And so the revenues he realizes from his exhibitions–currently there are two of them, a third one is in production–touring from one city to the next are invested in his Plastination City. After all, he is planning on writing a lasting chapter in the history of anatomy. His motto is "democratizing anatomy." And his goal he states as follows: "If 50 years from now there is a plastination museum in every large city, then my life as plastinator will have been worth it." And his plastinates will be used in teaching, not only at medical schools, but also at any facility that educates health care providers, from midwifery institutions to nursing schools to schools for massage therapists. "But to achieve that," he says, "I have to produce cheaply. Otherwise, no one will be able to afford the plastinates." Currently, says the doctor, the production of a whole-body plastinate costs him 40,000 euros. In mass production he believes he will be able to decrease this to 10,000 euros. And body slices would then be available from 10 euros up. "Dissecting a human body certainly is more unusual, but definitely not more difficult than assembling a computer, a TV set, or a car," he says. "It is not more difficult than complex assembly line work." So, he adds, there is nothing to stop industrialization of the process.

At the time of this writing, Plastination City swallows up about the equivalent of 125,000 euros a month, the salaries of the roughly 200 employees start at the equivalent of 240 euros. He wants to grow five times bigger. "If, some day, I have 1000 employees here," von Hagens calculates, "I will be able to produce an entire body in one day." Not to mention the numerous body parts and body slices...

"Plastination City"

What If No One Will Buy the Dead?

But, Doctor, what if you are stuck with your dead? Von Hagens gives a dismissive gesture. "Then we will have to create the need," he says optimistically–and immediately mentions an example of possible marketing: "Every year, there is a conference in the U.S. at which 40,000 radiologists meet. That's where we will have to go to show what we have."

But what if you run into production bottlenecks? If, let's say, everyone is interested in brain slices, but no one wants a hand? "That requires strategically planned production," von Hagens knows. Specifically: Cross-sections of arms are very attractive for hand surgeons because they are highly instructive. For medical students, however, who only study the various groups of muscles, longitudinal sections would be better suited. It would, therefore, be necessary to find out what the needs are. And if neither sections sell, entire arms would be plastinated for schools of acupuncture.

Plastination City has already passed its acid test: it saved von Hagens from bankruptcy. Here he produced within one year his second BODY WORLDS exhibition that became a major success in Korea. Record numbers of daily visitors: 22,000. After only a few months the exhibition was able to welcome its one-millionth visitor, while the parallel exhibition in London, UK, attracted not even half that number of visitors over the same period of time. Thanks to the Korean exhibition, von Hagens was able to pay back his million euro loans to Commerzbank, to whom he had pawned his plastinates–to finance the London exhibition.

The next item on the agenda is action. The visitors leave the storage bunker and head for the building next door. There, backbreaking work is performed in a brightly lit room: the dissection room. A vast fenestrated facade opens up on a dreamlike view of the Yellow Sea bay, only slightly clouded by a mild haze. In the front, ten metal tables are lined up. The corpses on them are wrapped in moist wool blankets to prevent them from drying out. Around each table five dissectors are crouching, men and women, all of them very young.

Armed with forceps and scalpels, they remove connective tissue, exposing muscles and organs. There is very little talking, everyone is

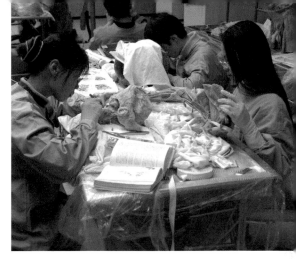

Very young dissectors

focused on the task at hand. Von Hagens recruits them directly after their graduation from the medical school where he is a visiting professor. Most of them are in their early 20s and live in the multi-story building that he erected for his employees. They sleep in bunk beds, four of them sharing a room. Compared to her student life, one of the dissectors says, those are luxurious conditions. "At the university, there were eight of us to a room." Still, she will move out soon to find an apartment in the city that she will share with her boyfriend. In von Hagens' dorm rooms the sexes are strictly separated.

"Look at how precisely they work," von Hagens praises his people. "In Germany, I am a star dissector, in China, I am only a meager average." The Chinese, he enthuses, cut with a precision of 1/250 of an inch.

The Fascination of Being Cut Up

His enthusiasm catches on. "How dedicated," enthuses Phil. The following day he will steal away from the group to return to this place. While the others are being led through the city on a sightseeing tour, Phil will be sitting at one of the metal tables, from 9:00 a.m. to 3:00 p.m., watching the dissectors skin an old woman, millimeter by millimeter.

The body donor describes the process as follows: "It is not like cutting pork, you cannot hack. It is quiet work, almost meditative. The dissectors have to proceed very gently. And I like the idea of someone being gentle with me when I am dead." Von Hagens phrases it a little more soberly: "The fascination of plastination lies in its visual attractiveness. Unlike decay, which is associated with visually stressful processes, plastination makes it possible to calmly look death in the eye."

Von Hagens arrived in China via detours. When he had his breakthrough in Japan in 1995, where the BODY WORLDS exhibition was shown for the first time and attracted a total of 2.5 million visitors, the Chinese noticed the German physician as well. Five Chinese universities offered him a visiting professorship–he, who in Germany had tried in vain for years to find a museum that would dare to show his specimens.

The reason he picked the seaside town of Dalian is its location. Dalian is home to the second largest port in the country–corpses from Germany, therefore, can quickly be transported here by ship. So far, he has shipped about 70 of them here, says von Hagens. The trip takes six weeks. But it is also the climate of Dalian that is much better suited for anatomy than, for example, that of the much warmer Shanghai further south. "Sufficiently cold in winter, not too hot in summer," von Hagens summarizes the advantages of his chosen home, "so that Chinese bodies, if they reach the anatomical institute within two to three days, will remain plastinatable, too." So he says. Meaning: and will not rot. In addition, the 100-year-old city is ruled by a young, fresh spirit. Dalian advertises itself as the "Northern pearl." Its clean streets are a source of pride. And the girls from the North are considered the most beautiful in the country. The only problem is with the Chinese population's willingness to donate. So far, only 46 Chinese have agreed to be taken to Plastination City after their deaths. First and foremost among them are intellectuals, who want to distinguish themselves from the masses through this decision. Von Hagens' seven-

Not afraid of the body's interior

employee "body donation department", in charge of recruiting Chinese donors, found most of them at the so-called "English corners," meeting places in public parks where, on Sundays, people meet who are interested in learning English, and where they freely practice conversation. Visits of the corpse recruiters to Chinese old age homes and universities so far have proven unsuccessful. The people in this country are too superstitious, von Hagens complains, and too traditionally minded. In China, the common form of burial is cremation. But that can be changed, the doctor is convinced, once his exhibitions are shown here, too.

Inside a back room off the dissection room sits the machine that enables von Hagens to snatch any tissue from decay and to preserve it for good: the vacuum pump. The vacuum pump trick is the core of his invention that he patented more than 20 years ago. The dead body is placed into ice-cold acetone, minus 23 degrees Celsius, 9.4 degrees Fahrenheit–acetone is nothing other than nail polish remover–until every cell of the body is saturated with it. Then the body is transferred to the pink silicone bath and the pump is started. This lowers the atmospheric pressure and the acetone begins to evaporate. It escapes from the body, leaving the cells and thus creating negative pressure. "And this negative pressure," explains von Hagens, "sucks the silicone into each cell." Graphically he forms a kissing mouth with his lips. "Just like the baby sucks milk from the mother's breast, you see? And has everyone seen the acetone bubbles rise?" And off we are again, on to "Bunker 2."

Chess Player or Goalkeeper?

"Bunker 2" houses the heart of the company: the "positioning" department. Here, the preserved plastinate is given its new shape. The bodies are posed, "as lively as possible," arranged for the eyes of a visually spoiled lay public. Their new roles: Chess player, Goalkeeper, Basketball player. Recently, a sorcerer riding his innards like a broom. In the end, von Hagens thinks of them as "anatomical works of art." Unique examples of the doctor's handwriting.

Stable girl Sophie, parking garage manager Phil, and the other donors eventually will also be posed like that, and they know it. They watch fascinatedly as 20 employees of the "positioning" tract bring dead muscles, nerves, and blood vessels into anatomically correct positions, using thousands of tiny needles, before the plastinate is hardened for good with gas. The doctor himself reserves the right to select the final pose—will the corpse become an athlete or a wizard? In exchange, the boss gives his all. "Sometimes he grabs a folding cot and spends the night in order to wake every hour to look at the plastinates," reports 28-year-old Zhao Xia to the group of visitors. "He says that his mind is inspired by the unusual." The petite, short woman has been the boss of "Bunker 2" for two years now. Behind her, two arms and two legs are dangling.

The draped bodies do not leave the positioning department until the doctor has succeeded at making the dead look almost livelier than during their lifetimes. "Every millimeter counts," he says, "and every angle—from the position of the chin to that of the smallest finger." So far the doctor has not been able to teach this sense of shape to any of his employees, no matter how hard he has tried. "It will be years, I think, until I have introduced them to my way of thinking." A race against time, for if von Hagens cannot

Body donor meets plastinate

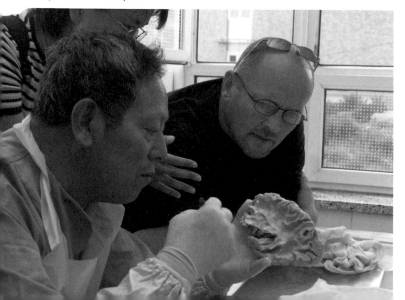

pass on his skills before he dies, not much more is likely to remain of plastination than what he placed on the small wooden table in the living room of his three-room apartment as a deterrent: the catalog of a competing exhibition. One of his first students produced it with the help of Japanese investors. The student had left von Hagens after he had trained him for one year in Germany. What is shown in the catalog, however, is not exactly flattering for plastination. Cheap copies of von Hagens' originals. Limply standing figures lacking any dynamics.

Postmortem Vanities, Shed

"When I saw von Hagens' exhibition," body donor Robert promotes the cause in front of the rolling cameras of a local Chinese TV station reporting about the visit of the Britons, "I knew immediately that I wanted to be part of it some day." For the interview, the cameraman has placed him in front of a camel; the animal has been skinned. And halved down the middle. Body donor Robert, who has a nervous twitch of his nose, has asked von Hagens in private to make him the star attraction when the exhibition moves on to the U.S. He claims to know something about the media. In a corner of the skinning room next door stands a young man, illuminated by neon light. He is made solely from skin, his organs are already in Korea. He himself will never make it into an exhibition. His skin is too reminiscent of death, von Hagens decided. "Too pale. We will sell him to a university."

After lunch in the cafeteria it is time for a discussion. A 38-year-old Chinese man, an accountant, shocks the English guests. He donated his body for egoistic reasons. To him, plastinates are like shrines, and he wants to be remembered by his family in this way. "And I would like it best if the Professor himself would plastinate me!" Von Hagens points out to him that he is almost 60 and hopefully will abdicate first. Laughter. "I am a body donor for only one reason," the Briton Raimond says, "and that is because I see it as a waste of resources to leave my body to the worms." And Phil says: "It is not immortality that I am after. When I die, people should have a beer in my honor." None of the eleven body donors wants to retract his or her decision. "But what will happen to you, Gunther, when you die?"

one of them wants to know. Will he be wearing his distinctive hat once he is made into a plastinate? "Well," says von Hagens, "only a year ago I would have said that I would prefer to be sliced in order to be able to teach in many different places at the same time. Since then, I have shed my post-mortem vanity." He will leave the decision to his descendants.

On the drive back from Plastination City to the Hotel, body donor Claire suggests to the group that they should exchange e-mail addresses for Christmas cards. And so they could attend each other's funeral services. Hunchbacked Richard, 51, a discharged janitor still living with his parents, admits at the end of the sightseeing tour that he had planned to ask Gunther for something, but that the group had advised against it: Whether he could take a piece of skin home. As a souvenir.

"Making Gold from Shit"

A Declaration of Love to a Great Friend and Teacher

I was only 21 when Gunther von Hagens made me his chief of communications and press spokesman. The two and a half years I spent as one of his closest colleagues turned into the most exciting challenge any young person could imagine. Ruthless management training by the least conventional self-made man of Germany, a valuable friendship included.

Actually, I never had wanted to meet Gunther von Hagens. In 1999, when his exhibition was shown in Basle, Switzerland, I had asked his then press spokeswoman for just a regular dissector whom I would be allowed to watch at work for a day. The master himself, after all, had had enough press coverage already. And what I had learned about him in the course of my preparatory research did not really make meeting him seem tempting. "He brags about being able to skin a human body with a single cut, without lifting the scalpel once from the skin," I had read in an article by a fellow journalist. "He sometimes catches himself," a female colleague wrote, "dissecting people in his mind, for example those who enter his field of vision on the trolley, as if he were envisioning their deaths already." I did not want to be turned into such imaginary dissection material. And I was not isolated in my assessment.

During an editorial meeting of Toaster, the largest independent youth newspaper in Switzerland, when I was editor-in-chief, none of the 30 participants was eager to meet a certain Prof. Dr. med. Gunther von Hagens, much less get to know his taboo breaking exhibition BODY WORLDS. Even the biologist of the editorial team declined: "I have dissected plenty of frogs at university." And so I set out, rather unsuspectingly, to enter the entrails of von Hagens' plastination universe.

When the dissection guru *in persona* welcomed my photographer and me in Heidelberg and guided us for a day through his mortuary and other production sites, it was only the first of innumerable surprises that I would experience during my excursion to "planet Gunther." And when this often flamboyant guy suddenly revealed himself as a sensitive and extremely witty conversation partner, who, when engaged in a dialog, does anything but preach doggedly or waffle on narcissistically, and instead listens attentively, trying to give precise answers–that was the second surprise.

The fact that, even after a packed all-day tour that even included the last body freezer of his company, I did not run out of questions during the subsequent drive to his Basle exhibition–that I even was glad for the four-hour traffic jam because it allowed me to grill him even more–that I found, even as a young journalist with six years of professional experience under my belt, somewhat remarkable, for it is anything but natural. Most people will begin repeating themselves after one hour at the most, especially when they, as Gunther von Hagens has, have built a life's work on which everything hinges. But that is not true for Gunther von Hagens. He knows how to spin the threads of his thought so that it feels as if one were walking on a seductively red carpet.

I let myself into his world and groped my way, thread by thread, towards the center, always following the question: who is this (allegedly megalomaniac) man? I wanted to know whether he was the world's best anatomist, and he vehemently denied it. Instead, in the back seat of his car, he tried to describe to me what his greatest strength was: a novel way of thinking, a novel way of seeing and making visible the human body. And he started to explain to me his approach to planning his plastinates: Before dissecting, he imagined shooting arrows from every direction into every point of the body, envisioning which tissue the arrow would have to penetrate and which would be next. That way he had reached novel, never before seen insights into the human body, giving laypeople access to their interior and occasionally even forcing professors of anatomy from renowned universities to admit that they had not known the body from this or that point of view.

Hired on the Trolley

My article on Gunther's microcosm was written while I was vacationing in Cypress. On the beach, at a restaurant, before going to sleep; I would carry my laptop everywhere–as if von Hagens' habit of melting all the places in this world into an open-plan office had already been passed on to me. In retrospect, I have to thank my siblings for their patience and tolerance. The article that I finished on my flight home began as follows:

When the German professor of anatomy Gunther von Hagens (54) dies, he wants to be cut in slices. With a band saw. Into millimeter thin slices. Whether longitudinal, from head to toe, or in cross-sections–that is a decision he wants to leave to his wife. The cutting, too, by the way. For his wife, Angelina Whalley, is not only younger than he is, but she is also a physician. And so chances are that one day she will fulfill her husband's last wish with her own hands.

And this is how it will work: As soon as von Hagens has expired, he will be loaded into the car. After only about five minutes of driving time, however, it will be time to get out again. Because the room of the "Institute for Plastination" where the dissecting, sawing, and plastinating takes place is only a stone's throw away from Gunther von Hagens' row house in Heidelberg, Germany. Discreetly a little out of town, for security reasons surrounded by a high fence. So. Whalley will place her husband on sawhorses and cut open his leg to gain access to his main artery. Overnight, she will pump ten to twenty quarts of formalin into his blood vessels that will stop the decay. The pumping will take no more than six hours, provided von Hagens is not suffering from major calcification of the arteries.

The following morning von Hagens' skin will feel somewhat tighter, and his body will look as if he had gained 40 pounds over night. Von Hagens' body will now be ready for the freezer where he will be frozen at minus 70 degrees Celsius (minus 94 degrees Fahrenheit). Only then will it be on to the band saw. [...][1]

---

1. *Toaster Junge Monatszeitung, November 1999 edition, p. 6ff.*

This article apparently was a hit with Gunther von Hagens, not that I had intended it. A few weeks later, when I invited him and three other guests to a one-hour radio talk show, he greeted me immediately with the title of my article: "Forget about getting buried–get cut up!" And he broke out into a hearty laugh that is characterized by the fact that he shows his entire upper row of teeth. From then on everything went at lightning speed. The informal "Du" came all by itself, he addressed me in this informal way, I returned the treatment, it never had to be formally agreed upon. He offered me the job as his press spokesman during our trolley ride to the radio station. The following Monday, I accepted. If I had been superstitious, however, I might have reconsidered. For during the train trip from Basle to Zurich after the talk show, my train suddenly slowed down and then stood still for what seemed like an eternity. For the first and only time during my career as train traveler a man had thrown himself in front of the train I was riding on–not even an hour after I had interviewed Gunther von Hagens.

Hobby: Self-Castigation in the Media

Today I believe that his enthusiasm for my article originated in his fascination of my turning the tables. For once it was him whom I–at least in my mind–put on the dissection table. That fits well with the almost childlike joy that he finds in staging the public side of his persona in the media, garnished with a shot of craziness, and then have himself torn to pieces by his critics. This is a characteristic present everywhere in Gunther's relationship with the media. One might even speak of a malicious, almost masochistic fun in feeding himself to the press hounds, in being food for them. There is nothing he enjoys reading more than a well-written damning review. For he knows what journalists want, what they need to spice up their stories: a juicy quote here, an unusual image there. And the media will bite. Why should he show the photographer of the national news magazine *Der Spiegel*, who traveled all the way to von Hagens' institute in Kyrgyzstan just for this story, only the conventional vessel gestalt specimen, if, only one freezer over, he has one with a (post-mortem) erection to display?

What is often lost in these media productions are the many other facets that are equally representative of Gunther's character: the fine, the lovable, the differentiated. For example, I have never met such a comprehensive thinker as Gunther von Hagens. As strictly as everything from A to Z in his existence that is booked up from morning to night and is completely tailored for efficiency is subjugated to his mental baby "plastination" like an army of recruits on the parade grounds of a barracks–as widespread is his horizon as far as society and human life in general are concerned. His curiosity about the many large and small topics of being is insatiable. A relationship between Chinese grammar and the Chinese way of thinking? Gunther points out numerous connections. A new study on the happiness-inducing effects of male sperm that suggests that women who have un-protected sex are less susceptible to depression? Gunther has read it and, as always, has memorized the most important points. A new discovery in brain research that nerve impulses–e.g., for lifting one's arm–are already triggered before one has "thought out" this command? Whether this means that we do not have any free will, that free will is merely an illusion–that, too, one can discuss with Gunther at length.

Buddhist Gunther?

I will not forget one of our working walks in Cologne alongside the Rhine river–we often fled the hustle and bustle of the exhibition to be able to talk about important issues without being interrupted–when I asked him how he imagined the infinity of the universe. He took out a 100-mark bill and shaped it roughly to resemble a Möbius strip, a never-ending loop on which you can endlessly walk straight ahead without walking in a circle and without ever reaching the end. The image reminded me of Einstein's theory of bent space. We agreed, however, on the smallness and limitedness of our minds and were aware of the model-like character of most attempts at an explanation. And in that there were overtones of a great modesty of the declared agnostic Gunther von Hagens, humility even, uttered by someone who emphasizes again and again that he reserves the right not to have to commit to something. An attitude of openness that shows as well in his interpretation of the meaning of life: *"Life has no meaning other than what we give it,"* says Gunther. A sentence that I often thought about, for it begins rather soberly and throws us humans back onto ourselves. Its dynamic unfolds in the second part: *"...other than what we give it,"* which points to the almost unlimited potential for filling the meaninglessness with meaning. Or, to use Gunther's most important motto: "to make gold from shit." Whoever is able to stand the initial sobering, caused by the pointlessness of one's existence, can then turn it around into a *carte blanche*, into an invitation to completely take charge of shaping one's own life–and who does that more consistently than Gunther von Hagens?

Over all those years during which I have accompanied him–for a long time close-up, occasionally from far away, and today only here and there–I never really understood why he builds the meaning of his life around plastination or what drives him from within. Until at one point I realized that it is not really important, and that there probably is not even a truly meaningful explanation for *why* he does just what he does. What is of critical importance is that he has decided on, and consistently pursues, his goal. I began to see something Buddhist in this approach, for in Buddhism the path is the goal, as they say. In Buddhism, being present and appreciating every moment is a daily task, living in the here and now.

So, Gunther von Hagens turns out to be a Buddhist–without being aware of it himself? Several aspects suggest that to be so. For example, his detachment from the image that others have of him. No matter how much he likes to occasionally fan the flames to provoke this image, he still can live with being perceived differently from what he is like. He spends most of his time in China, anyway, where no one recognizes him in the street. His attitude towards material things also fits the Buddhism hypothesis. He does appreciate money in order use it meaningfully, as a means to an end, in order to create something, to effect something. But any kind of luxury, aside from some technical toys to which he succumbs, is absolutely foreign to him. In China he as a three-and-a-half-room apartment on the seventh floor of a house that does not even have an elevator. Clothes or fashion need not worry him, either, for he adopted an outfit that he wears as consistently as a monk wears his habit. Even in winter he does not take off his black sandals. And whenever we went out to eat, he could not bear—thanks to his Prussian-thrifty upbringing—to leave food on his plate, not even one single time. His need to finish eating food is even so strong that he regularly ate my leftovers if I did not finish my meal.

Being Able to Sleep on Command

Another unforgettable item are the woolen blankets that Gunther had for us in his carryon luggage when we had to spend a 16-hour stopover in Moscow on a trip from Kyrgyzstan to China. He handed them to me and to a journalist who was traveling with us—just like a mother bird magically pulling straw from her beak so her babies can make their own nest—and headed purposefully for the first floor of the transit building. There, he said, passengers would pass by only rarely, so it was ideally suited for sleeping. Then he showed us how we should hook our feet into the handles of our carryon luggage so we would wake up should anyone tamper with it. After less than three minutes Gunther and I were sound asleep on the hard floor, just like two homeless guys in their regular spot. The journalist, the poor guy, never closed his eyes, and after a few days spent with us in Kyrgyzstan the first signs of sleep deprivation were noticeable in him. If you want to survive Gunther's marathon trips unharmed, you have to be able to fall asleep in any place, at any time, day or night, on command.

*Sleeping person
with hat in transit*

"With all due respect to Gunther's uncomplicated nature," you might object now, "but what about that unspeakably vain hat he always wears? How does that fit in with the above proclaimed Buddhist modesty?" Well, in order to dissolve that supposed contradiction you have to gain insight into the special relationship that exists between Gunther and the image he shows to the public. He consciously accepts that the finer gradations of his personality are almost always lost on the media, as I have mentioned before. He sees his public image mainly as belonging to his invention. And between him and this image a relationship has developed similar to that between the author of a novel and his main character who, after a while, also seems to develop a life of his or her own.

The Professor in a Ballet Outfit

As long as it will heat up the discussion about his exhibition–and in doing so, as Gunther believes, will propagate the "democratization of anatomy"–he is always ready to sacrifice any vanity he might harbor, such as the desire to look good in public (and especially in public) that any regular person has. And he is ready to do so, even when he risks losing his scientific reputation or making a fool of himself.

One of the most delectable public scenes happened at the "Love Parade" 2001 in Berlin. Gunther absolutely wanted to present BODY WORLDS on one of the floats that would be making their way through hundreds of thousands of people. Our original idea was to have dancers turn into plastinates. We hired make-up artists from the Babelsberg film studios for the making of the costumes. But when we saw how miserably they failed in creating realistic reproductions of plastinates, Gunther bought white ballet outfits and handed out paint and brushes to his Heidelberg anatomists so they could paint muscles, organs, and the like onto the outfit. The result, proudly presented by Gunther to the spontaneously assembled departmental managers of the Berlin exhibition, looked, to say it politely, as if pre-school children had encountered finger paint for the first time.

The reaction was uncomfortably long lasting silence. Eventually, someone asked: "And who is supposed to... *wear those?*" Without answering that Gunther disappeared into one of the neighboring offices for a few seconds. Moments later, he reappeared in the painted ballet outfit, making his body twitch to the beat of imaginary techno music until all of us broke out in booming laughter. With his uninhibited way of making a fool of himself he had, once again, won all of us over. And he kept his promise and wore the dress with the painted fig leaf covering his genitals–and thrashed about for eight hours in the brooding heat at the head of our BODY WORLDS float in the "Love Parade."

Not afraid of making a fool of himself: Gunther von Hagens in his self-painted ballet outfit atop the BODY WORLDS float at the Berlin 2001 „Love Parade"

Inside the Three-Million-Mark Tent

To me, the liveliest exhibition site clearly was the first one that I was in charge of: Cologne. On the one hand, there was the organizational challenge: When I started my job in 2000 my department consisted of merely one *iMac* and a phone–and the task was to set up a professional, smoothly running media office. Within a brief period of time we had recruited seven employees who, in addition to other things, took care of about 50 journalists a day. But Cologne also was unique with respect to the locale. Gunther had had a tent for three million German marks built on "Heumarkt," a large traditional square in the heart of the old part of town. The tent created a true circus atmosphere, but was equipped with sophisticated technology and even was home to a "Garden of Eden" that was tended to by several gardeners and in which the plastinates were presented.

Never had the exhibition been closer to the people, never had we been more immediately exposed to a place. Our offices were improvised, sepa-

BODY WORLDS inside the tent at Cologne's Heumarkt:
Never had the exhibition been closer to the people or more integrated into the city than here:

rated from each other by partitions. We heard every step of the attending public, almost every breath of the, on average, 5000 visitors a day. It rarely turned noisy, remained just as quiet as in previous exhibitions. Visitors often are deeply engaged in thought as they pass through the exhibition, in almost meditative contemplation. During the summer it got really hot in the tent, up to 40 degrees Celsius (100 degrees Fahrenheit), and the lines outside grew longer and longer, soon almost wrapping around the entire tent. Visitors waited in line for up to ten hours to get into the exhibition. There were even cases of cheating, because some of the workers in charge of managing the lines could not resist the offers of up to 400 German marks from some of the waiting to smuggle them inside.

I also remember how one night the press office phone rang at 2 a.m. We were busy folding 6000 copies of press releases because the machine that was supposed to take care of that had broken down. The voice at the other end of the line did not even sound surprised that the phone was answered

To this day the most successful act of „democratizing anatomy" à la Gunther.

by a real person in the middle of the night–and asked with all naturalness whether we would be open on Good Friday. To me, this seems to illustrate, in an exemplary way, what kind of entrenched institution we had become in Cologne. And it was as if the caller had had a premonition: Towards the end of our Cologne days we remained open around the clock.

The words BODY WORLDS continue to be a magical term in Cologne, where I, unlike in the other cities where the exhibition went, made some good friends whom I still visit often. In Cologne, we achieved, in a very tangible way, what Gunther means by democratizing anatomy: Although (or perhaps to some degree, because) the churches left nothing untried to keep the people of Cologne away from the exhibit, the people came in droves– determined to form their own opinions about the controversy. In their direct way, the Cologne citizens often addressed Gunther, grabbed him when he tried to rush unrecognized through the exhibition to attend a meeting or to get to his office, and peppered him with the questions they had. He often called me to join in if the discussions became especially exciting. And even the mayor showed up within a quarter of an hour after I had spontaneously called him to ask whether he would like to greet the one-millionth visitor.

Former Secret Police as Company Spies

Given all the good stuff I have to say about Gunther, you might wonder, and rightly so, where his weaknesses lie. That he, too, is not free from faults hopefully will be understood. Liking someone, however, also means generously ignoring those faults. I remember, for example, how appalled many employees were when we found out that Gunther, who himself had spent almost two years in a GDR prison, had hired former GDR secret policemen to spy on the exhibition staff–they had even written evaluations in their former civil servant's style. That is only forgivable if one knows how often Gunther already had been betrayed by his employees, and often just by those he had trusted most. Just think of Sui, his former Chinese General Manager, who had worked for the competition for an entire year while being employed by Gunther. And the secret police guys, thank God, soon were gone again, anyway. They had started so many intrigues that they had soon maneuvered themselves off the playing field.

Another weakness of Gunther's pops up when bad news has to be conveyed, such as the cancellation of projects that he already had euphorically planned. In such cases he likes to utilize the good cop, bad cop routine common in American TV crime shows,. He does this together with his wife Angelina, with her having to assume the bad cop role. For no matter how quick-tempered he can be in factual matters–for example, about a waste of money–he hardly ever can manage to tell someone what is bothering him or what he does not (any longer) want.

Corpses on the Bottom of the Sea?

In closing, I would like to tell you about the most exciting of the many research tasks that I completed for Gunther. It will take us a little away from him, but I believe that the freedom and the opportunities for personal development that a boss gives to his employees or a teacher to his students say much about the boss or the teacher himself. And I had plenty of freedom. His only condition was that everyday business was taken care of properly. The research task that I would like to talk about took me to Singapore. I was with Gunther in China when an e-mail arrived that made even him, the usually calm plastinator, catch his breath. As near as I can remember it went like this: "We are sorry to have to tell you," wrote the transportation company that usually shipped Gunther's specimens in containers to China, "that the vessel with your load had an accident in the Singapore Strait. Approximately 10 percent of the containers have sunk or have become contaminated with oil. Whether your containers are affected we currently cannot say."

Aboard the ship in question had been dozens of fixed and pre-dissected bodies[2] that Gunther had sent from Heidelberg to Plastination City in China by boat. These specimens were to be turned into a second, parallel BODY WORLDS exhibition, and it was of financially vital importance. The consequences from a loss of the shipment would have been devastating: Two years of preparatory work in Heidelberg would have been lost from one moment to the next, and the production of the second exhibition would have been delayed by years. Not to mention the dead body donors who had donated their bodies to him in order to have a useful post-mortem existence, but certainly not in order to rot at the bottom of Indonesian seas like sardines in oil-contaminated containers... In short, it would have come close to a real-life version of Gunther's nightmare in which body donors complain to him about not having been dissected well enough. I dropped everything and flew straight to Singapore to find out what had happened to "our" bodies. There were no leads. The shipping company apparently had tried hard to cover up the accident. The aforementioned e-mail message

---

2. As von Hagens' former press spokesman, I have to add that he himself would no longer be speaking of "dead bodies" in a legal sense as soon as the corpse has been "fixed,", i.e. has been prevented from further decay, and has been repurposed (in this case for an anatomical purpose) and no longer is the "object of individual grieving." However, for reasons of a richer imagery, to keep the language powerful, I stick with the words "dead body" and corpse, just as I–inspired by German language usage authority Wolf Schneider–say atomic energy rather than the (harmless sounding) nuclear energy and genetic manipulation instead of genetic engineering.

arrived two weeks after the accident; industry practice would have been to inform customers the following day at the latest. But there were other things that suggested foul play. The accident had happened in a very embarrassing manner. The container ship had, at its top speed of 22 knots, run onto a reef that is noted in each and every nautical chart. The reputation of the company seemed to be at risk, after all, it was one of the large French shipping companies. After my arrival in Singapore, I tried to contact them, but they remained adamantly silent about the accident and even claimed that our containers had never been aboard their vessel …

This was followed by a constant back and forth that lasted for days. It seemed that the shipping company was buying time by simply hanging up on me–and eventually also on Gunther, who had gotten involved from Kyrgyzstan. Gunther and I were speechless, especially since this (lack of) crisis management and the non-communication were the exact opposite of the public transparency we had always practiced.[3]

3. When, for instance, Spiegel magazine (issue 4/04, p. 36ff.) suggested in its cover story "Dr. Death–The Horrendous Deals of Corpse Exhibitor Gunther von Hagens" that Gunther was "apparently also" accepting victims of execution in China, he immediately had all bodies stored in Plastination City checked overnight for signs that would support this theory. A few days later, at a nationally announced press conference with more than 250 journalist including 25 camera teams from all over the world, he announced that in seven of the more than 600 bodies head injuries had been found. While he thought it highly unlikely that they were victims of executions, he had decided to cremate those bodies because a violent death could not be precluded with absolute certainty.–He certainly could have gone the easier route of simply declaring the accusations that Spiegel magazine was unable to prove as stupid speculation. Instead, he answered questions at this press conference until the very last journalist had either left or run out of questions.

Stefan Rathgeb (2001), photo: Henri Wagner

Plastinates at the Ship Junk Yard?

After a few days of research I located the ship that had had the accident at a junkyard for shipwrecks that resembled a military restricted area. No helicopter pilot was ready to fly me over it, all the captains of the cutters waved me off when I asked them to take me there. Finally, a shrewd and impressively corpulent manager of a limousine company found a way of getting me in there in order to inspect the ship with our containers. She had learned from an insider that on a certain evening that week a boat named "Captain Omar" would arrive at the shipyard for repairs. She ordered a white Mercedes limousine for me, sat down beside me and told me to leave the talking to her, she would pass me off to the guards at the entrance as a superintendent, because they were not allowed to check superintendents. I probably should add that back then I was barely 23, looked even younger and liked to wear my hair a little longer than the average citizen, definitely longer than superintendents, at least the superintendents I was able to envision. My companion thought that the limousine would keep them in check, and off we went. Believe it or not, the guard, armed with a machine gun, bought it. He did look at me a little longer than usual and asked me "Are you the superintendent?" But when I nodded he waved us through, and the tinted-glass window of the Mercedes was rolled up quickly.

As soon as we were inside, I began to understand why this place was as guarded from the public as a North Korean atomic lab. Looking for our ship with Gunther's containers, we drove past miles and miles of an underworld of dead ships. Burnt out cruise ships, damaged freighters, passenger ferries that had had accidents, all of them lying there like beached whales and in dire need of a complete overhaul. Flying sparks and bright lights everywhere. And seemingly tiny men in gray overalls, welding and hammering, and cranes moving individual parts. A view into a dark world, far from public life. Covered up boat accidents, mentioned, if at all, only in a few lines in the local media; how rarely one reads about them.

Eventually we found "our" ship, the "CMA CGM Normandie," the French flag still waving at its stern, the bow completely compressed. The containers, however, had already been removed, and so we left this ghostly place with the only certainty (and photographic proof) being that the accident had actually happened.

"CMA CGM Normandie"

A few days later I found out that the containers that had not sunk had been shipped to Malaysia aboard smaller transportation boats. After I had applied a lot of pressure and had shown them the facts that my research had yielded, the shipping company agreed that I could inspect the containers. However, they wanted a flat fee of 4000 German marks per day and 500 dollars for each container they would have to move to make ours accessible. In view of the mountains of thousands of containers we decided not to accept this offer. With this admission, however, we finally had at least indirect proof that our containers were not among the sunken ones. It would be many weeks, though, before Gunther was able to receive them in China, because an adjuster of the insurance company had to be present at their opening.

I will remember that nine-day research trip to Singapore for a long time to come. I decided to exemplary describe it here in a little more detail so that you can understand why being Gunther von Hagens' press spokesman was anything but a common office job. Working for him in that position meant always being up-to-date on the latest developments and stories that came out of his "plastination" enterprise. When I stopped working for him to undertake a major journalistic research project on the topic of capital punishment in the U.S. state of Texas that specializes in it, my to-do list at Gunther's still included a trip to Australia where a Buddhist monastery had asked to buy one of his plastinates. It was to help them in their meditations on transitoriness. My job would have been to convince them to win over one of their own as a body donor in return...

His Aftershave as a Souvenir

Naturally, I could go on and on telling these stories. But I want to end with a personal detail. Whenever I think of Gunther, I, of course, think of the person I experienced, of the boss he was, and of the friend he became. But a person who is important to us, who has accompanied us on an important part of our trip through life, will also always become an image, a representation of a mental principle that we internalize, that we make part of ourselves to a certain degree. In Gunther's case this has been especially true for me. To me he represents self-discipline, but also joy of life. And most of all enormous productivity. Whenever I have to brood about an article for hours, I quickly visualize him. I see him clearly in my mind, sitting aboard a plane, the only one with his reading lamp on, focused on his laptop, studying Chinese, while everyone else in the cabin slumbers peacefully. It does not take more than three seconds before I feel a surge of energy clearing my mind and making my fingers dance on the keyboard. Or, when I suffer defeat, I think of his motto and drive myself to turn shit into gold–to make something great of it after all, to keep working on it without allowing myself to be discouraged. And whenever I have an important public appearance to make, or critical negotiations to attend, I splash a few drops of his aftershave that he gave to me onto my cheeks–and the dynamic unfolds from within.

Bazon Brock, born 1936, Prof. em. University of Wuppertal; Dean of faculty for more than 12 years; Head of research family "Culture and Strategy." Since 1995 Professor of Non-normative Aesthetics at the universities of Hamburg, Germany; Vienna, Austria; and Wuppertal, Germany, after his studies in the fields of German studies, philosophy, art history, and political sciences at the universities of Hamburg, Frankfurt, Germany, and Vienna. Since 1957 Brock has organized 1600 happenings, action teachings, and exhibitions; since 1968 he has created and managed schools for visitors at the outstanding international documenta exhibitions in Cassel, Germany; he wrote and performed and produced numerous movies, radio plays, and TV shows. For the past 9 years he has hosted Germany's only long-running TV show on fine arts of today. He has published five volumes of collected works (DuMont Verlag, Cologne, Germany) as well as books on subjects such as aging as a problem for artists and future societies, imaging arts and sciences, the history of looking at floors and grounds. His relationship with Gunther von Hagens is characterized by mutual friendly respect.

Bazon Brock

In the Following

Never, not even in the greatest art shows, has one seen people focused on the object of their viewing quite in a way as could be observed in front of von Hagens' plastinates. Amazement, awe, shudders of deep inner emotion were so unforgettably expressed by the viewers because every viewer was looking at him- or herself in the viewed object. One could sense that the viewers never before had been as close to themselves as when they were confronted with the body plastinates. This was a true illustration of the, often only allegedly reflexive, reflexive modern age in the arts.

"Shudders, amazement, growing quiet," is what the German weekly news magazine *Stern* noted as the experience of viewers in its extraordinary report on the Mannheim exhibition in March 1998. The statement was not exactly a match for the characterization of the plastinator as "master of the macabre" that *Stern* itself even used as a headline. This discrepancy between the reaction of the audience and the public racket created by media people, churchmen, and judges of taste was generally characteristic of von Hagens' effect on the European public. Sometimes von Hagens enhanced this discrepancy when he referred to his works as pieces of art. The fact that he insisted on the humanistic unity of arts and sciences, as it was perceived in the time of da Vinci, helped only minimally, for this currently re-emerging unity, in the age of imaging arts and sciences re-appearing in the shape of the life scientist who, in using computer graphics to visualize complex molecules and subsequently using these visualizations for further scientific investigation, simultaneously is creating works of fine sciences and fine arts, so far has only been recognized by a few individual artists and scientists, but not by the larger institutions of the arts and sciences.

The poses of von Hagens also gave cause to trite, i.e., unproductive misunderstandings. His conspicuous physiognomy underneath his felt hat, worn indoors as well as outdoors, has been criticized as an unjustified transfer of the portrait of Joseph Beuys to von Hagens' head. So, on the one hand, we have to remind ourselves again and again that no one will be anchored in the collective memory who does not resemble others. Everyone who makes a lasting impression on the collective memory optimally represents a combined set of recognized patterns, also referred to as gestalt schemes. One example is the German tennis player Boris Becker who early in his career represented the large-eyed gestalt scheme of Alexander the Great and Goethe, and who later illustrated the same gestalt scheme that made Vincent van Gogh, also as portrayed by Kirk Douglas, the personification of the ingenious artist, driven by pressing doubts and fear of self-destruction. Both Beuys and von Hagens represent the schema of embodiment of the spiritual ascetic whose self-confidence is an expression of his or her radical nature. This is a characteristic that has made many representatives of the modern age, unjustly, seem like fanatics. They are not, or not only, fanatics in the sense of Stefan George's sentiment that anything we do is done with fanatism, but in the sense that they inspire people to become "fans," to become their converted followers. And indeed, the effects of Beuys and von Hagens can be determined by looking at how converted followers formed groups around them.

On the other hand the accusation that von Hagens is copying the representational type "Joseph Beuys" has to be corrected by pointing out that the *imitatio*, the following, has been a genuine concept of the modern age, ever since Dürer's self-portrait and self-interpretation in the painting known as Imitatio Christi has been turned into an imitation of Dürer practiced by the artists following him. And, without doubt, von Hagens sees himself appropriately as following the humanist grand masters of the time of Dürer, such as da Vinci or Vesalius. It would be a welcome development if another contemporary representative such as von Hagens joined the *imitatio*, the fellowship, of Joseph Beuys, besides good old Stüttgen.

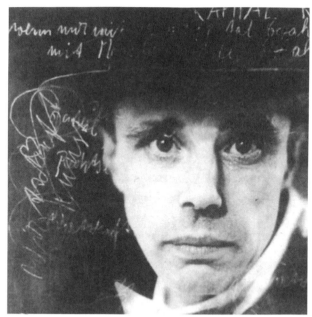

Joseph Beuys (1921–1986)

Gunther von Hagens (2001)

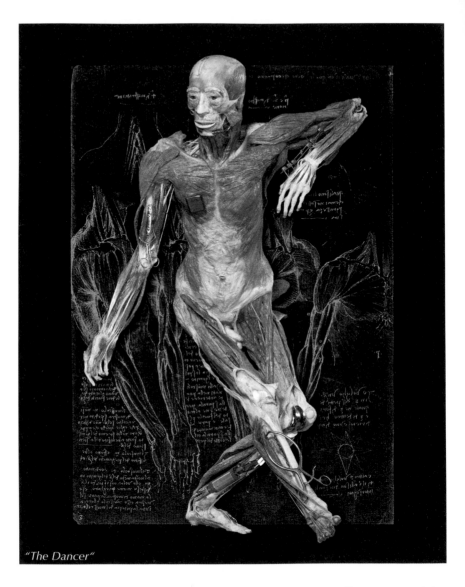

"The Dancer"

Yes, this much is true: Gunther von Hagens is, especially in view of the problematic aspects discussed above, one of the outstanding exponents of contemporariness in the arts and the sciences, in the public as presented by the media, in his self-image as founder and entrepreneur, and as addressee for fans/party liners/comrades in arms. He leads his team like a coach with the status of a guru, his Chinese institutes make him a successful founder in the business of science. He preserves his personal autonomy by practicing a monk-like life style and by way of his intrepid, even radical nature. This nature causes (provokes) passionate debates about the arts and the sciences the likes of which otherwise can only be found in the areas of the geneticists' interference with germ-lines, the applications of astrophysics, or man-made ecological disasters.

On another occasion I attempted to pay tribute to von Hagens through the literary sketching of attitudes, namely relating to the privy councilor Dr. Behrens, who heads the sanatorium in Thomas Mann's Magic Mountain. Dr. Behrens is the person who confronts Hans Castorp with himself–both in the physical sense, by showing him the x-ray images of his diseased lungs, but also in a figurative sense, in discussions that force the young engineer to truly reflect on himself. Here, on the occasion of his 60th birthday, I suggest to Gunther von Hagens that he might modify the privy councilor's activity based on the template offered in "Doctor Erich Kästner's Medicine Chest for the Treatment of the the Average Inner Life" as quoted below, thus continuing the creation of a truly reflexive work–humans reflecting on humans:

A fluorescent screen served as his easel. | Deeply touched, I stood to attention. |
He drew and drew, and told me that | he was drawing my orthodiagram.
Ceremoniously, he then brought out | a mirror, showed it to me |
And said: "In this mirror you can see | your roots."
I watched as he described | my anatomy, and how it worked. |
I saw my diaphragm in action | and saw my breathing ribs as well.
And in between those ribs, strangely beating | a shadowy growth. |
That was my heart! It looked exactly like | a twitching stain of ink.
I must admit, I was distraught. | Awestruck, I stood as still as a stone. |
That was my heart, the one that belongs to you, | beloved Hildegard?
Let us forget about what happened, | and let me go into a monastery. |
Who never saw his heart in a mirror, | will not be able to comprehend.

Franz Josef Wetz *has been Professor of Philosophy at the Schwäbisch Gmünd teacher's college since 1994. He studied philosophy, German studies, and theology and obtained his doctorate at the Gießen university in 1989, for which he received the university's prize for outstanding thesis. He achieved Habilitation (the formal qualification required for professorship in Germany) in 1992. He met von Hagens in the context of the controversies surrounding the BODY WORLDS exhibition and has accompanied him on his path and his work ever since, at an ethical-philosophical and a friendship level.*

Franz Josef Wetz

Pushing the Envelope

Gunther von Hagens is an envelope-pusher–an intellectual adventurer of the type humankind occasionally needs. Any society, however, would fall apart if all of its citizens were such types: it simply would die of their extreme personalities. At the same time, a society without any envelope-pushers is just as impossible–if it were made up only of average people it would go under as well: Wherever the new, at the risk of failure, is not attempted, development no longer happens, only stagnation and then decay. Progress is possible only if the traditional, if rules, dogmas, and bureaucracy, if everything that is common, settled, and set in stone, as important as these things usually are, occasionally is challenged. This sometimes requires breaking hitherto unquestioned taboos. The breaking of taboos sometimes is the price demanded by creativity.

I am not going to write from a peeping Tom's perspective about Gunther von Hagens. He and I met at the end of the 1990s in the context of the discussions about the ethical, legal, and religious permissibility of the BODY WORLDS exhibition. At the center of the debates about the Mannheim exhibition and the subsequent exhibitions in German-speaking countries were the terms "human dignity" and "rest in death." It was notable that in non-German-speaking countries, where the exhibition was shown in several places, these terms played only a minor role. Many opponents of the exhibition, to this day, see BODY WORLDS as a violation of human dignity, more precisely as a violation of the dignity of the dead. But, as often is the case in discussions about human dignity, this sublime construct of language remained–in spite, or perhaps because, of its luster–vague and incomprehensible for the most part. Just like an oracle, human dignity presents itself whenever invoked, but often has only dark epigrams to offer as answers to our urgent questions.

With skull in bookcase

Gunther von Hagens tried to remedy this situation by studying this highest legal good more intensely, and in doing so he came across one of my books that deals extensively with the concept of human dignity. This was followed by an invitation to the Heidelberg Institute for Plastination, which I gladly accepted. The actual purpose of the visit was to ask me the simple question of whether I would be willing to think about the dignity of the dead, which I had not treated in my book since it stops at the dignity of the dying. This seemed to be an interesting task, and I immediately undertook it. What surprised me back then was the bourgeois setting in which the plastinator and his personal spokesman, Thomas Knuth, received me: a cozy eat-in kitchen, where they served coffee and cake–the sole unusual item was the skull on one of the shelves. Politely, curiously, and attentively, Gunther von Hagens listened to what I had to say before he offered me a tour of his Heidelberg "workshop"–an offer I gladly accepted, for until then I had never seen a plastinate. The masses pouring into the Mannheim exhibition had kept me away; I did not see BODY WORLDS until its Vienna, Austria, showing.

Once my essay for the exhibition catalog on the "dignity of the dead" had been written, there were several more encounters with Gunther von Hagens on various occasions. They always were cordial and interesting, and we always discussed the ethical permissibility of the exhibition. A truly personal contact between us, however, did not evolve until the Cologne exhibition. At that time, the discussion about crossing limits, breaking taboos, dignity of the dead, and rest in death reached a hitherto unknown level. The BODY WORLDS exhibition split the media, the experts, and the general population into two camps. The debate was rekindled and fanned again and again mostly by high-ranking officials of both major German churches. But also artists, medicine ethicists, jurists, and colleagues from the medical field had critical things to say. The fact that someone had handled his responsibility in a way that he alone deemed right was perceived as an affront to bourgeois moral standards.

Over the past years Gunther von Hagens has often had to both answer matter-of-fact criticism as well as withstand personal insults. What is remarkable is the quiet and calm with which he has borne all of this up to now. There were, however, in addition to numerous religious believers, also a notable number of theologists, philosophers, medicine ethicists, scholars of the law and the arts, anatomists, and doctors from all fields of medical specialization in Cologne who were and are convinced of the ethical, legal, and aesthetic justification for the exhibition.

The opponents insisted that it was unjustifiable, even scandalous, to display dead bodies as exhibits to a mass audience. The exhibition, they claimed, was disturbing the rest of the dead, was violating human dignity and offending against the common decency and the reverence with which one ought to treat the dead and which are owed to their loved ones. In addition, they alleged, it was tasteless to degrade the human body and its structure to mere play materials, to make it into an artistic exhibit. Aside from that, most whole-body plastinates were nothing but macabre kitsch, inspired by anatomical illustrative art of the early modern age, stimulating a very dubious aesthetic pleasure. The BODY WORLDS exhibition, according to its critics, was not about education, but about death as a spectacle, about cheap thrills, the craving for sensations, a need to feel cold shivers, even about the desire to look at dead bodies as present in today's culture of peepers and rubberneckers. As had been expected, eventually we also heard the term "robbing the dead" in this context. Others doubted the legality of the exhibition which, after all, did not only question basic val-

Menschenwürde

Kunst oder Leichenfledderei?

"KÖRPERWELTEN" SPALTET DIE GEISTER

war bereits in mehreren
schen Städten ein große
blikumserfolg. Der Mü
ner Kreisverwaltungsrefer
Wilfried Blume-Beyerle ha
jedoch betont, dass in an
anderen Städten nie ein
rechtliche Prüfung stattge-
funden habe.

Menschenwürde

Nach dem bayerischen
Bestattungsrecht müsse
Leichen aber hi

Kunststoffe ersetzt. Die Zellen und
das natürliche Oberflächenrelief
bleiben dabei in ihrer ursprüngli-

Professor Gunther von Hagens will auch in München Leichen in der Öffentlichkeit sezier

„Das grenzt an Leichenfledder

"Lebensziel Menschenmu-
seum": München

Entrüstung über „Leichenfledderei"

Stadt soll öffentliche Autopsie verb

Die Ankündigung
Heidelberger
natomen Gunther
on Hagens, er
m Februar in M
chen eine Leich
entlich obduzi
hat einen Sturm
Entrüstung ent
Der Evange
Arbeitskreis d
hat die Staa
rung aufge
das Vorhabe
hindern A
Ärzteschaft
Spektak
Kreise
ferat e
tion z
bis
Vo
Geiß
bis 1
Hage
"Körper
zu seher
körper

Menschenwürde

Von Pastor Ulrich Wöhler

"Die Synod
schen Land
stützt das E
desbischöfli
mann zum E
nität des Ste

Leichenfledderei oder doch Kuns

Eine Gruppe aus dem Wetteraukreis besuchte die nicht unumstrittene Ausstellung „Körper

KÖLN/KEFENROD (xy).
Eine Schau zum Schaudern,
nfledderei.

nen ausgelöst. Vor allem von kirch-
licher Seite kamen die Bedenken,
damit werde die menschliche Wür-
de verletzt. Trotzdem pilgern täg-

Totenruhe und Menschenwürde

„Körperwelten" sind in München nicht zu sehen: Verstoß gegen Menschenwürde

München. Wegen Verstoßes
gegen das Bestattungsrecht
und die Menschenwürde
wird die Leichenausstellung
„Körperwelten" des umstrittenen Anatomie-Professors
Gunther von Hagens in München untersagt. Der Stadtrat
billigte am späten Abend mit
breiter Mehrheit bei nur acht
die Verbots-

Wander-Ausstellung sollte
von Ende Februar an in München Station machen.

Auch eine von dem Pro-
fessor ursprünglich ange-
kündigte Leichensektion
wird auf Grund des Stadt-
ratsbeschlusses verboten. Al-
lerdings hatte von Hagens
von diesem Plan bereits Abstand genommen.

war bereits in mehreren deutschen Städten ein großer Pu-
blikumserfolg. Der Münch-
verwaltungsreferent
werle hatte

Von Hagens hatte
Kritik an einer Leich
tion betont, es gebe
Grund" für ein Verbot
der Verstorbene zu L
sein Einverständnis
che gegeben habe,
üdevoll, dies

den. Hagens Ausstellung die-
ne aber nicht der Wissen-
schaft.

Als zweites und wichti-
geres Argument führte der
KVR-Chef die Menschenwür-

»Ein Verstoß gegen die Menschenwürde«

München verbietet Ausstellung »Körperwelten«

München (dpa/lby). Wegen Verstoßes gegen das Bestattungsrecht und die Menschenwürde wird die Leichenausstellung „Körperwelten des umstrittenen Anatomie-Professors Gunther von Ha-
in München untersagt. Der Stadtrat billigte am späten Abend

„Körperwelten"-Schau untersagt

ünchen sieht Verstoß gegen die Menschenwürde

ues of our constitution but also violated applicable burial laws. Yet others opposed making money from death, the subordination of moral standards and religion to commerce. They also denied the educational power of the exhibits, which, they asserted, would only serve to give medical laypersons quick access to extraordinary sensual impressions, but would not impart any anatomical knowledge to them.

So, while the opponents obstinately emphasized that BODY WORLDS in the end was only about superficial gratification, its proponents insisted that BODY WORLDS facilitated a deeper experience of the body. It goes without saying that the human body, just as planet Earth, has long since been discovered, investigated, and cartographed. Thus, BODY WORLDS cannot serve to discover anything new, but merely to understand that which is known. It opens up anatomy to a broad audience. In addition, the exhibition is a space that invites contemplative viewing and existential modesty. Without doubt it still is event- or experience-oriented. But that is not a valid objection, for it is just because of this characteristic that it seduces its visitors to discover their own self via the study of the bodies of others. It has been demonstrated that for many visitors the accent is shifted from the mere looking at bodies to a deepened experience of the self. Gunther von Hagens' intention for the exhibition is primarily to confront humans with life, which he demonstrates through the dead, and less about a culture of death. That is why we can say: This unusual kind of "sightseeing" facilitates an extraordinary kind of "lifeseeing!"

The discussions in Cologne did not die down quickly. They quite often took me to this city on the Rhine river, for interviews, talks, and panel discussions, and during such times I got to know Gunther von Hagens better and better. I came to know a man who was able and willing to incessantly discuss the points at issue that had come up–be it late at night or early in the morning. To him everything was about BODY WORLDS, just as there still

Left: Newspaper headlines about BODY WORLDS and the public autopsy in London with key terms such as "Menschenwürde–human dignity," "Leichenfledderei–robbing the dead," "Totenruhe–rest in death," "Körperwelten–Body Worlds," and "Kunst–art."

The Cologne exhibition in 2000

is hardly any other topic for him today. Only two representative discussions of our many, many conversations from back then shall be mentioned here. After a radio show broadcast by the Cologne-based WDR station, during which the main question at issue was whether or not plastinates are dead bodies worthy of protection, we met in the exhibition office where we once more plunged into the question of the state of death of the plastinates: What kind of dead body is a plastinate, after all? It was during that night, which we spent sitting together, exchanging thoughts into the wee hours of the morning, that we came up with the idea of creating a table of the dead that would distinguish between corpse or dead body, wet corpse, and dry corpse. Back then Gunther von Hagens arrived at the–for me extremely informative–conclusion that plastinates belong to the subset of artificial dry corpses. As such, they are comparable to dried specimens, mummies of pharaohs and skeletons that usually are allowed to be publicly displayed. With great seriousness and in deep, sincere reflection, we struggled to answer this question that hitherto had only partially been solved and was of such a tricky nature. This asceticism in the concentration on what is essential, without getting sidetracked by additional issues, is something that I saw quite often in Gunther von Hagens back then.

At the same time, however, he is able to take a back seat in the discussion, to ask very focussed questions, and to listen attentively, as is demonstrated by another conversational situation: After the opening ceremony of the Cologne exhibition, we met at the hotel to end the day together with several experts from the fields of law and medicine. Gunther von Hagens steered the conversation to a new project that he already was envisioning: the plastination of a horse and rider. Immediately, a controversy on the pros and cons of this project sprung up: how would such a plastinate be useful, after all, and would it not do further damage to the exhibition's reputation? Patiently, Gunther von Hagens followed this debate, but he hardly participated. The debate never reached a definite conclusion, and that alone was reason enough for the plastinator to stick with his idea and to put it into action.

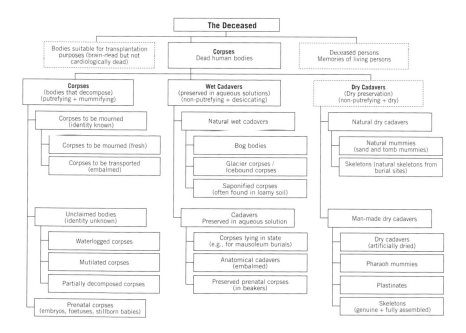

Diagram: The dead, the body, and the corpse (according to Gunther von Hagens)

His energy for such demanding projects is generated by the build-up of tension between his enthusiasm for a project and the inherent risk, which on some occasions lets the plastinator rise above himself. The intensity with which he analyzes everything related to BODY WORLDS–not only the technical questions of plastination, his main field of work, but also the ethical-aesthetic and legal questions, on which he regularly consults with experts–is remarkable. This incredible intensity is only possible if one considers it an obsession, a term that is usually interpreted negatively, but with-out obsession the difficult, even unlikely goals in the world could never be reached. In many other respects, too, Gunther von Hagens is very similar to extreme athletes such as rock climbers and mountaineers. What is critical to them is neither effort nor reward, but the joy of doing something that often demands superhuman feats from them. It is their complete devotion to and total identification with their projects that enables their extraordinary performances. Whether in sports, in economics, in science, or in the arts–there is no stronger incentive than self-determined enthusiasm. One is tempted to say that Gunther von Hagens is the Reinhold Messner of anatomy. For just as the extreme mountaineer was tempted by the very hostility to life of the highest mountains to climb them without oxygen supply, later even alpine style, and eventually to go it solo, seemingly hopeless proj-ects enhance the plastinator's readiness to perform. He is one of those people who will neither be satisfied nor bearable until he has reached the outer limits of his capabilities and possibilities.

Add to that what Reinhold Messner calls real utopia: grandiose visions and daydreams that are not pipedreams. Never before have I met someone who has worked so determinedly and fearlessly on realizing his ideas. As with any mountain climb, the implementation of an extreme idea begins in the mind, where it is carried by both the extreme athlete and the plastinator for quite a while–at home, while half asleep, on trips–until it finally can be made one with reality and tested by experience.

Gunther von Hagens is a person who allows himself to do what he cannot stop himself from doing. So he insists on being himself, the autonomous creator of his own life story, without clinging to the bourgeois myth of complete self-transparency. I know him as a reader of neurophilosophical essays that explicitly do not attempt to escape the fascinating eeriness of experiencing oneself as foreign and unavailable. Nevertheless, the self-driven, unconventional adventurer for whom taking the road less traveled, the self-determined freedom from a certain place, long since has become the stuff of daily life, believes in the possibility of the autonomous shaping of one's existence. Is this an inner discrepancy or even contradiction one sees here? In any case, autonomy, self-sufficiency, self-assertion, creativity, uncompromising discipline, strict time management and self-control, as well as an obsession that is prepared to take risks are essential components of his existence. From this magma of virtues of being that reflect each other, this envelope-pusher opens up resources for the individual modeling of his self. In his model of his self, the plastinator himself invents his own duties—as demands on himself. In doing so he remains at the same time obviously transparent and enigmatic. The former makes him vulnerable, the latter usually prevents attacks on him from reaching their goals.

The restlessness of his day-to-day business often endangers the required focusing on what is essential. That is why von Hagens regularly withdraws from daily life to work on new ideas. For example, he wrote the concept for his essay "On Gruesome Corpses, Gestalt Plastinates, and Mandatory Interment"—escaping from anybody's reach—in my kitchen, where he stayed from morning to late at night, surrounded by a few books, a laptop, and several quarts of milk as his only means of nutrition. Naturally, his hat remained on his head as well.

In Berlin, 2001

There is no question that Gunther von Hagens is not only obsessed and extremely disciplined, a man who like all extreme athletes loves going one step further than anyone else has before, but he also is very ambitious. He is a person hungering for success and recognition, a man with a pronounced need for self-improvement–as are others. This hunger forms part of his motivation. But he does not deny the ambitiousness that drives him to top performances at times. The satisfied need for recognition enhances self-esteem in humans!

In addition, he enjoys himself in the role of *enfant terrible*: He likes being a confusing public disturbance. The directorial character of his being is made obvious by his outer costume alone. He utilizes a vast range of self-promotions to adequately express his need for conspicuousness. Without doubt this supposed breaking free from the constraints of bourgeois order is the flip side of his desire to present elitist instances of success within the social space and in the public discourse. But his image cultivation is mainly a means of promoting BODY WORLDS. An inherent danger of such self-promotion is that the discussion may quickly focus on the producer of the exhibition rather than the exhibition itself–as has happened in Munich and Frankfurt, both Germany. There, his life on the fringes of bourgeois society suddenly became the ticket to the center of society!

His commercial needs play a role similar to that of his image cultivation. Gunther von Hagens is, at the same time, both a talented organizational manager and a sales strategist. His recipe for success is the conscious combination of high and low culture, the combination of cultivation with commercialization. However, there is no alternative to this, for every single exhibition constitutes a major investment. In addition to time and energy, an exhibition requires a lot of money. Thus, it is hard to understand why many of our contemporaries have difficulty reconciling his character as moneymaker with his character as plastinator. In their eyes, there is a clear either-or between for-profit culture and not-for-profit culture! The latter usually is subsidized by tax money, associations, sponsors, and patrons of the arts. It normally is dependent on these subsidies, which most often come from tax revenues. Wherever these are not available, an enterprise has to make its money in the free market. To reproach BODY WORLDS for doing so is, from a micro- and a macroeconomic viewpoint, completely absurd. In an economic system such as ours, professional marketing can be seen only as praise that may be misinterpreted as criticism.

But no matter how strong his craving for money and recognition, Gunther von Hagens at the same time is extremely undemanding. The plastinator himself is not modest, but he lives a modest life. Because there is hardly any personal life for him, there is also hardly any money taken from the business for personal use. His obsession makes him re-invest most of his money in his projects. He hardly needs any to cover his living expenses–less than most people I know, as strange as that may sound.

The Berlin exhibition, trumping even the already successful Cologne exhibition, was a real source of joy for Gunther von Hagens. In Berlin, the public interest was even stronger and the discussion about the permissibility of BODY WORLDS even more intense. The entire debate started, for the n-th time, all over again. I encountered Gunther von Hagens ever more frequently at panels and in the studios of TV and radio stations, where each of us used his own arguments to fight the critics. The discussions were not always good, sometimes even frustrating, but then again they were interest-ing, informative, and exciting. My nicest memory of that time is that of a joint radio appearance that lasted several hours (with musical interludes) on an evening show by the ORB station, broadcast on the weekend of the opening of the Berlin exhibition. Already exhausted from the many interviews that day, we drove out together to the radio studio that night, by then somewhat weary of the aggressive debates about human dignity, rest of the dead, robbing the dead, and commerce. So it was very pleasant for us that the host explicitly did not want to have those debates again, and carefully avoided these topics. He was most interested in the motives and goals that Gunther von Hagens was pursuing with the BODY WORLDS exhibition, and in how Gunther hat gotten into plastination, and how I had hooked up with the plastinator. In the course of this pleasant discussion, I gradually realized that the academic relationship between the plastinator and me, which had always been about the ethical dimensions of

BODY WORLDS in Berlin, 2001

BODY WORLDS, had in the meantime turned into a friendship. Today that friendship is almost exclusively about the ethical permissibility of BODY WORLDS, which is due to the fact that for Gunther von Hagens there is hardly any other topic besides plastination and anatomy.

He is willing to take almost any risk for BODY WORLDS, another characteristic he shares with extreme athletes. For Gunther von Hagens is, in addition to and before everything else, an envelope-pusher, sometimes even a dare-devil. We refer to someone as an envelope-pusher who consciously goes to the limits of his or her own possibilities and sets more and more ambitious goals in doing so. Envelope-pushers never stand still, but try to expand the limits further out, little by little, by taking yet another step, even a tiny one. Naturally, there is a lot of stress and effort for such a person to maintain his or her balance, but it also is thrilling, because every instance of this pushing the envelope, of going to the limit, is associated with significant hazards and risks. As confirmed by rock climbers and mountaineers, and hikers crossing deserts of ice and sand, every successful trip to the limit increases self-esteem and self-assurance, the necessary prerequisites for taking the next step. These activities usually are carried out by people with a strong, venturesome attitude and a craving for records. Basically, whatever has been achieved is no longer sufficient. The sense of achievement does not last, it is short lived. Again and again an envelope-pusher believes that he or she has to dare to do something new that will fascinate him or her and others. Usually, these people are guaranteed at least some public recognition, but at the same time there will be critical voices declaring them crazy. And often these voices are those of their peers. Whether in extreme sports, in science, or in the arts–taking a new path does not necessarily endear one to one's colleagues, as Gunther von Hagens has experienced again and again.

But if you make adventure your profession and take on the world as some kind of adventurous playground, you have to be prepared to encounter resistance and possibly to even be thwarted by it. Those who hesitate, who doubt, and who wait and see, avoid such hazards carefully. Gunther von Hagens, on the other hand, finds indecision repugnant, even though a straight-forward approach does not necessarily lead to the goal, especially when it is associated with pushing the limits. The most difficult situation for BODY WORLDS that I witnessed close-up happened in Munich, Germany, when the city banned the exhibition and was determined to prevent its opening. The Bavarian authorities tried, with a clear gesture, to silence this *persona non grata* and to put him in his place. Eventually, it seemed, a law enforcement agency was succeeding at getting the usually mellow plastinator agitated, turning his hitherto unrestrained restlessness into cluelessness. But if your idea of life is to get through venturesome activities, you must not be surprised when hopeless situations arise! And once more the plastinator did not succumb to hopelessness. Just like an envelope-pusher in the great outdoors facing an approaching natural disaster, he was utterly determined to resist the superior strength of the authorities and to conquer fate. He did not lack in his readiness to fight, if possibly in his forcefulness in view of these ruthless obstacles. But what had he, ready as he was to go to all extremes, which he could use in his fight against the authorities, other than his persistence? That meant risking life and limb, putting his company in a dangerous position. In spite of the ban, he had the exhibition set up in Munich, hoping that the lawyers, in their search for regulating and liberating words, would reach a settlement that in the end would not let BODY WORLDS down. However, the prospects for such a result were rather grim if one took a sober look at the actual endangerment to the company and at his own possible strategies. The entire enterprise was being put at risk in this envelope-pushing, limit-crossing, high-risk activity–this was a game, a gamble that no longer aimed for the special kick as white-water rafting or parachuting with a snowboard does. The dizzying thrills had been replaced by anxious worry. The situation was serious, if not dramatic. There was nothing in it anymore that would compare to the search for excitement by extreme mountaineers, surfers, and white-water rafters, i.e., to the longing for an escape from a daily life that is perceived as not sufficiently exciting. But adventures often are no longer exciting when they become reality; then they frequently turn into pressing worries and exhausting drudgery. They usually are exciting only beforehand, in the planning stages, or afterward, as memories.

Although it seemed that the BODY WORLDS exhibition had been abandoned to ruthless law enforcement agencies, and although the thrill of the self-sought hazard had evaporated, Gunther von Hagens–as gamblers and adventurers routinely do–put all of his eggs in one basket in proceeding with his plans to open the Munich exhibition after all. In doing so he developed an amazing trust in the idea that fate once again would be kind to him. So he presented himself as an adventurer as described by Georg Simmel: "The adventurer to some degree relies on his own strength, mostly however on his luck, and actually on a strangely undifferentiated unity of the two. The strength, of which he is sure, and luck, of which he is unsure, subjectively are combined into a feeling of safety for him." And indeed, as it had many times before, it all worked out–as it were, at the last minute.

For the opening of the exhibition that had been set up at von Hagens' risk had been scheduled for 5 p.m. The Bavarian higher administrative court granted permission for this opening on the very same day at 12:30 p.m. Depressed tension and exhaustion were immediately transformed into enthusiastic exuberance!

No envelope-pushing without risk! Risk is a prerequisite to adventure. In general, risk is part of any intense life. Just like there are those afraid of risk, there also are people among us who are ready to take risks. Gunther von Hagens is one of the latter. He can hardly imagine a life without passion and risk. Venture is a part of mountaineering and climbing as much as it is part of tightrope walking or bullfighting—but it also is part of science and business, and of running an enterprise such as BODY WORLDS. And one cannot help feeling that the envelope-pusher Gunther von Hagens has conducted some of his past activities not only in spite of the associated risk, but because of the associated risk. An example is the public autopsy in London, the first one in 200 years, that caused quite a stir, and with which he not only risked the exhibition, but also his reputation. Certainly he was back in the headlines overnight, especially in Germany, and in addition he gave to his critics a huge opportunity for harsh criticism. However, he usually does not put himself or his enterprise into hazardous situations blindly or with suicidal intentions, but for the most part conducts these risky endeavors with much deliberation and consideration. He

"Rearing Horse with Rider", wrapped

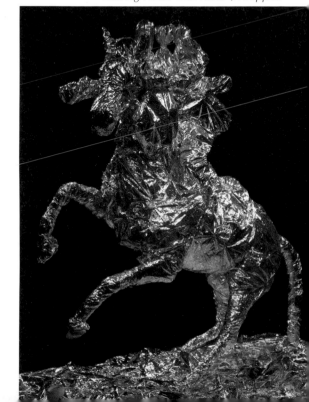

estimates the level of hazard associated with what he has in mind by discussing it with his closest co-workers and with experts before leaving the safe ground of the mere idea in order to implement it in uncertain reality. It goes without saying that in spite of all sober assessments, there always will be a residual risk; misestimates can never be completely precluded. Nobody knows whether the residual risk is too great, and how far one may venture into the hazardous zone in question. Gunther von Hagens is one of those envelope-pushers who like to test and to cross limits, who are inspired by a prickling sense of risky adventure without ever loosing their confidence of being up to the challenge.

Balint distinguishes between two character types: the philobat, who has high self-confidence and who seeks out and enjoys risk; and the ochnophil, who tends to avoid danger, clings to a safe place, and seeks protection. Gunther von Hagens clearly is a philobat personality who does not flee reality, but engages it, and who has developed both trust in his own strength—accomplished by growing competencies that are adequate to the tasks at hand—and confidence in the world's readiness to be conquered.

Public autopsy in London, in 2002

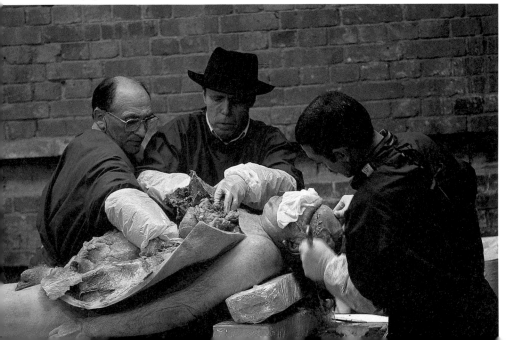

Goethe once described these two character types. On the one hand, in the shape of the daredevil, hungry-for-life, and curious Faust, who is even ready to seal a deal with the devil in order to get to the last secrets behind things. Goethe contrasts him with the dry, indoor scholar and bookworm Wagner, a fearful scholar afraid of risks, who is free of even the tiniest drive for the extraordinary and the courage to push the envelope. He prefers safety and comfort to adventure. Faust understands Wagner when he notes: "By one impulse alone you are impressed. Oh, never learn to know the other!" This is followed by the famous part about the "two souls" who Faust feels dwelling in his breast: one of them longing for safety, peace, and contentment, and the other who wants, just like a bird, to lift off from the ground and to break through all boundaries and limitations. And it is the latter that characterizes Faust more strongly than anything else.

The same is true for Gunther von Hagens—the inventor, scientist, artist, grumbler, and troublemaker as I know him. It is typical of creatively demanding people with a strong need for recognition that they occasionally, recklessly, ignore the conventional, the common, the known, in order to venture forward into new areas of thinking and acting. Gunther von Hagens embodies this personality type. He is creative in many ways—as anatomist, as business man, and as self-promoter, and as such he is a many-talented person.

Making use of one's creative powers and exhausting one's own capabilities are the highest forms of human self-actualization that provide great fulfillment and meaning to the individual. Gunther von Hagens exploits his talents almost unsparingly. He neither spares himself nor his co-workers nor his audience, and least of all the authorities. His restless urge for creativity and originality that will today not be satisfied by yesterday's achievements, again and again puts new demands on himself and lets him seek out ever-new fields of action in which he then wants to express himself without limits. In order for such restless striving to yield success, it has to be accompanied not only by obsession and the willingness to take risks, but also by patience, discipline, and endurance. The boldest idea is good for nothing if the working asceticism required for its implementation is lacking.

In Gunther von Hagens, I have met a person who needs both for living: The limelight, popularity, publicity on the one side, loneliness and seclusion on the other. The latter is his personal realm, which the plastinator–when, for a change, he is not busy with BODY WORLDS or plastination–fills with learning languages and playing the violin. But a personal life in the conventional sense simply does not exist for him, as anyone visiting him at home in Heidelberg will immediately realize. For his dwelling is a place of business masquerading as a place of living. His kitchen, for example, is a place for heated discussions rather than for heated pots!

He generally does not seem to need a home in the traditional sense. To him, apartments are mainly places to sleep and to work in. So one may say: Gunther von Hagens is a nomadic personality, characterized by mobility, flexibility, urbanity, and open-mindedness. He is a restless wanderer who likes to make himself at home in his habits, yet always keeps one foot on the threshold, but without having to take every opportunity to be somewhere else than where he currently is. And still, he is afraid of comfort because it leads to lethargy. What he does not like: sitting around inactively! Uniform everyday life, the bourgeois working life with all its routines, to him is rather repelling, although he himself has by no means left all routine behav-ior behind, and regularly brings his turbulent life back on track. And yet, he spends his life, for the most part, in self-chosen placelessness. He does not seek a home, neither in his native culture nor in foreign cultures. But his permanent on-the-go being does not serve as some kind of cure for the melancholy that for some is associated with a settled way of life. The nomadic aspect of his existence cannot be romanticized, because feelings of an existential homelessness are rather foreign to him. He is an adventurer, but not a dropout, he is a cosmopolitan plagued by neither homesickness nor wanderlust. Unlike the romantics, he is restlessly driven, without the longing or the melancholy desperation of inner conflict or estrangement. A nomad is immune to homesickness because he finds his way around everywhere and is at home everywhere and nowhere. He practically is at home in homelessness. There are numerous people who are forced by political, economical, or discriminatory reasons to live unsteady lives. As opposed to them, Gunther von Hagens can afford to be homeless and to revolt against confining domesticity and standardized biographies. It seems that he was born with his compulsive restlessness. He even has always known how to turn his yearning for restlessness into a work ethic. Always searching for paths less traveled and alternative routes, to him every place at which he arrives is, in the literal and the figurative senses, a place that already bears the next leave-taking in itself. A home to him is not a space limited by walls and enclosures, but an open road. His homelessness he cushions by living inside his work.

2nd printing

© 2007 Arts & Sciences
Verlagsgesellschaft mbH, Heidelberg, Germany

Printed in Germany
Design: die werbeaktivisten, mArc schumacher, Ladenburg, Germany
Editing/copyediting: rhet publica, Pfullingen, Germany
Translation from German: Dr. U. Walter Translation Services, Bremen, Germany
Printing/binding: Himmer AG, Augsburg, Germany

Photograph and illustration credits:
All photographs and illustrations are, unless otherwise noted,
from the archives of the Institute for Plastination, Heidelberg, Germany,
or from personal sources.

ISBN 978-3-937256-07-8